Seeing Through Language

THE LANGUAGE LIBRARY

EDITED BY DAVID CRYSTAL

SEEING THROUGH LANGUAGE

A GUIDE TO STYLES OF ENGLISH WRITING

Ronald Carter and Walter Nash

Basil Blackwell

Copyright © Ronald Carter and Walter Nash 1990

First published 1990

Basil Blackwell Ltd
108 Cowley Road, Oxford, OX4 1JF, UK

Basil Blackwell, Inc.
3 Cambridge Center
Cambridge, Massachusetts 02142, USA

British Library Cataloguing in Publication Data

A CIP catalogue record for this book is available from the British
Library.

Library of Congress Cataloguing in Publication Data

Carter, Ronald
Seeing through language : an introduction to styles of English
writing/Ronald Carter and Walter Nash.
p.   cm. — (The Language library)
Includes bibliographical references.
Includes index.
ISBN 0–631–15134–6 — ISBN 0–631–15135–4 (pbk.)
1. English language — Style. I. Carter, Ronald. II. Title.
III. Series.
PE1421.N37 1990   90–200
808'.042—dc20   CIP
Typeset in 10½ on 12 pt Baskerville
by TecSet Ltd, Wallington, Surrey
Printed in Great Britain by
T. J. Press Ltd, Padstow, Cornwall

Printed and bound in Great Britain by Marston Lindsay Ross International Ltd, Oxfordshire

CONTENTS

PREFACE

The title of our book is designedly ambiguous. It announces that we 'see through language' by understanding its workings as the instrument and channel of communication; but it also hints at ways of 'seeing through' language when language is the mask or cover of underlying purposes and ideologies. In the one case, language is regarded as an enabling facility, a sufficient access to meaning; in the other, 'meaning' goes beyond language, and language is an accessory code, to be deciphered by the initiate. One kind of 'seeing', we would like to say, complements and indeed involves the other.

These are not particularly original propositions, especially now when in our schools and colleges there is an increasing interest in the study of the English Language, in Literary Theory, and in the provision of all kinds of courses bridging disciplines in the humanities or even making links between the humanities and the sciences. The tendency of such studies is to challenge the narrow concept of 'English' as the appreciation of canonical literature, and to suggest that English, because it examines the making of meaning, is a subject for the whole curriculum. We are conscious, however, that many students are as yet ill-prepared for the linguistic and textual explorations we propose in this book. In many schools there is no established tradition of language study, and undergraduates in most English departments are consequently averse to the exacting and systematic study of Linguistics, which, as they see it, involves them in theoretical considerations remote from their felt experience of language at work. They are nevertheless aware of a lacuna in their intellectual repertoire.

Our aim in this book has been to enable such students to develop a fuller awareness of language, an articulate awareness. It would please us if, given that awareness, a student should feel impelled to pursue the further studies that seeing through language promotes: not only in stylistics and literary criticism, but in the general study of communication, in sociological studies, in so-called 'media studies', in the examination and development of professional or vocational skills in oral and written English. We acknowledge our responsibility, as university teachers of English, for helping our fellow citizens to master the diverse practical functions of their native language, and yet, because we have constantly felt the impulse to avoid simple models of language and communication, our book is neither 'functional' nor 'anti-functional'. Written language serves a rich variety of purposes, and we have accordingly considered a range of texts wide enough to include insurance documents, travel brochures, car maintenance manuals, the poetry of Hardy, newspaper editorials, popular fiction, dialogues in the novel, political speeches, and the literary criticism of T. S. Eliot.

We hope that we have at least demonstrated the possibility of seeing how the functional, social and aesthetic uses of language may be linked in a study which has as its aim the enhancement of creativeness, a liberating creativeness, in the student. It is specifically for this reason that we turn, in our final chapter, from a concern with textual analysis to the complementary topic of textual *composition*. Our aim in that chapter is to challenge the romantic, 'inspirational' view of writing, which considers that talent is to be treasured but not tampered with, and to encourage a sense of composition as a process which can be studied, practised, and improved in the light of an informed understanding of the structure of language and its manifold workings. To this end a final section of the book includes exercises based on the material of all four chapters, but particularly designed to integrate the study and practice of writing.

Ronald Carter
Walter Nash

Acknowledgements

Parts of this book have appeared in earlier versions in published forms as follows. Parts of 2.2 to 2.4, appeared in *Prose Studies* 6.2 (1983) and *Language Topics* (eds. R. Steele and T. Threadgold; Benjamins, Amsterdam, 1988); parts of 3.1.1 appeared in M. Ghaddesy (ed.), *Registers of Written English* (Frances Pinter, London, 1988) and in *Vocabulary* by R. A. Carter (Unwin Hyman, 1987); parts of 3.3.3 appeared in *Language in Popular Fiction* by Walter Nash (Routledge, 1990). In all cases the material has been revised and updated for inclusion in this book. We also acknowledge the use of examples in 3.2.1 which first appeared in B. Moeran's article in *Language and Communication* (1984) – full details are cited in the bibliography to this book.

The authors and publishers wish to thank the following for permission to use copyright material: Alister Cameron for letter to the *Guardian*, 8.8.89; Carcanet Press Ltd and New Directions Publishing Corporation for 'This is Just to Say' from *Collected Poems 1909–1939 Volume 1* by William Carlos Williams: copyright 1938 by New Directions Publishing Corporation; the Controller of Her Majesty's Stationery Office for excerpts from the Queen's Speech to Parliament, 6 November 1985, as recorded in *Hansard;* Margaret Hotine for letter to the *Guardian*, 8.8.89; the Independent for extracts from the 18.11.87, 1.7.87, 24.10.87 and 9.11.87 issues of the *Independent*; the Listener for a review by Meredith Oakes, 13 October 1983, in the *Listener;* Ewan MacNaughton Associates for extracts from the 23.11.85, 22.4.83 and 14.11.85 issues of the *Daily Telegraph;* Peter C. Main for letter to the *Guardian*, 8.8.89; New Statesman and Society for competition entry by Stanley J. Sharpless, *New Statesman*, 1.11.85; the New York Times Company for 'the Drug Bandwagon' by William Safire, 11 September 1986, *New York Times*: copyright © 1986 by The New York Times Company; Christine Reynolds for an extract from 'The Love Song', *Love Story*, May 1989; Solo Syndication for extract from 8 October 1983 issue, *Daily Mail;* Times Newspapers Ltd for extracts from the 7.11.85 and 4.11.87 issues of *The Times*: copyright © 1985 and 1987 by Times Newspapers Ltd; Michael Toomey for letter to the Guardian, 8.8.89; Tourist Development Corporation, Malaysia, for an extract from advertising material.

1

Language and Style

'Our teaching still privileges literature to the detriment of all other types of discourse. We must be aware that such a choice is purely ideological and has no justification in the phenomena themselves. Literature is inconceivable outside a typology of discourses.'

Tzvetan Todorov, 'The Notion of Literature'

1.1 INTRODUCTION

Our aim in this opening chapter is to try to clarify what we understand by the title and subtitle for the book: *Seeing Through Language: A Guide to Styles of English Writing*. The main aim of the book as a whole is to offer discussion and analysis of a wide range of English texts. We anticipate that readers of the book will mainly comprise students and teachers from different backgrounds in language, literature and communication studies who may be united by interest in different styles of English writing. However, in the manner of almost all books on language our examples and exercises draw on some methods and models of description from modern linguistics. We recognize that few of our potential readers will have undertaken much analysis of language, particularly in pre-university studies. We aim therefore to operate at an introductory level and try not to assume too much knowledge *about* language even though every mature speaker of English has remarkable depths of knowledge *of* language. But if our main aim of offering analysis of a wide range of texts is to be fulfilled, then discussion of language will have to be linguistically detailed wherever it is relevant and necessary to be so. These analyses follow in Chapter 2 and 3.

In order to prepare the ground for the main analytical chapters, this opening chapter discusses some theoretical issues and seeks to explain our own theoretical and procedural assumptions. As stated above, we aim to focus on the words used in the title of the book and try to answer the following questions:

What is style?
Is style a literary concept?
Why is 'styles' preferred to 'style'?
What is meant by 'seeing through' language?
What is the relationship between style and ideology?
Why are the terms 'writing' and 'literariness' preferred to 'literature'?
What is the relationship between style, writing and composition in English?

Two main arguments are presented in the first chapter. The first argument is that the language of texts cannot be adequately explored by focusing only on one particular feature of organization such as grammar or phonology. Above all, description must try to account for the ways in which written texts function in contexts and as part of a dynamic process between writer and reader. The way language is patterned in such contexts involves attention to the organization of language beyond grammar, that is, beyond such relatively small units of language as the sentence and towards larger units of organization across speaking turns (in the case of spoken language) and across such textual structures as paragraphs (in the case of written language). Recent advances in what linguists term discourse analysis have begun to make this possible and have allowed a multi-levelled approach to texts *in toto*. We argue that richer analysis of texts can be facilitated by attending to their discoursal and contextual properties. Our second main argument is for an approach to the analysis of texts which synthesizes linguistic and literary concerns. We object here to the widespread view that literary language should be privileged by being somehow specially set off against other language uses, and argue instead that differences are due rather to the distinctive functions of the different text *conventions* which frame language in particular contexts, and to which readers respond in different ways. Thus, two main focal points in this chapter are: (1) arguments for the importance of text convention and for the enlargement of the scope of stylistic description, with its existing strengths in grammar and phonology, to include contextual factors – especially the relationship between writer and reader, and (2) a descriptive strategy which sees literary texts as subject to procedures of analysis which allow the distinctive properties of *all* texts to be discussed. A regular technique of arrangement in this book will therefore be one of comparing and contrasting a number of different styles of writing. In this respect the book differs from previous books in this field which have been devoted to *either* literary or non-literary styles. This chapter and the book which follows from its theoretical premises argues that such distinctions are at best arbitrary and can prevent full appreciation of both the range and the quality of English writing.

1.2 STYLE AS DEVIATION

One of the most widespread definitions of style is that we recognize it because it stands out in some way. You notice a distinctive way of doing things, whether this is a particular style of fashion or a style of playing tennis, because it is *marked* in relation to more standard or *normal* ways of doing it. It can be especially marked sometimes because the style concerned involves a break with particular rules of the 'game' or with conventions associated with the process. This view of *style as deviation* has been particularly prominent in discussions of literary style. It has entailed many elaborate accounts designed to demonstrate how the use of language in a literary text differs from 'normal' uses of language outside a literary context.

In discussions of literary style, 'normal' usually has the meaning of most frequent in the statistical sense. The most frequently used language will be usages that are the most expected; literary language will therefore either involve many unexpected abnormal elements; or unexpectedness will result from a text being organized in such a way that normal usages are made to be deviant through such devices as 'coupling' (Levin, 1962) or 'parallelism' (Jakobson, 1960:368). Good examples of *deviation* in a conventional literary context would be the rule-breaking styles of writers such as e.e. cummings or Dylan Thomas. An example from another (earlier) period would be this stanza from the nineteenth-century style of Gerard Manley Hopkins:

> There lives the dearest freshness deep down things;
> And though the last lights off the black West went
> Oh morning, at the brown brink eastwards, springs –
>
>   ('God's Grandeur')

Good examples of *parallelism* would include anything which involved repetition. This can range from lexical parallelism, as in the following example:

> What is this life, if full of care,
> We have no time to stand and stare.
> No time to stand beneath the boughs
> And stare as long as sheep and cows.

> (W. H. Davies, 'Leisure')

to a more complete parallelism in which whole structural units are marked by being placed in a relationship of congruent repetition. A striking example of this structural parallelism is found in the first and last stanzas of William Blake's 'The Tyger' (in which one key word is replaced):

> Tyger Tyger, burning bright
> In the forests of the night;
> What immortal hand or eye,
> Could frame thy fearful symmetry?
> . . .
> Tyger Tyger, burning bright
> In the forests of the night;
> What immortal hand or eye
> Dare frame thy fearful symmetry?

Such a conception of style has its roots in theories of Russian and Czech Formalists developed in the 1920s and 1930s. Central to many Formalists' views of how style works is the process of what has been termed 'automatisation' and 'foregrounding':

> By *automatisation* we thus mean such a use of the devices of language, in isolation or in combination with each other, as is useful for a certain expressive purpose, that is, such a use that the expression itself does not attract any attention: . . . By *foregrounding*, on the other hand, we mean the use of the devices of the language in such a way that this use itself attracts attention and is perceived as uncommon, as deprived of automatisation, as deautomatised . . .(Havránek, 1932)

In a classic paper Mukařovsky (1932) argues that poetic language aims at 'the maximum of foregrounding' that is, 'the aesthetically intentional distortion of linguistic components'. For him: 'The distortion of the norm of the standard is . . . of the very essence of poetry.' Furthermore, Mukařovsky extends Havránek's inference that foregrounded usages attract attention to themselves, by arguing that this special, 'poetic' language does not communicate in a way which is comparable with the normative, standard language. In fact, its main function is to be self-referring and primarily to communicate about itself: 'In poetic language foregrounding achieves maximum intensity to the extent of pushing communication into the background as the objective of expression, and of being used for its own sake; it is not used in the services of communication, but in order to place in the foreground the act of expresison, the act of speech itself.'

There is little doubt that foregrounding occurs or that degrees of expectation do play a significant part in determining particular effects. But one major difficulty with the notion of foregrounding concerns the problems encountered in attempting to measure what *is* expected or normal and thus *how* foregrounding actually takes place. A person doing stylistic analysis is hardly likely to have time enough to carry out statistical analysis for every deviation that he or she perceives. The likelihood is therefore that the view of the 'norm' will be an impressionistic one.[1] Although detailed work has been undertaken in defining grammatical norms, this too runs into problems associated with the impracticability of determining relative frequencies of occurrence. There is also the problem of what to do with a sentence, or sentence set, which may be grammatically normal but is felt to be lexically deviant. Somehow areas of deviational *overlap* need to be made both theoretically and practically explicable.

A further note of caution concerning deviational notions of style should be sounded. It may seem curiously paradoxical to put it in the form of the question we do, but: *how deviant is a deviation?* We are, in fact, asking here what kind of departure from the norm or norms of language in a text actually constitutes a deviation. Some stylisticians have remarked, justifiably in our view, that style results more regularly from 'deflections' than from 'deviations'. Deflections, according to Sinclair (1966) and Halliday (1971), can be defined as structures which contain elements not quite in their usual order. There may be no grammatical rule-breaking involved; only a slight displacement of the expected sequence serves to mark the language stylistically.

For example, the fronting of the adverbial phrase in the second of the following declarative sentences compares with the more 'normal' first sentence. The sentence is not grammatically deviant but it is stylistically marked, 'deflecting' attention, as it were, to the potential thematic significance of the fronting:

1 We go on holiday in August.
2 In August we go on holiday.

Indeed, to take this argument one stage further, if we accept that there is more to literary language than mere linguistic oddity, is it not also possible that in certain instances style can result not so much from deviation as from achievement of, or a positive appeal to, a norm?

Finally, we should note a paradox inherent in much of the preceding discussion: if we are unable to account adequately for the background norms by which style might be measured, how is it that so many writers on the subject talk so confidently about foregrounding?

Some studies have, however, recognized the complexities attendant on an adequate definition of norms. For instance, Riffaterre (1960) and (1964) and Halliday (1964) recognize that there are norms built into the very 'stylistic context' in which the language is used. In other words, for Riffaterre, 'style' emerges from the contrast between perceptible stylistic devices and the norms set up within the language of the work as a whole. Deviation is thus described in relation to (a) a norm present in the text (syntagmatic) and (b) a norm absent from the text.

An example of a norm being established within a *stylistic context* might be that set up in a poem of five stanzas where every sentence in the first four stanzas was in the interrogative mood. An interrogative norm would thus be established *internal* to the text; its prominence would mark this norm or macro-context over against other language structures in the poem even though the interrogatives are well-formed and do not deviate from use external to the poem. If in the fifth stanza a shift in mood occurred from the interrogative to a declarative or to an imperative structure then internal deviation or, in Riffaterre's terms, the setting up of a micro-context could be said to have taken place. Attention is subsequently drawn to the resulting communicative import of the shift within the stylistic context.

One problem with Riffaterre's theory, as with many deviation theories, is the inevitable concentration on stylistically active or foregrounded features to the exclusion of a consideration of items and structures which, though not 'deviant' can play an important role in the creation of a communicative effect. For Riffaterre style would appear to be something added rather than something integral to the message. However, by recognizing a 'dual' kind of deviation Riffaterre *is* able to offer a richer and more powerful explanation of the stylistic problems he poses than would appear to be possible by operating with a single norm/deviation framework. The postulation of a stylistic principle internal to a text- or convention-dependent view of style, or, more accurately, of *styles* rather than style; indeed, there is nothing in Riffaterre's definitions that would preclude such a concept being applicable to *all* texts, and not exclusively to 'literary' texts. Since their formulation in the early 1960s, Riffaterre's insights have proved to be consistently helpful in the course of attempts to define 'styles' of writing.

1.2.1 Style as Ornamentation: Style in Context

Opposed to, but as we hope to show, also connected with 'style as deviation' theories there are a number of theories that may be loosely termed 'style as ornamentation'. (For a description of these within a historical context, see Chatman, 1971.) Under this group of definitions style is seen to provide an emphasis or *stress* for the message. It is an extra which essentially cannot alter the meaning of an utterance; that is, if the order in which words occur in a sentence is altered then it is claimed that the meaning is not necessarily altered too. It follows from this that differences in linguistic form are no more than *ornamental* and that all style does is give an emphasis to content. Once again, we have a version of the statement that 'language expresses and style stresses'. But is the notion of an isomorphism of linguistic form and content preferable? Not necessarily. For example, the subject matter framed by a sentence is not always wholly contained by that sentence. Of the following two sentences Leech (1969:10) is able to claim the second to be pompous because the subject matter is not conventionally treated in a formal style:

1   The bus we got on was the one he had got off.
2   The bus we boarded was the one from which he had alighted.

Certainly, the meaning of (2) here is more than what the words refer to. Indeed, it is not difficult to imagine a communicative context where the words could be construed as a sarcastic insult and therefore have a very different meaning from (1). Thus, it would appear a not unreasonable claim that an ornamentalist view of style is applicable only if sentences are seen in isolation from their function in a context of use by participants. Variations in meaning can occur when changes are made in a contextual or situational dimension, although, needless to say, context alone does not confer meaning.

What seems to be emerging here is a view of style as *relational*. Style is not definable by reference to either content, a single 'neutral' norm, to linguistic form or to context but to some relational construct which produces a nexus of effects within *each* dimension. Thus, neither theories of style as deviation nor theories of style as ornamentation are entirely suitable. What is certain is that it is dangerous both to make too easy a correlation between deviation and 'literary meaning' and to assume any context-free notions of style.

1.2.2 *Style and Levels of Language*

In order to provide some more concrete indication of the nature of the general conclusion reached in the preceding discussion we should examine the following half dozen sentences. Our main position is that more than one *level* of analysis is required in stylistic investigations. For example, it will be observed that the four sentences here are not deviant grammatically:

1 They are all over there.
2 She lived unknown, and few could know
    when Lucy ceased to be
  But she is in her grave and, oh
    the difference to me.
3 I shall wear the bottoms of my trousers rolled.
4 The oat was merry in the wind.

However, if the first sentence (1) were to appear in the exchange:

a: Where's the cat
b: They're all over there.

it is likely that, though not deviant grammatically, the sentence would be interpeted as a 'deviant' reply. That is, although explanation might be given by reference to conversational rules such as those of 'shared knowledge', it would appear not to conform to normal rules of reference ('the cat' – 'they'). The case of the second sentence, from one of Wordsworth's Lucy poems, demonstrates that poeticalness is not inherently dependent on grammatical deviance. Here, we would argue, the words become overlaid with patterns such as graphological shape, rhyme and rhythm which confer points of emphasis not available from within the poem's grammar. This might be illustrated by the way in which each syllable of the word 'difference' is drawn out to parallel the rhythmic structure of the second line; or the way in which 'be' and 'me' are linked semantically as well as phonologically almost to reinforce that Lucy is, for the speaker, the whole of existence (the exclamation 'oh' at the knowledge of her death – 'know' has the same effect). Here it could be said that meanings are modulated by the conventions of reading this mode of discourse. With the third example what might appear to be an ordinary, norm-adhering statement becomes charged in its context (T. S. Eliot's 'The Love Song of J. Alfred Prufrock') with meanings produced by its 'deviant' place in the total 'stylistic context' of the poem. Such factors as the conformity of the sentence to certain lexical and grammatical norms may indeed be a significant feature in its aesthetic effect. Finally, sentence (4) shows how a sentence can be deviant lexically, or anomalous semantically, without being odd grammatically.

It may thus be seen that, as Widdowson (1972) puts it, 'grammatical sentences may be used for deviant communicative acts' (e.g. here, sentences (1) and (4)) and that communicative effects depend on more than grammar for their working. This is not to deny the significance of grammar in the formulation of meanings but rather to stress that appeal needs to be made to other levels of analysis too. However, if one example is re-examined and one grammatically deviant sentence added to our list then another perspective emerges:

4 The oat was merry in the wind.
5 Because the ice-cream man ice-cream sells.

In (4), as pointed out previously, the anomalies may be resolved by seeing the sentence as operating in a particular context, say, in a farming community to denote the ripeness of the corn. That is, recognition of the interpenetration of lexis and context is necessary. In (5) recognition of a context of foreign language teaching of German, the particular technique of literal translation (to indicate verb placement after certain sentence binders in that language) along with a foreign language 'text convention' of lexical repetition of collocates and word families, allows a 'deviant' sentence to become normal. Figure 1.1 offers a diagrammatic summary of the above points concerning levels of language in the organization of text.

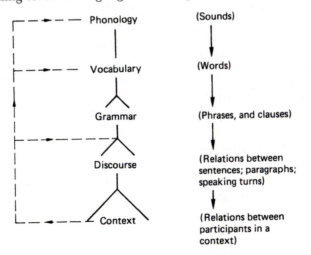

Phonology	(Sounds)
Vocabulary	(Words)
Grammar	(Phrases, and clauses)
Discourse	(Relations between sentences; paragraphs; speaking turns)
Context	(Relations between participants in a context)

Figure 1.1   Levels of Language

In general outline, then, our position is one close to that of Sinclair (1982):

> . . . the notion of a special language of literature is unhelpful. The set of conventions appropriate to the interpretation of a literary text is not necessarily the same set as that set appropriate to an advertisement or telephone call, but the total inventory of conventions is shared and the method of interpretation is the same no matter what the register.

This position is not really far removed from Mukařovsky (1932) who, while in our view mistakenly seeing a dichotomy between standard and poetic language and backgrounds and foregrounds in literary texts, recognizes none the less the need to specify literary conventions as themselves constituting some kind of norm of usage:

> The background which we perceive behind the work of poetry as consisting of the unforegrounded components resisting foregrounding, is thus dual: the norm of the standard language, and the traditional aesthetic canon. Both backgrounds are always potentially present, though one of them will predominate in the concrete case.

What, then, is the nature of the literary context? What is the part played by literary or, more broadly, text conventions? What kind of rules do they obey and in what kind of relationship do they stand to grammatical rules or to other norms? What role in the context is fulfilled by communicative codes existing between speaker and hearer or, in this case, author and reader? How close is this view to Riffaterre's 'stylistic context' outlined above?

1.3.2 *Style and Text Convention*

In this section we make what we consider to be a point central to the argument of this chapter and, by extension, to the book as a whole. We postulate here that it is only by recognizing the particular and context-specific conventions of a text that description of style becomes possible.

It is not that the writer does not have the choice of making his or her own meanings, but that the constitutive conventions fundamentally restrict the set of elements available for combination in specific texts. And, of course, the constraints vary according to the type of writing involved. In fact, when seen in the context of conventions and textual norms Tzvetan Todorov's essay (1973) devoted to a definition of literature and style and cited in the epigraph to this chapter comes to offer a sharp theoretical prime:

A particular type of discourse is in turn defined by the list of rules which it must obey. The sonnet, for example, is characterized by extra limitations on its meter and rhyme. Scientific discourse in principle excludes any reference to the first or second person of the verb, as well as to any but the present tense . . . It has become equally obvious that there is no common denominator for all 'literary productions' . . . each type of discourse usually referred to as literary has nonliterary relatives which resemble it more than do other types of literary discourse.

The main inference that can be drawn from this is that the danger inherent in opposing literary and other uses of language can be extended into setting literary discourse apart from other modes of communication. As Todorov states, the opposition between literature and non-literature can be replaced by a 'typology of the various types of discourse'. There are conventional regularities in the use of language in many contexts and situations; if stylistic differences in texts are to be accounted for perhaps one of the main constituent factors will be the function of these codes and conventions and the use of language either in association with them or in breaking with them. In the broader area of 'literary competence' Culler (1975; 1981) has shown how experienced readers bring with them to the text a number of conventional operations that they perform as part of their reading competence.[2] Dependent as it is on reader expectation and writer awareness of reader expectation, this competence underlies and, Culler argues, is thus a significant part of the meaning created by readers in particular texts. Much research still needs to be done in this area, but the process is in certain of its components relatively determinable.

Some of the procedures determining how the reader 'naturalizes' a text, that is how he/she encodes and recodes the literary utterance in terms of a previous structural knowledge of literature and as part of the way he/she releases meaning from a text, can be illustrated by the following much cited poem by William Carlos Williams:

This is Just to Say
I have eaten
the plums
that were in
the icebox

and which
you were probably
saving
for breakfast

Forgive me
they were delicious
so sweet
and so cold.

In another context, the language might constitute a banal domestic note or interlude; here largely as a result of the visual signs of 'poemness' in the graphological construction of the message such factors, Culler would argue, as the reader's consequent expectation of totality and significance in the message, his natural preparedness to imagine a coherent enunciative situation by fitting the participants into a fictional construct (the outer context), together with the effect on semantic structure of such conventions as line-breaks, enjambment, run-on lines, metrical patterns, etc. (the inner context) are significant contributory elements in the determination of the poem's meaning – even if such meaning might here reside primarily in a questioning of relative modes of significance. As a further example, the following lines from Robert Lowell's, 'Mr Edwards and the Spider':

Faith is trying to do without
faith

demonstrate that typographic space and capitalization can accentuate the split between preposition and object and thus contribute an extra dimension to the meaning of the words. (Here one effect may be to underline that real Faith involves progressive attempts to give up lower-order – lower-case – kinds of faith.)

There are, of course, many other conventions and, as stressed above, the charting of a reader's conventional expectations is still in its initial stages of development; but such an approach to a poem as a discourse with its own specific determinants on how it is to be received is one which, we believe, promises more than accounts of poems in terms of 'special' linguistic properties. *It thus seems reasonable to pursue the question of the differentiability of literary language more in terms of those conventions of the transmission and reception of its language that distinguish it from other circuits of communication.* If so, a basis might be said to exist for the establishment of a norm of expectation within the context of the text itself. Such a norm or set of norms may be seen to be more fundamental to, yet may be also inclusive of, the kind of text-internal norm adumbrated in Riffaterre's writings (see 1.2 above).

Before concluding this section on text conventions, which has focused on a reading of poems (or what Todorov might call poetic discourses), we would like to underline the main points made about conventions by examining an example of non-poetic writing and its attendant text conventions. In the text shown in Example 1.1, which is a weather forecast extracted from a national newspaper, there are some main governing conventions to be noted. Because they are generally familiar and, unlike a poem, read without any active recognition, is no reason for not attempting to chart these conventions. Thus:

1 The forecast usually contains a *summary* of the expected weather for that day across the whole country together with an outlook in which expected weather conditions over a period of one or two days is reported.
2 The country is divided into regions and region-specific forecasts are given. The typographic layout is designed to provide easy information access.
3 Maximum temperatures are cited in Fahrenheit and Celsius, e.g. *15C, 59F*. The figures follow standard abbreviations and typography.
4 Abbreviations are common but are encoded in an easily recognizable form, e.g. *Wind S, fresh to strong*.
5 Sunrise and setting times are cited.
6 World weather is summarized by temperature and a four-point code.
7 Finally, at a more specific linguistic level, there are linguistic forms, especially those of vocabulary, which belong more or less exclusively to this 'discourse' of weather-forecasting, e.g. sunny *intervals*; wind *moderate; outbreaks* of rain; early fog *patches; occasional* rain. (The italicized lexical items and their particular place in the noun phrase of which they are a part tend to form fixed phrases associated with weather-forecasting.)

Of course, different newspapers adopt different conventions and there is no one single formula. And we are dealing here with written not broadcast (television or radio) forecasts which are oral and scripted. But at the level of text conventions this extract shares a number of common features with other forecasts. Compared with a poem, however, there are no main reading processes activated by a reader other than the extraction of required information and there is certainly no need to enlist the conventions to aid in the interpreting of the message or to provide any additional meaning. It is interesting, however, to ask how far these conventions might be displaced before readers either started to read it as something other than a weather forecast or even dismissed it completely.

Weather

MAINLY dry, sunny intervals in places. Outlook: Cloud, occasional rain, becoming brighter.

District Forecasts

1, 2, 3, 4, 5, 6, 7, 8, 9, 15: Dry, sunny periods developing, early fog patches. Wind S. light. Max 16C 61F.

10, 11, 12: Dry, sunny intervals. Wind S. moderate. Max 15C 59F.

13, 14, 20, 21: Rather cloudy, rain or drizzle at times. Wind strong, locally gale. Max 14C 57F.

16, 17, 18, 19: Mainly dry, sunny intervals. Wind S. fresh to strong. Max 16C 61F.

22, 23. (Orkney and Shetlands: Mainly cloudy, outbreaks of rain. Wind S. strong to gale. Max 13C 55F.

 Sun rises 7.18 a.m. sets 6.15 p.m. Moon rises 4.53 p.m. sets 1.31 a.m. tomorrow. Lighting-up times (London) 6.45 p.m. to 5.49a.m. High water (London Bridge) 9.5 a.m. and 9.57 p.m. Tomorrow 10.28 a.m.

World Weather at noon yesterday

C—cloud, F—fair, R—rain, S—sun.

	C	F			C	F			C	F			C	F			C	F
Amsterdam	S	16	61	Cairo	F	27	81	Innsbruck	S	19	66	Malaga	C	17	63	Reykjavik	F	4	19
Athens	S	24	75	Capetown	S	23	73	Jersey	S	17	63	Malta	F	24	75	Rome	S	24	75
Barcelona	F	21	70	Florence	S	22	72	Jo'burg	S	21	70	Nairobi	C	28	79	Stockholm	C	9	48
Belgrade	S	22	72	Funchal	C	20	68	L.Palmas	F	25	77	New Delhi	S	31	88	Tel Aviv	F	28	79
Berlin	C	15	58	Genova	C	17	63	Lisbon	F	20	68	Nice	S	23	73	Tokyo	R	18	64
Biarritz	F	20	68	Gibraltar	C	22	73	London	S	16	61	Oslo	S	9	48	Venice	S	19	66
Brussels	R	13	55	Helsinki	R	7	45	Madrid	F	17	63	Paris	S	18	64	Warsaw	S	17	63
				Hong Kong	C	26	79	Majorca	R	20	68	Prague	R	20	68	Zurich	S	16	61

8 Channel Islands

Example 1.1

This is not the place to discuss the specific differences between the discourses or to explore the relative literariness of 'literary' texts. This is undertaken much more extensively in Chapter 2 of this book. Our aim here is simply one of re-emphasizing that: texts are convention-bound; that reading styles of writing is controlled in different ways by such conventions; that all texts generate interactive contexts for the reading of such conventions; that both writers and readers have expectations concerning the intersection of style, text convention and context.

1.2.4 Summary: What is Style?

In this short section we begin to answer the question 'What is style?' by summarizing the main points reached in our argument in this chapter so far:

1　Style in language cannot be explained by reference to only one level of language such as grammar or vocabulary. Although grammar is the level of language organization which linguistics can describe most completely and has therefore tended to figure prominently in discussions of style, style results from an interplay of language organization at several levels. This book is characterized by stylistic analysis at different linguistic levels. (See especially Chapter 3 which introduces a range of different descriptive frameworks relevant to different levels of language organization.) Throughout the book style is seen as a *textual* phenomenon.

2　One of the most important levels is that of context. By context in this study is meant (a) a stylistic context, i.e. the 'inner' contextual conventions in which the language is set – these have also been termed *text conventions*; (b) the 'outer' contextual constraints which affect any message which has a sender and a receiver (a writer and a reader); this has also been referred to as the *interactive context* in which text conventions operate. (Questions of writer/reader relations are taken up at 1.4.1.)

3　Definitions of style which, however powerfully argued, seek to explain style in terms of deviation from a norm are inadequate. Firstly, norms are very difficult to standardize. Secondly, stylistic effects can result from various degrees of adherence to as well as departure from a norm.

4　The notion of a special language of literature or literary style is not a helpful one. It cannot be defined as any one singular concept and cannot be defined in relation to a single norm. It is generally more productive to see style as *relational* and examine how a piece of language works in context in relation to the operations of language in other contexts. In this book we do not attempt to provide a 'typology of discourses' but we do attempt to discuss style *beyond* the literary.

1.3　LITERARINESS

In this chapter so far we have argued that no one language or style should be privileged over others; we have argued that differences in language use are best measured in terms of the different text conventions within which styles are read by readers; and we have shown that attempts to describe a 'literary' style or to locate an essential poeticalness in language have tended to be somewhat narrowly based. One further argument which we have not mentioned is that of *style as evaluation*. Although it is impossible to conceal our own preferences and prejudices – and this can be seen even in the selection of texts for discussion – we are aware that use of the term 'style' (in the singular) can suggest that some uses of language are evaluated as 'better' than others. The notion owes much to popular usage in expressions such as 'they've got style' or 'that was written with real style' or 'they won in style'. And so on. By insisting on the terms *styles* (in the plural) and preferring the term 'literariness' to 'literature' (which like 'style' receives dissociating and problematizing quotation marks), we are, however, open to charges of relativity. Pluralizing style can, after all, suggest that anything goes.

It is not an overt aim in this book to evaluate pieces of writing. However, discussion and analysis of texts in this book is regularly undertaken by means of juxtaposing and comparing similar and dissimilar texts. We have already seen how discourse conventions are best explained *in relation to* each other and that style was argued to be a relational term. Traditional definitions of literary style (such as deviation therories) have been made by comparison with non-literary style. Indeed it could be argued that stylistics is (or should be) an essentially comparative discipline. However, an examination of style as relational should not automatically lead into relativity. Indeed the very process of comparison forces compelling questions upon us even if the questions transcend in a number of respects those posed in the introduction so far. For example: *is* there a literary language? is there more to literature than language? is the notion of literature a tenable one? is there a fixed dividing line between literary and non-literary discourse? how important is the way in which readers decide to read a text? are certain conventions more likely to provoke 'literary' readings than others? to what extent are some of these questions non-linguistic ones? Such questions are raised here not because answers can be explored in this section of the book. They are raised in order to show that we do not dismiss the notion of a poetic function of language, the notion of language use which is definably literary as opposed to non-literary.

We are also aware that describing something as *poetic*, no matter how hard we might try to present this neutrally, necessarily involves an inherent evaluation on the part of readers. We are part of a culture in which 'literary' and 'poetic' are terms of negative and/or positive value.

This exploration of 'literary' language is continued in Chapter 2 which contains an extensive relational study of different texts with regard to the degrees of *literariness* they may be said to manifest. The term literariness is an important one in this book and is widely employed. There is space here only for a preliminary defining example of what we understand by this term. It can be most effectively explained by reference to the way language is used in the following advertisement:

You can't see through a Guinness

The advertisement is of course accompanied pictorially: in this case, this is a picture of a bar with two glasses of beer placed on the bar counter. The beers are of two different types – one is a light, lager-type beer, the other is Guinness beer which is a dark and opaque liquid. Through the transparent light beer we can see a distant game of cricket being played which those in the bar are all engaged in watching. In this context the caption *You can't see through a Guinness* acquires extra significance. In particular, a further semantic overlay accrues to the phrasal verb *see through*, which has two meanings in English: literally, to 'see through' is to look through something which is transparent and which does not impede vision; the second sense is that we 'see through' people or things which intend to deceive or which are deceptive or duplicitous. By extension, therefore, beer which is transparent can be seen through as not genuine. The *real* beer is therefore the Guinness beer. It is a beer we can trust.

Plays on words, semantic ambiguities – call them what we may – as well as figures of speech such as metaphor, or rhythmic patterning or allusiveness are generally regarded as belonging to a special and separate domain of literary language. The example of the Guinness advertisement demonstrates that this is not *exclusively* the case. Metaphor is an even more pervasive feature of language use, found in everyday conversations, articles and newspaper headlines such as:

Slums Are a Disease, Claims Minister

Rhythmic and phonological patterning occurs in many children's playgrond games while allusiveness is again a pervasive feature of advertisements. This is explored extensively in an article by Brian Moeran (Moeran, 1984) on advertising as 'cultural discourse'. Moeran shows the kinds of allusive or intertextual continuity exploited with varying degrees of subtlety by advertisers. Two examples he cites are, firstly, for the range of Smirnoff vodka advertisements with their patterned sequence of slogans:

I thought St Tropez was a Spanish Monk . . .
Accountancy was my life . . .
I thought Kama Sutra was an Indian restaurant
    until I discovered Smirnoff.

and the series of Heineken lager advertisements which began with:

Heineken refreshes the parts other beers cannot
reach

and which is alluded to in:

Renault reaches the parts other cars cannot reach.

The main point to be underlined here is that features of language use more normally associated with literary contexts are found in what are conventionally thought of as non-literary contexts. It is for this reason that the term *literariness* is preferred to any term which suggests an absolute division between literary and non-literary. It is, in our view, more accurate to speak of degrees of literariness in language use. This view is substantiated further in our next chapter, though it is extended in Chapter 3 where, for example, the language of canonical literary texts (3.4) is examined alongside advertising language (3.2).

1.4 STYLES OF WRITING IN ENGLISH

It may now be clearer why we have chosen the sub-title *A Guide to Styles of English Writing*. In this book we do not follow the pattern of many books in stylistics, which is to apply linguistic analysis to literary texts. Previous work in this field, with which both authors of this book have been closely involved (e.g. Carter (ed.), 1982), is characterized by a selection of texts for discussion which are drawn from a canon of authorized works. This canon of texts is one from which there are regular and, some would say almost automatic, choices for study in many university or college departments of English Studies. In a number of respects such *literary stylistics* is ancillary to and supportive of this discussion of canonical texts. Neither, however, have we determined to practise a purely *linguistic stylistics*, the practitioners of which are more interested in the linguistic structure of texts than in using linguistic analysis to support interpretations.

Instead we have sought to combine discussion of canonical literary texts, such as poems by Browning and Hardy and extracts from prose fiction by Galsworthy, with non-canonical texts such as samples of popular fiction, little-read nineteenth-century writers such as George Sanger, and non-fictional writing such as advertisements, instructional manuals and encyclopaedia entries. Our view of literature is not that of literature with a capital 'l' but of literature in one of its basic senses of written material – the sense retained in the use of the term in the 'literature' of an academic subject or in travel or insurance 'literature'. However, potentially awkward questions concerning why some texts are canonical and others non-canonical will not be avoided and, as we have seen in the previous sections, the notion of *literariness* in language use is one which can provide a basis for examination of such issues. In any case, we hope it is now clear why we prefer the term 'writing' to embrace these many senses and to include the wide range of varieties of English writing examined in the book. We hope it is also clear why the term 'styles' is preferred to the more normal 'style'. Although the singular form is often no more than a collective noun it is important to remove not only any evaluative suggestion of a preferred style but to retain a sense that there are some styles which are more appropriate than others and that in particular contexts certain conventions have to be adhered to. Our subtitle *Styles of English Writing* is intended to emphasize that our primary concern is not evaluative, to underscore our basic recognition of the plurality of

English writing and to suggest (by omission) that the term 'literature' is not an unproblematic category.

One further point needs to be made in connection with the use of the term *English* writing, for it is a term which is easy to use in a restrictive or even parochial and unreflective way. The restrictive sense of the term would be to refer to English writing as the writing produced in English in England. It needs to be continually pointed out, however, the that are many literatures in the world which are written in English but which are produced a long way from England. There is English literature written in the United States, Australia and South Africa; and less obviously, there is English literature written in countries in which English is an institutionalized second language, e.g. India, Singapore, Nigeria, Kenya, or The Philippines, and where it is produced by writers for whom English is not a mother tongue. Less obviously still there is Irish, Scottish and Welsh writing in English as well as literature in English such as West Indian English poetry produced by writers of British English nationality with differing ethnic backgrounds. We do not explore this particular aspect of the diversity and plurality of writing in English as much as we would have wished. But it is important that students of styles of English writing are aware of this dimension to their study.

1.4.1 Style and Ideology

The assumption we have made in much of our discussion so far is that all readers process and analyse texts in uniform ways and then interpret them from the same linguistic, cognitive or attitudinal vantage point. Of course, we must not expect that universality is so easy to attain. Much more realistic would be an assumption that ideas do not merely float in the air; they are produced and reproduced in specific social and cultural contexts by language users who are positioned in different ways in these contexts. More pertinent still would be to recognize the ways in which ideology operates through language and serves to construct and reproduce political relationships in which language users have a key position. And we must recognize that authors and readers of 'literature' do not transcend such relations; they are ineluctably intermeshed with them.

What is understood by the term 'ideology'? Ideology has been taken to mean several things but it can be understood in two main senses. The first is that of a classical Marxist conception of ideology as 'false consciousness', in which ideology is a distorted image of the real network of inequality and asymmetrical power relations which exist in societies. The second sense is that of ideology as a socially and politically dominant set of values and beliefs which are not 'out there' but are constructed in all texts especially in and through language. Within this second sense we can explore the ways in which ideologies impregnate a society's modes of thinking, speaking, experiencing and behaving, are therefore a necessary 'condition' for action and belief within a social formation and hence are crucial in the construction of personal identity. To study ideology and its representation requires close attention to language and style. The particular focus, however, needs to be on the intermeshing of language and style in the *context* of social systems and institutions. Ideologies cannot be unmasked by linguistic analysis at a single level or with reference only to decontextualized sentences. Our view of stylistics with its attention to whole texts in context and to the context of communication between a writer (speaker) and reader (listener) is well-placed to try to reveal the ways in which writers exploit linguistic structures in order to address the reader/subject of the discourse and 'subject' him/her to a particular way of seeing (and believing). John Thompson (1984:64) has written of ideology as follows:

> For ideology operates, not so much as a coherent system of statements imposed on a population from above, but rather through a complex series of mechanisms whereby meaning is mobilised in the discursive practices of everyday life for the maintenance of relations of domination. It is of the utmost importance, therefore, to search for ways in which the theory of ideology can be linked with methods for the analysis of the discursive forms in which ideology is expressed.

This position is interestingly close to our own. Style is a textual phenomenon and should be studied both in terms of particular linguistic forms in a text and as the effects generated by those same forms on the consumer (the reader) by the producer of the text (the writer). In this nexus between linguistic forms and functions text conventions play an important part in a mobilization of meanings. Language and text conventions create asymmetrical relations between writers and readers which ensure that certain of the meanings mobilized prove difficult to resist. In this important sense style is political; questions of language and style are ideological questions.

   In addition to assuming provisionally that all texts are processed by all readers in the same way, we have also assumed in our earlier discussion in this chapter that writer–reader relations are always symmetrical. This position can now be countered and adjusted. We have to recognize that writers entertain, whether consciously or not, particular kinds of designs on readers and that these are in important ways realized by an exploitation of available linguistic choices and of available text conventions. A writer's stylistic choices enable or facilitate certain kinds of readings while closing off or suppressing others. Invariably, a particular kind of reader is constructed, or a particular position from which the dominant meanings of the text are intended to be read. In this respect writers are more powerful than readers who have consciously to resist the reading being offered to them. The easier route is to co-operate with the writer and reconstruct the required readings, avoiding in the process any ideological contradictions or differences in viewpoint.

There is space in this introductory chapter for only brief illustration of the kind of relations which exist between language and ideology. The illustrative texts – which are newspaper headlines – are conveniently short but they are complete texts. The following headlines are taken from British national newspapers in 1984 at a time when a national coal strike led to a not inconsiderable polarization of political positions. The three headlines are taken from (1) the *Guardian*, (2) the *Daily Express*, and (3) the *Morning Star*:

1 NCB chief fit after incident at pit.
2 Coal Supremo felled in pit fury.
3 MacGregor scraps pit visit in face of angry demo.

There are several stylistic features which merit comment here. These include: the characteristic conventions of newspaper headlines such as omission of articles, the deletion of a main finite verb, abbreviations (*demo*) and phonetic patterning (*pit/fit; felled/fury*); the formality differences signalled by lexical choices, e.g. *incident/demo* and by naming devices – *Coal Supremo, MacGregor, NCB chief*. And so on. Also relevant here would be features not immediately recognized when the headlines are laid out as above. These are such features as typography, the placement of the main caption in relation to pictures as well as to other headlines. Of some significance in this connection, for example, are the styles of sub-headlines which in some newspaper styles support the main caption.

But analysis of style in and for itself does little to reveal the contrasts between these headlines in terms of ideology. The relationship here between language and ideology is not a transparent one; it is signalled with some subtlety and works to subject the reader to a particular interpretation of events. In the case of healdine (3), for example, MacGregor is placed in the role of main actor in the clause and is made responsible (*scraps visit*) himself for the act of cancellation. There is no reference to his physical position or disposition. By contrast headline (2) represents MacGregor as acted upon (*Coal Supremo felled*) and underlines the lack of 'agency' by use of a passive verb and markedly emotive lexis (*felled/fury*). Headline (1) seeks to be altogether more neutral by use of the lexical item *incident*, and the use of a complement structure (*NCB chief (is) fit*) avoids a passive/active distinction with its necessary assignment of agency. In other words, each headline inserts a different view of events. In (3) there is no suggestion that those taking part in the demonstration are directly responsible for action by MacGregor whereas in (2) MacGregor is the object of an action which we assume is initiated by the fury of the miners at the pit. In the opposition between coal supremo and miners the headline subjects the reader to a position which is limited by a pre-ordained interpretation of events. In (1) there is no overt taking of sides although in the case of such struggles neutrality signals greater allegiance to those social and political forces which seek to maintain a status quo. In all three headlines there is a relationship between stylistic choice and text structure and the ideological construction of a particular reading position.

For a more detailed analysis of the relationship between language and ideology readers are referred to sections 3.1.1 and 3.5.1 of Chapter 3 in which newspaper reporting and political rhetorics are explored as styles of text. It is also important not to neglect the fact that there are historical as well as social determinants on ideology. Analysis from within a socio-historical dimension explores the relationship between ideology and the changing forms of power and control which meaning production serves to sustain. The forms change in history as a result of struggles for a discursive position from which meanings can be made. The making of meaning through words does not depend therefore on the words in themselves nor on an individual's inhabiting and creating meaning by means of trans-historical self-expression. Words change their meanings according to the social and historical positions from which they are used. The word *salvation*, which originally was used to mean an eternal release through faith in Christ, has come under the pressure of historically determined evolution to acquire a stronger sense of release from political despotism. The meaning changes in relation to changing ideologies.

There is insufficient space in this book for exploration of a historical semantics of texts; but there is a consistent attempt to 'see through' language to the historical and socio-cultural determinants on the ways in which we read. 'See through' language has at least two main senses here. The first is that of looking at language more closely. There is nothing particularly original in our claim that analysing language as it is used in a wide range of texts can help us account a little more systematically for the ways in which meanings and effects are made in the texts. Such a claim is a commonplace of stylistic analysis; but in many courses in literature and communication studies in particular, there is still a tendency to look *past* language at the more 'important' ideas or content that a text contains. In this first sense of 'seeing *through* language' our position is that language is central to ways in which meanings are constructed in texts and that is is important not to regard it as if it were merely a window on to something else. It is a medium which is active in the transmission of the message. This leads naturally on to the second main sense of 'seeing through language'. In this sense there is a greater social responsibility for stylistic analysis, although we recognize that such words can sound pompous and pretentious. Our view is, however, that it is important for readers of all texts, whether they be canonical literary, highbrow newspaper or pulp fiction, to recognize and, where necessary, resist the fact that particular uses of language can work to construe realities in particular ways. That is, particular linguistic or stylistic choices are not innocent value-free selections from a system; they work to conceal or reveal certain realities rather than others, establishing or reinforcing ideologies in the process and refracting (as opposed to reflecting) particular points of view. Seeing through language involves seeing both the manifold ways in which language can be exploited and the ways in which readers of texts can be exploited *by* language. We discuss these particular questions in greater detail in sections 2.5 and 2.5.1 of the following chapter.

1.5   WRITING AS PROCESS: TEXT AND COMPOSITION

One problem with stylistic analysis, however textually it might be based, is that any equation between analysis of linguistic form and an interpretation of semantic function is necessarily a somewhat arbitrary one. The problem leads to the question: how is it that different readers who are native speakers of the same language can make a text in that language *mean* differently? The problem has been posed since the practice of stylistics was originated: 'Thought tends towards personal, affective integral expression: *la langue* can only render the most general traits of thought by depersonalising and objectifying it' (Bally, 1925). An example of this kind of problem can be given by pointing to the very different interpretations produced by readers of texts in which a main finite verb is omitted. Such texts range from classic examples such as the opening to Dickens' *Bleak House*, to less well-known examples such as in concrete poetry by Edwin Morgan (e.g. 'Space Poem 3'), the opening to Isherwood's *Goodbye to Berlin*, or a poem such a Roethke's 'Child on Top of a Greenhouse'. The effect of such an omission is generally interpreted to be different from one text to another: in one text producing for some readers a sense of disorientation, in another producing for other readers a sense of dramatic suspense. And so on.

This book is no different in this respect from other introductory books in stylistics in that we make numerous interpretations of linguistic functions which aim to be retrievable, in that we hope we give enough linguistic detail for others to be able to retrace our steps; but in the actual equation between linguistic form and function the interpretative act will reveal no automatic or guaranteed meanings.

There are no easy solutions to such problems which are to some degree embedded in the very nature of language and in the processes by which meanings are communicated. But we should note that interpretations as described above are necessarily from the outside and made from the receiving end of the communicative act. The resulting tendency is often to regard texts as finished *products*. It is rare in stylistic analysis for the process to be explored from the transmitting end: such a practice would involve a 'stylistics from the inside'. In Chapter 4 below, which is devoted to style, composition and creativeness, there is extensive discussion of compositional *processes* and of the patterning and creative shaping of linguistic forms. The perspective in Chapter 4, however, is less that of the reader-to-interpretant but, more prominently, that of the intentions of the *writer*. We hope that the student of styles of English writing will benefit from this alternative perspective. Such an examination, coming where it does in the book, will not help us to overcome the form/meaning dichotomy and its associated arbitrariness; but it will hopefully reinforce a concern with *meanings* in discourse rather than a tendency to assume that there is one fixed meaning. Meanings and interpretations are constructed not pre-determined, and our hope is that Chapter 4 should serve to underscore awareness of creative and compositional processes in the construction of meanings and effects.

The general conclusions reached in the examination of compositional processes in our fourth chapter underline that the notion of *literariness* is a useful one in the stylistic organization of writing. It also adds a further dimension to the notion of *seeing through language* by exploring how writers construct a view of the world through choices among both the patterns of language and the textual conventions available to them.

1.6   Seeing Through Language: The Organization of the Book

The aim of this first chapter has been to open up and thereby try to make explicit some of the theoretical assumptions with which we have operated in writing and in organizing this book. As we have already stated, the pedagogical design of the book is *introductory*. There are few books which introduce students to a study of the language and styles of texts and we hope to provide an analytical toolkit which is both accessible and usable. The organization of the book is weighted towards examples of practical stylistic analysis in action; but we have not shied away from significant theoretical issues, especially those which enable us to demonstrate that texts cannot be analysed in isolation from a 'seeing through' to social and cultural practices.

The second chapter is almost exclusively devoted to a theme which runs throughout the whole book: the notion of literariness in language use. Again a wide range of styles and texts is analysed, from instruction manuals to encyclopaedia entries and from tourist guide books to canonical literary texts. The chapter is organized by the fact that the texts discussed are all linked by a common theme and a set of further analytical categories are suggested by which the texts might be arranged along a cline or continuum of *literariness*. Theoretical issues are prevalent in this chapter and the existence of 'literary' language problematized, although the main focus is on practical analysis of texts at an introductory level.

Chapter 3 is the most extensive chapter in the book, and is pivotal in a number of ways. We suggest some descriptive frameworks and analyses at different levels of language from vocabulary to discourse organization. These analyses are conducted at relatively introductory stages and should supply a useful basis, a rudimentary toolkit, as it were, for discussion of other texts beyond the pages of this book. In keeping with the position argued for in this first chapter, a range of texts in different styles and with different text conventions is discussed, sometimes by a process of contrast and comparison. What are conventionally regarded as literary texts are examined alongisde what are conventionally regarded as non-literary texts. The ordering and sequencing of the chapter is not entirely arbitrary, however. Passages are grouped according to demands of a particular topic (e.g. language and ideology) or, more commonly, they are arranged according to particular styles such as newspaper, literary or advertising style. We also consider formal styles of spoken English such as political speeches and debates which are essentially 'written' in rhetorical pattern and organization.

The fourth and final chapter takes the notion of literariness further by examining compositional processes in writing English texts and demonstrates why it is preferable to work with a notion of styles or of style as a concept which is relational, that is relative to both context and convention. The chapter takes as its starting point the kinds of determining influences on the creative use of language, and does so by considering the processes of composition from the position of the writer rather than from that of the reader. This chapter and the conclusion draw together the main threads of the book, especially its main design of inspecting literariness in language use and of styles of writing as relational constructs.

Finally, it is worth reiterating that we do not view it as the purpose of an introductory book in stylistics to lead directly into full-blown linguistic analysis. Our aim is to help to develop the habit of *Seeing Through Language* and to increase *awareness* of the uses to which language can be put. Detailed stylistic analysis may be at the end of the road for some students and we certainly hope to have provided sufficient interest and stimulus to encourage a move in such a direction. But our initial goal is to promote and enhance language awareness and awareness of language as a social and textual phenomenon.

Notes

1. Short (1973) has shown how grammatical norms can be established in terms of particular syntactic patterns but how in the area of semantics and lexico-grammatical relations (as well as collocations) the predictability of co-occurrences is less measurable. A useful introductory discussion of norms in relation to definitions of style is contained in Cluysenaar (1976: Ch. 1).
2. The notion of literary competence is a complex one. It is *not* an issue which we systematically engage in this book, although it is touched on in several places (e.g. 2.5.1). It is worth recognizing here, however, that 'competence' may not be a singular notion; rather it may be more appropriate to speak of competenc*ies* relative to different literatures as

well as to different contexts of reading. It is also to question who exactly a reader is. Is literary competence perhaps no more than a circular notion? If literary competence is that taught in educational institutions then 'literary competence' is an institutionalized competence and can only be defined relative to the 'privileged' group of readers with access to the right institutions. Culler's notion of literary competence, as advanced here, is an essentially static one and appears not to take proper account of a dynamic of changing social circumstances or developing socio-historical and cultural contexts.

2

Language, Style and Literariness

2.1 INTRODUCTION

Traditionally, books on language and style have tended to concentrate on *either* literary *or* non-literary varieties of language. We do not consider such texts to be mutually exclusive and do not see why the same analytical procedures and schemes cannot be applied across a range of texts. Indeed, it may be unhelpful or even impoverishing to impose sharp divisions between literary and non-literary texts. We have argued in Chapter 1 that style is a relational phenomenon and that literariness is a feature to be found in texts which are not traditionally or 'canonically' considered to be literary (1.3).

Thus, we have begun in theory, but if this or any other book on language and style is to be of value, we must try to realize some of these theoretical questions in practical demonstrations. The issue we accordingly take up in this chapter is an importane one, perhaps the governing concern of any investigator trying to understand the principles of style in writings ranging from the severely functional to the highly literary. The question is: *What do we mean by 'literariness'?* In this chapter we present two extensive demonstrations of the notion of 'literariness', in a 'cline' or gradation of stylistic and discursive qualities. This exercise (we claim no more for it than that) leaves us with the reflection that the attributes of discourse are not wholly accounted for by describing the language of the text itself. Writer and reader bring their own interests and predispositions to the making and interpreting of texts. The word *discourse* thus implies, strictly speaking, an interaction involving and transcending the *text*. In the chapters that follow this we shall be centrally concerned with *texts*, but our comments will frequently suggest broader considerations of discourse.

2.2　Literary Language: Some Definitions

As we saw in Chapter 1 (1.3), in one sense, literary language is the language of literature; it is found in literary texts and is, for many literary critics, an unproblematic category. Such a position cannot, however, be as unnegotiable as it seems to be, if only because the term 'literature' itself is subject to constant change. In the history of English 'literature', literature has meant different things at different times: from elevated treatment of dignified subjects (fifteenth century) to simply writing in the broadest sense of the word (for example, diaries; travelogues; historical and biographical accounts) (eighteenth century), to the sense of creative, highly imaginative literature (with a hieratic upper-case 'L') appropriated under the influence of Romantic theories of literature by Matthew Arnold and F. R. Leavis in the last one hundred years. For a fuller account of such semantic change in respect of literature, see Williams (1976), who also points out the semantic detritus of the eighteenth-century sense of the word in its use to describe the 'literature' of an academic subject, or in the collocations of insurance 'literature' or travel agents' 'literature'. Literature is subject to constant change; it is not universally the same everywhere and is eminently negotiable. Definitions of literary language have to be part of the same process.

The history of definitions of literary language in the twentieth century is a long and battle-scarred one with various interest groups competing for power over the property(ies); and each definition has itself inevitably assumed a theory of literature whether explicitly recognized or admitted to be one or not. We shall begin with Formalist definitions because they are historically anterior, but also because their influence is pervasive in the export of Russian Formalism into American New Criticism and its subsequent import into practical criticism in Britain.

As we have seen in Chapter 1, Formalist definitions especially those of the Russian and Czech Formalists, such as Mukařovsky, Havránek and Jakobson, assume a division between 'poetic' and 'practical' language, and to this extent, parallel common oppositions between 'scientific' and 'poetic' discourse. The Russian Formalists shared the belief of the Symbolists in the early twentieth century in the aesthetic autonomy and a historical separateness of art and literature from other kinds of discourse, but were unhappy about the Symbolists' vague subjectivity and impressionism when it came to discussions of literature.

Paradoxically, they wanted to set up a *science*, a *poetics* of literature which would seek to define the literariness of literature, that is, isolate by rigorous scientific means the specifically literary forms and properties of texts. Since there is no literary content, they argued – no subject matter which belongs only to literary texts – poetics should evince a concern with the *how* rather than the *what*. Thus, the early Formalists gave special attention to the linguistic constituents of the literary medium – language – and drew on the new science of linguistics for their theoretical and descriptive apparatus.[1] Their main theoretical position was that literary language is deviant language. It is a theory which has had considerable influence, and a preliminary examination was undertaken in Chapter 1 (1.2).

According to deviation theory literariness or poeticality inheres in the degrees to which language use departs or deviates from expected configurations and normal patterns of language, and thus defamiliarizes the reader. Language use in literature is therefore different because it makes strange, disturbs, upsets, our routinized normal view of things, and thus generates new or renewed perceptions. For example, the phrase 'a grief ago', the title of a poem by Dylan Thomas, would be poetic by virtue of its departure from semantic selection restrictions which state that only temporal nouns such as 'week' or 'month' can occur in this sequence. As a result, grief is perceived as a temporal process. Deviation theory represents a definition of literary language which contains interesting insights, but which on close inspection is, as we saw at 1.2, incomplete. For example:

1   If there is a deviation then this can only be measured if you state the norm from which the deviation occurs. What is the norm? Do we not mean norms? Is the norm the standard language, the internally constituted norms created within the single text, the norms of a particular genre, a particular writer's style, the norms created by a school of writers within a period? And so on. If it is the standard language norms then what level of language is involved? Grammar, phonology, discourse, semantics? This is an important question; because a deviation at one level may be norm adherence at another level. And there is a further problem in that our ability to measure and account accurately for deviations will depend on what levels of language linguists know most about. Since the greatest advances this century have been in grammar and phonology, Formalist poetics has tended to discuss literariness, rather limitedly, in terms of grammatical and phonological deviations.

2   What is defamiliarizing in 1912 may not be in 1922.

3   There will be a tendency to discover literariness in the more

maximally deviant forms – i.e. poetry rather than prose, avant-garde rather than naturalist drama, in e.e. cummings and Dylan Thomas rather than Wordsworth's Lucy poems or George Eliot's shorter fiction.

4   It presupposes a *distinction* between poetic and practical language which is never demonstrated. It can easily be shown that deviation routinely occurs in everyday language and in discourses not usually associated with literature. Similarly, in some historical periods, literature was defined by adherence to rather than deviation from literary and linguistic norms. (See work by Halliday, 1971, on the notion of 'deflection' as opposed to deviation as well as pp. 5–6 above.)

Yet the idea of literary language as language which can result in renewal or in a new way of seeing the familiar cannot be as easily discounted as this. But it needs greater theoretical and linguistic precision for the definition to hold and it needs augmentation by complementary definitions.

Another influential Formalist definition is associated with Roman Jakobson. Originally connected with the Russian Formalists, Jakobson subsequently moved to the United States and in a famous paper (Jakobson, 1960) he articulated a theory of poetic language which stressed the *self-referentiality* of poetic language. In his account literariness results when language draws attention to its own status as a sign and when as a result there is a focus on the message for its own sake. Thus, in the examples:

I hate horrible Harry *or* I like Ike

the verbs *hate* and *like* are selected in favour of 'loath' or 'support' because they establish a reinforcing phonaesthetic patterning. The examples cited (the latter is Jakobson's own) demonstrate that poeticality can inhere in such everyday language as political advertising slogans. We have already seen in our section in the previous chapter devoted to 'advertising styles' as well as 1.3 above that advertising languages shares some features such as creative ambiguities, punning, allusion and phonaesthetic patterning which are more usually associated with literary texts. We should note here, however, that Jakobson's definition assumes a distinction between 'poetic' and 'pragmatic' or 'everyday' language,[2] like that of all the Russian and Czech Formalists we have examined.

This emphasis on patterning and on the self-referential nature of literary discourse is valuable, but it should be pointed out that (1) Jakobson's criteria work rather better in respect of poetry rather than prose; (2) he supplies no clear criteria for determining the *degrees* of poeticality or 'literariness' in his examples. He does not seem to want to answer his own question as to what exactly makes some messages more unequivocal examples of works of art than others; (3) Jakobson stresses too much the *production* of effects, neglecting the process the recognition and reception of such effects. The reader or receiver of the message and his or her sociolinguistic position tend to get left out of account.[3]

2.2.1 Speech Acts and Language Functions

Accounts of literary language which attempt more boldly to under-score the role of the reader interacting in a sociolinguistic context with the sender of a verbal message are generally termed *speech act theories* of literary discourse. Speech acts are uses of language which, either directly or indirectly, commit the user or recipient to a particular *action*. Thus, I *promise to pay you £10* is a statement which has a real-world function in obliging the speaker to carry out what has been promised. Where the work of Jakobson and others can be termed 'formalist', these theories are more functionalist in orientation although one of their main proponents, Richard Ohmann, might be better described as a formalist disguised as a functionalist.

Ohmann's basic proposition is that in literature the kinds of conditions which normally attach to speech acts such as insulting, questioning and promising do not obtain. Instead we have quasi- or mimetic speech acts. As Ohmann (1971) puts it:

> A literary work is a discourse whose sentences lack the illocutionary forces that would normally attach to them ... specifically, a literary work purportedly imitates (or reports) a series of speech acts, which in fact have no other existence ... Since the quasi-speech acts of literature are not carrying on the world's business – describing, urging, contract-ing, etc., the reader may well attend to them in a non-pragmatic way and thus allow them to realize their emotive potential ...

Thus, the literary speech act is typically a different kind of speech act – one which involves (on the part of the reader) a suspension of the normal pragmatic functions words may have in order for the reader to regard them as in some way representing or displaying the actions they would normally perform. That is, a promise, or warning or threat by a character in a novel or by a person in a poem cannot be taken as a literal speech act. No one expects it to have any real-world effect. The statement 'come live with me and be my love' is the first line of a poem, not an invitation to the reader.

The notion of a displayed, non-pragmatic fictional speech act certainly goes some way towards explaining why we do not read Blake's 'Tyger' for information about a species of animal or Wordsworth's 'Daffodils' because we are contemplating a career in horiticulture. Or why we cannot be guilty of breach of promise when that promise is in a love poem rather than a love letter. (See Widdowson, 1975.) It also explains to some extent why Gibson's *Decline and Fall of the Roman Empire* is still widely read today or appears on literature syllabuses in numerous university and college English departments, when his statements about the Romans are, as history, either invalid or at least irrelevant.

Ohmann's theory suffers from an essentialist opposition between literary and non-literary which careful consideration does not really bear out. Pratt (1977), for example, has convincingly demonstrated that non-fictional, non-pragmatic, mimetic, disinterested, playful speech acts routinely occur outside what is called literature. Hypothesizing, telling white lies, pretending, playing devil's advocate, imagining, fantasizing, relating jokes or anecdotes, even using illustrations to underscore a point in scholarly argument, are then, by Ohmann's definition, literary. Ohmann's theory does not explain either the 'literary' status of certain travel writing, or Orwell's essays on the Spanish Civil War (and Orwell would have been extremely perturbed for people to read those essays as merely pretended speech acts); nor does it explain how Thomas Kinneally's *Schindler's Ark*, a piece of non-fiction, a 'novel' based on documentary research into real events and characters in a Second World War German concentration camp, won the Booker Prize for 'Literature' in 1982. Neither does it explain why detective novels, science fiction or popular romance (see pp. 99–115) which are fictional are not 'literary'; nor why the prose works of Milton or Donne, which are non-fictional, are literary.[4]

2.2.2 Literariness in Language

In the next section it will be argued that the opposition of literary to non-literary language is an unhelpful one and that the notion of literary language as a yes/no category should be replaced by one which sees literary language as a continuum, a cline of literariness in language use with some uses of language being marked as more literary than others. The argument will follow that advanced in Carter and Nash (1983) and Carter (1988), and illustrative material will be provided by a range of thematically connected texts which describe different aspects of Malaysia. Although the most immediate focus is on text-intrinsic linguistic features, it will not be forgotten that one crucial determinant of a text's literariness is whether the reader *chooses* to read it in a literary way, as a literary text, as it were. For example, Herrnstein-Smith (1978: 67) discusses how the first line of a newspaper article on Hell's Angels can, when arranged in a particular lineation, be read and interpreted for all kinds of different literary meanings:

Most Angels are uneducated.
Only one
Angel in
ten
has
steady work

(opening lines to magazine Report
in *Answer Back* (New York, 1983, p.33).)

See also related discussion in Eagleton (1983:1–17) and Fish (1980:Ch.14).

2.3 Describing Places: Analysis of Styles I

In this section some criteria for specifying literariness in language are proposed. Reference to the criteria will enable us to determine what is prototypical in conventional literary language use, as far as it is understood in its standard, modern average Western conception; in other words, they will assist in determining *degrees* of literariness, thus providing a systematic basis for saying one text is more or less 'literary' than another. The texts about Malaysia used in this discussion are labelled A, B, C and D.

Text A

Watch 'Little Asia' come alive in Kuala Lumpur, then relive the historical past of nearby Malacca.
Kuala Lumpur. Malaysia's capital city with an endless maze of colourful images. The people, the food, the sights, the sounds. All an exotic mix of European and Asian cultures. A pulsating potpourri of Malays, Chinese and Indians.
And there's more. To the south is the historic town of *Malacca*. Here, 158km from *Kuala Lumpur*, you can step into history and relieve the glorious past of this ancient port.
Fish, sail, swim or simply relax on the sandy, sun-kissed beaches of *Port Dickson*, only 100km away from *Kuala Lumpur*.

Or take a scenic drive from the capital city to one of several hill resorts, set in the midst of lush green topical jungles.

And it's all here in Malaysia. The country where great cultures meet, where the diversity of its history, customs and traditions is reflected in the warm hospitality of gentle, friendly Malaysians.

Come share a holiday in this wonderful land. Come to Malaysia. We welcome you now and any time of the year.

IT'S ALL HERE IN MALAYSIA.

Text B

Malaysia, East, part of Federation of Malaysia: inc. Sarawak and Sabah (formerly Brit. N. Borneo); less developed than W. Malaysia; p. concentrated on cst.; hill tribes engaged in hunting in interior; oil major exp., exploration off cst.; separated from W. Malaysia by S. China Sea; a. 77,595 sq. m.; p. (1968) 1,582,000.

Malaysia, Federation of, indep. federation (1963), S. E. Asia; member of Brit. Commonwealth; inc. W. Malaysia (Malaya) and E. Malaysia (Borneo sts. of Sarawak and Sabah); cap. Kuala Lumpur; a. 129,000 sq. m.; p. (1968) 10,455,000.

Malaysia, West (Malaya), part of Federation of Malaysia; consists of wide peninsula, S. of Thailand; most developed in W.; world's leading producer of natural rubber, grown in plantations; oil palm and pineapples also grown; world's leading exporter of tin; nearly half p. Chinese; a. 50,806 sq. m.; p. (1968) 8,899,000.

Text C

Malaysia: Escorted Tours

A Tour of Peninsular Malaysia to Singapore

Day 1 London/Kuala Lumpur

Leave Heathrow in the evening by MAS flight.

Day 2 Kuala Lumpur
Free to explore the old city remains with its domed mosques, Chinese shop houses and bustling markets.

Days 3 & 4 Cameron Highlands

Today you will see something of the daily life of rural Malaysia as you climb up into the cool invigorating Cameron Highlands. Tour the tea estates, flower gardens and see a tin mine before crossing the central highland to the east coast.

Day 5 Tanjong Jara

Enjoy the Kampong (village) life – serene and unhurried; see top spinning and kite making en route to Tanjong Jara.

Day 6 Kuantan

Morning at leisure. After lunch a short drive south brings you do the unspoilt resort of Kuantan characterised by its quaint villages on stilts.

Day 7 Kuantan/Singapore

Continue south to Singapore visiting a rubber plantation on the way. Walk the green carpet of an immaculate estate to see the rubber being 'tapped'. Arrive Singapore late in the evening.

Note
You may choose only one category of accommodation (standard or superior). If your choice is standard hotels, then it should be borne in mind that some accommodation in Malaysia will be simple and unpretentious.

(concocted text based on five Far East travel brochures published in Great Britain in 1988)

Text D

VICTOR CRABBE slept through the *bilal's bang* (inept Persian word for the faint unheeded call), would sleep till the *bangbang* (apt Javanese word) of the brontoid dawn brought him tea and bananas. He slept on the second floor of the old Residency, which overlooked the river.

The river Lanchap gives the state its name. It has its source in deep jungle, where it is a watering-place for a hundred or so little negroid people who worship thunder and can count only up to two. They share it with tigers, hamadryads, bootlace snakes, leeches, pelandoks and the rest of the bewildering fauna of up-stream Malaya. As the Sungai Lanchap winds on, it encounters outposts of more complex culture: Malay villages where the Koran is known, where the prophets jostle with nymphs and tree-gods in a pantheon of unimaginable variety. Here a little work in the paddy-fields suffices to maintain a heliotropic, pullulating existence. There are fish in the river, guarded, however, by crocodile-gods of fearful malignity; coconuts drop or are hurled down by trained monkeys called *beroks;* the durian sheds its rich fetid smell in the season of durians. Erotic pantuns and Hindu myths soothe away the depression of an occasional *accidia*. As the Lanchap approaches the coast a more progressive civilization appears: the two modern towns of Timah and Tahi Panas, made fat on tin and rubber, supporting large populations of Chinese, Malays, Indians, Eurasians, Arabs, Scots,

Christian Brothers, and pale English administrators. The towns echo with trishaw-bells, the horns of smooth, smug American cars, radios blaring sentimental pentatonic Chinese tunes, the morning hawking and spitting of the *towkays*, the call of the East. Where the Lanchap meets the Sungai, Hantu is the royal town, dominated by an Istana designed by a Los Angeles architect, blessed by a mosque as bulbous as a clutch of onions, cursed by a lowering sky and high humidity. This is Kuala Hantu.

Victor Crabbe slept soundly, drawn into that dark world where history melts into myth.

(Anthony Burgess, *Time for a Tiger*)

Medium Dependence   The notion of medium dependence means that the more literary a text the less it will be dependent for its reading on another medium or media. In this respect Text B is dependent on a code or key to abbreviations used and on reference to a map or illustrations (e.g. inc.; indep.; a.; p.; cst.; exp.; sq.;). To this extent it is similar to the newspaper weather forecast (discussed at 1.2.3 above) which also contains codes and abbreviations. To a lesser extent Texts A and C could probably be said to be medium-dependent in that they are, or are likely to be, accompanied by a photograph or by some means of pictorial supplement. By contrast, Text D is dependent only on itself for its 'reading'. It generates a world of internal reference and relies only on its own capacity to project. This is not to suggest that it cannot be determined by external political or social or biographical influences. No text can be so entirely autonomous that it refers only to itself nor so rich that a reader's own experience of the Malaysia it refers to (though, paradoxically, none of the places actually exist – there is no Kuala Hantu, etc.) is sovereign. Its sovereignty is that, relative to the other writing about Malaysia, this text does not head to be supplemented.

Re-registration   The notion of re-registration means that no single word or stylistic feature or register will be barred from admission to a literary context. Registers such as legal language or the language of instructions are recognized by the neat fit between language form and specific function; but any language at all can be deployed to literary effect by the process of re-registration. For example, Auden makes use of bureacratic registers in his poem 'The Unknown Citizen'; wide use of journalistic and historical discourse styles is made in novels such as Salman Rushdie's *Midnight's Children* and *Shame* and in numerous novels by Norman Mailer. This is, of course, not to suggest that certain stylistic or lexical features are not appreciably more 'literary' than others; but such items as 'twain', 'eftsoons', 'azure', 'steed', 'verdure', together with archaic syntactic forms and inversions, belong to a past literary domain. They are associated with what was considered to be appropriately elevated and decorous in poetic discourse and were automatically used as such, losing in the process any contact with a living, current idiom and becoming fossilized and restrictedly 'literary' in the process. Re-registration recognizes that the full unrestricted resources of the language are open to exploitation for literary ends. Text D, for example, exploits the language more normally connected with travel brochure and geography book discourse but re-deploys or re-registers it for particularly subtle literary purposes. Here the guide book style is regularly subverted, an ironic undercutting serving to suggest that the conventional geographical or historical presentation of the state is comically inappropriate to a world which is much more heterogeneous and resistant to external ordering or classification.

Interaction of Levels: Semantic Density   This is one of the most important of defining criterial categories. The notion here is that a text that is perceived as resulting from the additive interaction of several super-imposed codes and levels is recognized as more literary than a text where there are fewer levels at work, or where they are present but do not interact. There are different linguistic levels at work in Texts A, B and C but in D, we have a degree of semantic density which is different from that in the other texts and which results from an interactive patterning at the levels of syntax, lexis, phonology and discourse. The most prominent of these patterns is *contrast*; contrasts exist between a simple syntax of, variably, subject, predicate, complement (*The river Lanchap gives the state its name; This is Kuala Hantu* – both of which act as a kind of frame for the first two paragraphs), and a more complexly patterned syntax involving greater clausal complexity through parti-cipial and subordinate clauses, more embedding and simply longer sentences. There are contrasts, too, on the level of lexis between words of *Greek* and *Anglo-Saxon* derivation (*accidia, unimaginable, pantheon, dominated, brontoid, progressive* as opposed to *clutch, hurled, sheds, smug, fat*) which is simultaneously a contrast between mono- and polysyllabic, formal and informal lexical items. The contrast is carried further into semantic oppositions marked in the items *inept/apt, lowering sky/high humidity, blessed/cursed, soothe away/blare* and the opposition of *East* and *West* in 'smug *American* cars'/'*Los Angeles* architect' and 'call of the *East*' and 'pentatonic tunes'.

  Grammar, lexis and semantics are further complemented by effects at the level of phonology. Here the plosive 'b' and 'p' are predominant patterns (overlapping notably with the more formal and 'ancient' lexical items, e.g. *bulbous, pentatonic, pullulating, brontoid, pantheon, paddy-fields, pantuns, prophets*); but they exist in contrast with an almost equally predominant pattern of 's' sounds (*second, source, snakes, sleep, shave, tigers,* etc.). This interaction of levels, particularly in the form of contrasts, serves to symbolize or represent the unstated content of the passage. For example, one of the possible functions of these linguistic contrasts it to underscore the contrast between Victor Crabbe, an idealistic colonial teacher, and the alien ex-colonial territory in which he is placed; but between these contrasting worlds there also subsists a less clearly marked, more heterogeneous reality to which Crabbe is directly exposed.

Text D is, however, not the only passage in which an interactive patterning of different linguistic levels is foregrounded. Text A contains many such features from the phonetic symbolism of:

Fish, sail, swim or simply relax on the
sandy, sun-kissed beaches of Port Dickson

or the metaphoric and phonetic constellation of:

A pulsating potpourri of Malays, Chinese and Indians

or the syntactic and graphological self-referential deviation of:

IT'S ALL HERE IN MALAYSIA

or the parallelisms of:

relive the historical past
relive the glorious past

and the contrasts between past and present figured in the juxtaposition of present and past, Malacca and Kuala Lumpur, the past tense and the eternal present of moodless clauses (*The people, the food, the sights, the sounds*).

Across this spectrum of texts about Malaysia it is clear that where different levels of language multiply interact there is a potential reinforcement of meaning. More than one possible meaning is thereby represented or symbolized although any activation of meanings must be dependent on a reader whose literary competence permits 'reasonable' correlations of linguistic forms and semantic functions. In this respect Text D can be demonstrated to have greater semantic density than Text B, for example. The interesting case is Text A which, as we have seen, contains an interaction of levels. The existence of these texts illustrates one aspect of a cline of relative 'literariness' and enables us to begin to talk about one text being more or less literary than another.

Polysemy The main point in this section is one which has been widely discussed: the existence of polysemy in literary texts. In terms of this criterion of literariness Text B, by being restrictively and necessarily monosemic, sacrifices any immediate claims to be literary. The monosemy of the text is closely connected with the need to convey clear, retrievable and unambiguous information. This end is served by a number of means: the formulaic code of the headings, for example *Malaysia, Federation of;* the many abbreviations employed; the geographical and numerical explicitness and the extreme economy of presentation (giving as much information in as little space as possible). There is no indication that the text should be read in more than one way although the compositional skills which go into entries such as this in encyclopaedias and geography text books should not be dismissed. Polysemy is a regular feature of advertisements although there are no particular examples of this in Text A, which is perhaps best referred to as *plurisignifying* rather than polysemic in that it shares the capacity of many advertisements to be memorable, to promote intertextual relations and to provide a verbal pleasure which can result in frequent citation and embedding in discourses other than that for which it was originally intended. (See Moeran, 1984, especially his discussion of the Heineken beer advertisements.) Text D is, however, polysemic (in that individual lexical items carry more than one meaning) *and* plurisignifying. Polysemic lexical items in Text D can be: *call* of the East (actual sound and longing for); *smooth* . . . American cars (surface metal and, by extension, the personality of their owners) and *dark* world (lack of light and mysterious, uncivilized, etc.). And so on.

One characteristic of the polysemic text is then that its lexical items do not stop automatically at their first interpretant; denotations are always potentially available for transformation into connotations, contents are never received for their own sake but rather as a sign vehicle for something else.

Displaced Interaction The notion of displaced interaction serves to help differentiate the direct speech acts of Text C, in which readers will, if they take the advertised holiday, actually perform the actions described in the sequence depicted in the itinerary itself, from the more indirect or displaced speech acts transmitted in Text D. In D the reader is asked to perform no particular action except that of a kind of mental accompaniment to the text in the course of which he or she interprets or negotiates what the message means. The meaning may change on re-reading, of course; but this is unlikely to be the case with Text C or B, although in the case of Text A there is some scope for taking it in more than one way and this is a function of its potential literariness. Displaced interaction allows meanings to emerge indirectly and obliquely. What is conventionally regarded as 'literary' is likely to be a text in which the context-bound interaction between author and reader is more deeply embedded or displaced.

Discourse Patterning Criteria for literariness discussed so far have focused mostly on effects at sentence level. At the suprasentential level of discourse effects can be located which can help us further to differentiate degrees of literariness. Space prohibits detailed analysis at this level so the point will have to be underlined with reference to one example.

In Text D patterning at the level of discourse occurs by virtue of repetition of the particulars of place, which is concentrated in the long second paragraph. Reference to the river and town is made as follows:

> The river Lanchap gives the state its name.
> As the Sungai Lanchap winds on . . .
> As the Lanchap approaches the coast . . .
> Where the Lanchap meets the Sungai, Hantu is the royal town . . .
> This is Kuala Hantu

One of the possible effects of cross-sentential repetition here, reinforced by repeated syntactic patterns of clause and tense, is to enact the lingering presence and progress of the river and to provide for the appearance of the town as if the reader were actually engaged in a journey through the jungle towards the town. The short focusing sentence *This is Kuala Hantu* is thus discoursally interconnected with a number of related patterns out of which it has grown organically and, in terms of the content of the passage, actually grows. Although there is a related patterning around the word *Malaysia* in other texts (e.g. A and B, especially A) the discourse patterning does not reinforce or represent content to the same extent. (For further discussion see Hasan, 1971; de Beaugrande and Dressler, 1981: 165–61.)

2.4 Describing Cars: Analysis of Styles II

In this section extracts from four text styles are explored with reference to clines of literariness. The passages are connected by a single theme and like the texts at 2.3 present descriptions of different aspects of a single topic, here that of a motor car.

Passage A

Commence by replacing the hub-bearing outer race (33), Fig. 88, which is a press fit and then drop the larger bearing (32) into its outer member followed by oil seal (31), also a press fit, with lip towards bearing. Pack lightly with grease.

If the hub is to be fitted to a vehicle equipped with disc brakes, a concentric ring of Prestic 5686 must be applied between the shield and axle face. On hubs with drum brakes, apply sealing compounds between shield and back-plate.

Fit hub (28) to back axle (1) and fit the inner member of the outer race, also greased. Replace the inner nut (34) and tighten to remove all end-float. If discs are fitted check run-out. Slacken inner nut two holes and check end-float (0.004–0.006 in.) using a dial gauge.

The most prominent feature of this passage is that the lexical items are only effective in conjunction with another medium, that is, the technical drawing referred to as Fig. 88. It is generally apparent that the text has to do with the fitting of a hub assembly to the axle of a car; but its details cannot be properly understood without the accompanying diagram. Such 'medium dependence' (see 2.3) is not a characteristic of literary language, though there are certainly special cases (for example, the dramatic text, the film commentary) in which a verbal process is linked with another channel of communication. One of the ways in which such cases differ from the present example is that in them words function descriptively and inferentially, rather than directively. This text implies the relationship of the instructor and the instructed. It specifies performances and in that way is markedly non-literary. Literary language is sometimes axiomatic, carrying directives in the form of moral injunctions, but it never directs us to perform particular actions in current response to the text.[5]

In these two respects, then, Passage A lacks the property of literariness: it depends on a parallel, non-verbal, form of communication, and it treats the reader as an agent responding to a directive process. It is also unliterary in its restrictive *monosemy*, that is, its use of precise technical terms which are valid only in special application by a special type of audience. Some of these terms, like *end-float* and *run-out*, must be obscure to all but the motor mechanic; others, for example, *hub-bearing outer race, oil seal, axle face,* are difficult in the absence of the diagram with which they have an ostensive (= 'What's this called?') relationship. This brings us back to the question of 'medium dependence'. The uninformed reader of a workshop manual can struggle to come to grips with it by studying the text in relation to the diagram, and the diagram in relation to the text. In literary discourse, by contrast, there are vital and increasingly complex relationships between words; as we read, we try to follow these semantic networks and create in our own minds the experiential pattern they imply. This is a difficulty of a different order from that of discovering the meaning of a set of technical terms.

Passage B

1   The Company will indemnify the Insured against damage to or loss of the Insured Vehicle (and its accessories and spare parts while thereon while in the Insured's private garage).
Provided always that in the event of damage to or the total destruction or total loss of the Insured Vehicle the liability of the company under this Clause shall be limited to the market value of the Insured Vehicle immediately before such damage, destruction or loss or the Insured's estimate of the value of the Insured Vehicle (as last advised to the Company), whichever is the less.
If to the knowledge of the Company the Insured Vehicle is the subject of a hire purchase agreement any payment for damage to or loss of the Insured Vehicle (which damage or loss is not made to the vehicle by repair, reinstatement, or replacement) shall be made to the owner described therein whose receipt shall be a full and final discharge to the Company in respect of such damage or loss.

Here is another piece of ulitarian prose, like Passage A, and as devoid of literary resonances. Yet, by examining its presuppositions and its management of language, we may take a step towards the definition of literariness. This text supports itself, through its own verbal elaborations, and although it presupposes knowledge of a certain type of social convention (the exchanging of contracts) it at least does not rely on another medium or on the co-presence of some extra-textual object. It is syntactically elaborate; every sentence is stacked with co-ordinate and dependent constructions. It is also lexically elaborate, with abstractions designed to cover all lines of meaning and obviate most possibilities of misunderstanding.

Here, as in A, we have 'working language' appropriate to a special register, but one significant point of contrast presents itself. In A, vocabulary items are concrete, specific, and semantically disjunct, that is, each makes its own meaning without entering into complementary relationship with others. In B, by comparison, the items of vocabulary are companions or complementary elements in a semantic pattern. The Company, the Insured, the Vehicle, are characters in the document's unfolding 'plot'; while items such as *damage, loss* or *destruction* establish, through their communities and diversities of meaning, a broad central theme. Such 'plotting' of the vocabulary suggests analogies with literary process, though there are reasons (discussed below) why in B this elaborate cohesion does not achieve the character of 'literariness'.

In one particular sense, B is the least literary of all passages presented in this section. The feeling of speech is suppressed; and hence we lose all sense of the text as an interaction. It does not say 'listen, let me tell you'; it records a transaction – the Company promises to pay the Insured. One symptom of this transactional character is that the lexicon is designedly monosemic. Important terms like Company, Insured, and Insured Vehicle, are accorded proper-noun status (markedly by the initial capitals), having been defined elsewhere in the document. Where the vocabulary is elaborated (as in *repair, reinstatement* or *replacement*), this is done in order to specify the semantic components of a broad concept (for example, made good), rather than to institute some dynamic, text-informing process of branchinig associations and psychological connections. The elaboration of the vocabulary, noted above as a mark of 'literariness', is therefore literary here in semblance only. It has the 'analytic' elaboration of the thesaurus, which lists synonyms and equivalents, not the 'organic' elaboration of a poem or a piece of prose fiction, in which items of language progressively gather meaning in relationship to each other.

For these reasons (among others) B lacks the property of 'literariness'. This need not mean, however, that its language could never be available for literary purposes. In our search for emphasis and variation in style, we make continual borrowings from familiar registers (for example, the language of sport, the language of the theatre, the language of commerce). One consequence of this is a traffic in idioms and figurative expressions that gradually lose the colouring of their derivation and become standard turns of phrase; we may speak of being covered or securing something at a premium without being more than vaguely conscious that these phrases belong to the language of the broker. A second, perhaps more interesting, consequence of this 'register borrowing' is the restructuring of technical terms so that they enter into new relationships and acquire a special symbolic value in the context of the literary work. The crime novel *Double Indemnity* (made into a film with the same name) had for its plot a variation on the well-worn theme of murder for the insurance money. Accordingly, its title might be read simply as a technical term denoting a certain type of policy agreement. Yet, for the audience, it is bound to mean much more than this; the significance of indemnity and double is conditioned by the particular circumstances of the plot. The technical term acquires a new relevance; it is, so to speak, re-registered as an element in the language of fiction.

Such re-registrations are by no means uncommon. It would be possible, for example, to re-register the vocabulary of Passage B, by placing it in a somewhat different syntactic environment:

> The Insured found himself trembling uncontrollably.
> Where was the Vehicle? Lost? Damaged? Destroyed?
> What would the Company do when they heard? Would he
> be indemnified this time? Or would the liability
> fall on him?

This may illustrate how precise, functional monosemy might be transmuted into vaguely symbolic literary polysemy. It is possible in this case because the vocabulary of Passage B, precise and monosemic though it certainly is, consists none the less of abstractions and superordinates, that is, of generalized terms that can be related, if we so wish, to an altered set of implications and subordinates. Thus, Company, which implies 'board', 'Chairman', 'management', 'sales staff', 'shareholders', etc., can be semantically reconstructed so as to imply 'government', 'hierarchy', 'junta', 'party', 'overseas', and so forth; and Insured may be analogously reconstructed, to entail the meanings 'citizen', 'servant', 'slave', 'worker', etc. The imposition of a new thesaurus entry, by blending or realigning registers, is a typical literary act.

Passage C

> Have you had the great Sunday car washing ritual?
> Have you got better things to do with a car than run round it with a rag,
> and show it off to your neighbours?
> Then the Maxi is for you.
> Because the Maxi was made for doing things.
> In a Maxi, you can run your wife and kids around in real comfort.
> Or do 500 miles in a day without trouble, and save on your fuel bills.

And if you have to take the odd pram, chicken coop or chest of drawers
with you, you can do that, too.
Just drop the rear seat flat and slide it in through the wide fifth door at
the back.
In the front, you've got two fully reclining seats.
Which will turn into a full size double bed, should you need it.
You're not short of pulling power either. With a proven 1,485 cc.
overhead cam transverse engine, a five-speed gear box and our famous
front-wheel drive.

At this point in the cline, the quality of literariness begins to be more
evident. Passage C has some points in common with the 'functional'
texts that precede it, but it also makes important linkages with the
novelist's language of D below.

Consider first the layout of the text. The line-by-line presentation is
in some respects merely functional, a visual device that makes for easy
reading and fulfils the purposes of salesmanship by giving separate
weight to successive points or recommendations. This layout,
however, has an additional and perhaps more important aim: it
'scores', i.e. suggests the phonetic contours of, a dialogue or speech
event in which the reader is the silent partner. The reader observes
while the writer persuasively demonstrates. This persuasive function
accounts for some notable features in the grammar of the text, for
example, the direct address to the reader through the second person
pronoun, the use of questions, and the typographical interruptions
(part of the quasi-colloquial 'scoring') that separate subordinate from
principal clauses, for example 'In the front you've got two fully
reclining seats. Which will turn into a full size double bed, should you
need it'. The syntax becomes expressive, through ellipses and
deletions that bring subordinate elements into thematic focus (for
example, 'Then the Maxi is for you').

As with many 'literary' evocations of speech, the apparent
casualness is suspect. There is evidence of a conscious design, not only
in the syntax but also in the rhythms of the passage, for example:

Have you got
              better things to do   with a car
    than
              run round it   with a rag
    and
              show it off   to your neighbours?

The cadencing of the prepositional phrases (*with a car, with a rag, to your
neighbours*) can hardly be accidental; nor, surely, are we meant to
overlook the phrase-contouring alliterations ('run round it with a

rag'). Clearly, the sound of the text is important – or rather, it is part
of the copywriter's intention that we should in some sense 'perform'
the text, not necessarily by speaking it aloud, but at least by rehearsing
it inwardly. Thus rehearsed, it suggests a quasi-conversational process
(someone talks to us, asking questions, giving directives) and also a
quasi-poetic pattern of rhythmic phrases and phonetic echoes
(someone recites to us). It is worth noting that the 'recital'
characteristics are less evident as the piece moves towards its
conclusion.

There is, furthermore, something like a poetic complexity in the
vocabulary, typified by the polysemic game which the writer plays
with the expression *run (a)round*. This occurs at two points, the first
instance being in the second line of the text, in the clause *run round it
with a rag* (i.e. 'clean it'). We note the alliterative framing of the
construction; we note also the ironic understatement, the ambivalence
of *run* (quick and easy? long and strenuous?), the humorous
incongruity of the expression, in the context of the preceding *ritual* (to
which it is alliteratively bonded). The reader, we additionally note, is
expected to know something about British cultural conventions; to
share in the banter of the text, he must know that on Sunday, the day
of rest, the day of churchgoing (ritual), the English are in the habit of
washing their cars, in a quasi-religious zeal for respectability. An
expression like *run round it with a rag* is thus a point of convergence for
several expressive lines; alliteration, ambiguity, allusiveness, all come
to a focus in one deceptively off-hand phrase. But the game does not
end there. Presently the copywriter introduces a teasingly echoic
construction: *you can run your wife and kids around in real comfort*. There is,
of course, a grammatical distinction here, in that 'run around' is a
phrasal verb (as contrasted with the verb plus preposition in *run +
round*), and is also a transitive verb, taking an object and expressing a
goal-directed agency. The meaning of *run* is now 'convey rapidly', and
the beneficiaries of this 'running' are not *your neighbours*, to whom the
results of your labours are pointlessly shown, but *your wife and kids*, who
are carried *in real comfort*. Discernibly, if perhaps not very ambitiously,
the text puts up the kind of challenge that may meet us on any page of
a short story or a novel: to perceive the implications consistently and
intricately developing with the verbal pattern of the text.

A further characteristic of Passage C is its idiomatic span, which is
fairly broad, ranging from the casual note of conversion (*have you
had . . .?*) to the formality of documented language (*should you need it*).
Its norm, however, is the casual/colloquial: *the Maxi is for you, save on
your fuel bills, the odd pram, you've got, you're not short of*. These suggest a

familiar warmth of address towards the reader, a species of *tutoiement* that goes along with the *you* pronoun and the carefully 'scored' sentences. Technical monosemy is restricted to the final sentence, and even in that context there is an element of literary play, with the adjectival counterpointing of the formal-documentary *proven* (*a proven 1,485cc.* etc.) and the informal-colloquial *famous* (*our famous front wheel drive*). What is generally clear is that the text has two objects: to engage the reader personally, and having done that, to supply 'information' about a product. This duality of procedure is something not apparent in texts such as A and B. We recognize it as a characteristic of publicity and propaganda; we may also perceive affinities (albeit crude) with the organization of literary language that offers the possibility of 'reading at more than one level'.

Passage D

> A minute later Dixon was sitting listening to a sound like the ringing of a cracked door-bell as Welch pulled at the starter. That died away into a trebel humming that seemed to involve every component of the car. Welch tried again; this time the effect was of beer-bottles jerkily belaboured. Before Dixon could do more than close his eyes he was pressed firmly back against the seat, and his cigarette, still burning, was cuffed out of his hand into some interstice of the floor. With a tearing of gravel under the wheels the car burst from a standstill towards the grass verge, which Welch ran over briefly before turning down the drive. They moved towards the road at walking pace, the engine maintaining a loud lowing sound which caused a late group of students, most of them wearing the yellow and green College scarf, to stare after them from the small covered-in space beside the lodge where sports notices were posted.

Passage D does not need to be analysed in great detail, since the basic terms of discussion have been established and readers can extend them to this extract for themselves. The basic point to underline is that attention to the fine detail of linguistic organization here guarantees a place for this text further along the *cline of literariness*. It involves recognition that the lexical items deployed are more *polysemic* in that they are selected as much for the resonance they create, the associations they produce and the interaction they generate semantically (in conjunction with syntactic and phonetic contouring) within, across and beyond the text itself. Examples might be 'beer bottles jerkily belaboured' which depends crucially on complementary phonetic and syntactic patterning, and in the case of 'belaboured' produced a shifting set of transitions between what are, for these readers at least, colloquial items (*jerkily, cuff, lowing*) and more formal

terms (appropriate in the context of literary/academic vocabulary)
such as *involve, component, belaboured, maintaining..* It is also worth
recording, too, how the metaphors and analogies in the text are
organically related by belonging to the same semantic domain of
sound:

> a sound like the ringing of a cracked door bell
> died away into a treble humming
> beer bottles jerkily belaboured
> a tearing of gravel
> maintaining a loud lowing sound

The resulting semantic density and the creation of satiric/ironic effect
allows more to be conveyed than the description of a car being started
and driven from a college courtyard. There is little restrictive
monosemy, the text acquires a degree of sovereignty (or 'medium
independence') and words are not being held, however creatively and
skilfully, within any one domain or register, nor within a direct
author/reader channel of communication.

2.5   STYLE AND IDEOLOGY: THE INTERESTED WRITER

We have commented in the previous chapter on the relationship
between language and ideology and we have undertaken preliminary
discussion of some ways in which ideologies are mediated through
particular linguistic choices and patternings. (See 1.4.1.) However, so
far our discussions of literariness in this chapter have focused on
text-intrinsic features and we have not considered the wider social and
cultural contexts into which all such texts have to be inserted. Our
argument is that literariness is primarily a linguistic and textual
property and that it is valuable to be able to recognize such properties
of texts. But we would not want to suggest either that our analysis is
disinterested or that examining texts along clines of literariness means
that the texts exist in a vacuum, in isolation from the sociolinguistic
conditions under which they are produced and are read. There is
insufficient space for detailed analysis but in returning to questions of
ideology here we give particular attention to the *interests* of readers and
writers. The argument in this sub-section is that our interests as
readers are in proportion to the extent of our investment in the texts.
Investment in a channel of communication between a writer and a
reader is unlikely to be a disinterested one or one concerned merely
with the neutral transmission of a message. Writers and readers expect
returns. We begin with the investments of a writer.

Writers are concerned in varying degrees with: first of all persuading readers to pick up the text and to read it (and in this respect such non-linguistic factors as cover design, typography and pictorial effects can be crucial); second, they are concerned with prompting readers to act in accordance with a set of behaviours whether directly or indirectly enjoined. For example, readers should be able to follow car maintenance instructions in a clear step-by-step sequence without discovering ambivalences; or they should be able to act to buy a car or to take a holiday without inspecting the nature of the product too closely. In particular, many writers want to gain a reader's attention and to persuade him to action or to a particular view of things *without* disturbing a routinized commonsense view of the world. They want to represent the world as essentially unproblematic, as a locus for an untroubled transaction or a tension-free transition from one place or one set of events to another. The reader might need to be persuaded but this cannot usually be done by displacing the reader from a secure place in the normal scheme of things. If readers are to do anything then it has to be in their interests.

For example, in the case of Text C in 2.3 above (the extract from a brochure advertising touring holidays in Malaysia – which, in fact, closely accords with the text conventions of an itinerary) the language used serves both to promote constant reassurance and to offer positive evaluations of Malaysia and of the anticipated sequence of events in that country. In particular, lexical items which might have possibly pejorative connotations in other contexts are negotiated into assuming distinctly positive values:

> *Quaint* villages on stilts
> The *unspoilt* resort of Kuantan
> Kampong (village) life – *serene and*
> *unhurried*
> Accommodation in Malaysia will be
> *simple and unpretentious*
> . . . you climb up into the *cool*
> *invigorating* Cameron Highlands

This process is paralleled in Text A in 2.3:

> *lush green tropical* jungles
> *scenic* drive
> *sandy, sun-kissed* beaches
> *the glorious past* of this ancient port

The adjectives here gloss over or obscure the potentially 'uncivilized' by (Western Europe standards) nature of life in Malaysia, the possibly slow and primitive level of services, the debilitating heat on the plains (as opposed to the Highlands), the dangers to health for those unaccustomed to 'tropical' encounters, or the succession of bloody colonial wars which mark the 'glorious past' of Malacca. Even the rubber plantations offer the 'domestic' comfort of a *green carpet.*

In Text A the particular cultural character of Malaysia, constituted by the different races which make up the population of the country and which is a regular source of disturbance, is referred to. But cultural and ethnic differences are harmonized into alliterative euphonies such as:

a pulsating potpourri of Malays, Chinese and Indians

an exotic mix of European and Asian cultures

an endless maze of colourful images

We should note, too, how assumptions, awkward questions, ideologies are kept in place and undisturbed by the very selection from the stylistic options open to the writer. The reader is subjected to the role of passive spectator of this untroubled and comforting inventory of impressions. The sequence of verbless clauses serve, as it were, to leave the pattern of imagistic impressions unanchored to anything. They do not occupy a dynamic of relation, process or action. Instead, an almost dream-like quality is imparted to the images. The picture can be maintained by acting to purchase the holiday. The 'rewarding experience' offered in the advertisements is there to be bought.

In Text A the picture of general, free-floating pleasure is deliberately left without any specific focus. It works as a generalized appeal to all who may be interested in a visit to Malaysia. The specific holiday in Text C or the appeal to a particular car in Text A (2.4, p.43) are targetted in a more individualized way; and this is realized through a greater density of personal pronouns which directly address the reader and foster a greater sense of personal involvement. In Passage C (the advertising for the Maxi) the *you* is represented particularly precisely, membershipped, as it were, as belonging to a specific gender and to a specific social group:

You can run your wife and kids around
in real comfort

And if you have to take the odd pram,
chicken coop or chest of drawers with
you, you can do that, too.

Have you had the great Sunday car washing
ritual?

The identity of the addressee here is constructed as male, married with children, likely to be land-owning or self-employed (how many of us regularly have to transport a chicken coop?), and to be more probably engaged in an agnostic Sunday occupation of cleaning the car than attending the 'ritual' of a church service. The inherent sexism of the appeal makes no concession to a woman purchasing or owning such a car. With a few limited exceptions this advertisement for cars is one of many which are male-gender, middle-class and macho-oriented (note the sexual innuendo in the juxtaposition of *pulling power* – and its associations of sexual conquest – with the *double bed*). It is in the interests of many writers to use language to frame the reader socially and ideologically. It is clearly in the interests of the writer of this piece of advertising copy to construct an image of an ideal reader for this passage who is so deeply enmeshed in male, middle-class ideologies that the very position passes unnoticed, or unresisted by its readers. The text is in one sense successful simply because it does not question commonsense or 'natural' images and their attendant reading positions. The text reproduces existing ideologies by not questioning the fact that men normally buy cars, that men are attracted to certain qualities and behaviours associated with a car and that men will be the most likely readers of such texts.

The car advertisement here maintains an effective balance between a specific appeal to buy and the construction of a generalized convenience and indulgence. Against such a background the (male) reader is reinforced in the security of a designated social, cultural and ideological role. However, in the case of the particular holiday described in Text C 2.3 (the holiday itinerary) it is necessary that neither reader nor writer feels the complete absence of restraint or obligation proposed in the more generalized invitation of Text A (2.3). Almost buried in a Note are a set of prescriptions which attempt to modulate the perspective of Malaysia and begin to suggest the outlines of a contract between writer and reader. A sequence of modal verbs inserts qualifications (*it should be borne in mind*), provisions (*accommodation in Malaysia will be simple and unpretentious*) and restrictions (*you may choose only one category of accommodation*). The modals in other parts of the text (e.g. Today you *will* see) regiment in accordance with the itinerary; but they do not regulate.

Even greater restraints and controls are exercised in the text which is extracted from a car insurance document (Text B, 2.4, p. 44). Here the interests of the writer are served less by personalized address or socio-cultural membershipping than by an impersonal transmissive mode. In our discussion of this passage on p.44 we commented as follows: 'every sentence is stacked with co-ordinate and dependent constructions. It is also lexically elaborate, with abstractions designed to cover all lines of meaning and obviate most possibilities of misunderstanding.' Re-reading the text in the context of social and ideological practices might lead us to another interpretation of this text's design. It has the designs *on* its readers which serve to obscure and conceal as much as to clarify. The text appears to cover every contingency and eventuality; on the surface, the reader is given reassurance that he/she is 'covered' and protected. But it is in the interests of the insurance company not to over-specify and to allow a deliberate undertow of indeterminacy. This generates sufficient space for legal disputation and for alternative readings of this document. In other words, if the language is a little vague in places, the text is open to interpretation. It attempts literally to 'obviate *most* possibilities of misunderstanding' and to 'cover' most if not all lines of meaning. For example, in the second paragraph the syntactic and lexical elaborations do not make it clear whether the Insured or the Company are responsible for determining the market value of the car in the event of total destruction or loss. It is likely that the liability of the Company is limited to its *own* assessment of the car's value unless the owner undervalues his/her own car in which case the Company is empowered to pay the lower figure without informing the Insured. We invite readers to put their own interpretation on this particular paragraph:

> Provided always that in the event of damage to or the total destruction or total loss of the Insured Vehicle the liability of the Company under this Clause should be limited to the market value of the Insured Vehicle immediately before such damage, destruction or loss or the Insured's estimate of the value of the Insured Vehicle (as last advised to the company), whichever is the less.

Power is knowledge. Here power is invested in the legal copywriter who has sufficient knowledge of legal procedure not to encourage such readings between the lines. The suppression of agency in the decision-making process concerning estimates of value (that is, who decides?), together with a syntactic elaboration which appears to allow for all possibilities, subject the reader to a kind of acquiescence. This acquiescent reading position is based on inadequate access to knowledge and information.

Among many other possible interpretations of the language of this paragraph we might conclude by asking how *total* is a 'total' loss or a 'total' destruction. Is there such a thing perhaps as a 'partial' loss? What is the liability of the Company in the event of partial destruction? How are estimates of value made in such circumstances? Once again, the main agents in the decision-making process are those with the power which knowledge of the law accords and the Insured has to remain a mere subject in the legal kingdom, the extent of the subject's challenge limited to the extent of the interpretive power he/she is able to or can afford to muster.

This legal text exerts its own form of control. It has greater controlling provenance than the holiday itinerary. It is a control which keeps must subjects acquiescent and ideologies intact. The contract is one which owners of motor vehicles have no choice but to enter as they are legally required to be insured.

So far, we have drawn no equations between the extent of a text's literariness and its relationship with societal power structures and ideologies. It is not within our analytical remit to analyse (in this book) the nature of such complex relationships. But it would defeat our general argument if literary texts or, to put it more appropriately, texts possessing according to our definitions the greater degrees of literariness, were left out of account in this section. In any case, Text C in 2.3 (p.37) – the extract from Anthony Burgess's *Time for a Tiger* – is an especially interesting and illuminating instance.

The linguistic design of this passage operates to order the world in a different manner from those passages we have examined in this section so far. As we noted in our commentaries on this passage (pp. 38–39 and pp. 40–42) one of the effects of the passage is to use text conventions to frame the description of Kuala Hantu as if the style were that associated with a tourist's guide to the region. Climatic, topographical, botanical, agronomic and historical information is blended together and supported by lexical items which have the tenor of academic text books (e.g. *heliotropic, pantheon, pullulating*) and which impart due seriousness to the text casting the reader in the role of the serious explorer rather than the casually interested tourist. However, the writer's aim appears to be to present a picture of Kuala Hantu which is not the expected or conventional portrait. Instead, the even surface is fractured into a more heterogeneous discourse. As discussed above (p. 39) this is in part realized by a mixing of different stylistic levels several of which exist in contrast or opposition to one another.

For example,

Simple syntax	v.	elaborate syntax
simple lexis	v.	complex lexis
Anglo-Saxon-based words	v.	Greek-derived words

are reinforced by semantic contrasts such as

East	v.	West
blessed	v.	cursed
lowering sky	v.	high humidity

And so on.

We have already suggested that one possible function of such patterning of language is to suggest a contrast of realities between Victor Crabbe's experience and the kind of experience awaiting him in the Malaysian interior. It is not a settled world, though on the surface it may appear so. It is a world on the verge of breaking with the colonial past of which Crabbe is a representative, a teacher teaching English within an education system imported by British colonial powers. Crabbe's insertion into this world (symbolically, perhaps, he has not woken to it yet) is not unproblematic. His encounter with Malaysia is not smooth and trouble-free. The ideologies he represents do not provide the means by which cultural difference can be harmonized. Anthony Burgess's interests are not invested in keeping things the way they are; instead he seeks to work at the interface of contrast and difference to explore and question the extent to which existing controlling ideologies might be supported or modified or challenged. It is not an easy progress. Even the name Victor Crabbe (Victor = signalling power and glory; Crabbe = signalling slow sideways movement) is not auspicious. The linguistic fracture and the resulting stylistic unevenness projects the reader, at this opening juncture of the novel, into a fictional world in which underlying social and cultural practices are subjected to scrutiny. Consequently, as the novel progresses it is likely that readers will be encouraged to view realities from alternative perspectives, to uncover rather than to cover and to probe *beneath* the surface of things.

We have returned to our discussion of the defamiliarizing role of literary texts at 2.2. We might conclude by suggesting that a further mark of literariness is the critical and defamiliarizing conjunction of style and ideology. Instead of reproducing existing ideologies, it could be said to be a mark of literary texts that they serve to provoke readers to penetrate the ideological formations which control the ways we think, feel and behave. Ideology is nearer the surface in some texts than others although it is not necessarily any more easily uncovered. As we have seen, this may be precisely because such texts present such an obvious and commonsense picture of the way things are that the picture goes unchallenged and unresisted. In texts such as *Time for a Tiger* the reader has to work harder, to recognize the role of language in fracturing a commonly understood representation of things and to accommodate the discomforting message that all is not as even or as unproblematic or as 'obviously' true as it may seem.

2.5.1 The Interested Reader

A legitimate objection to the discussion in sections 2.3 and 2.4 above is that both the role and the relative position of *the reader vis-à-vis* the text has been underplayed. One major problem is that of regular agent-deletion in discussions of the reading process; and the above discussion is not innocent of such a practice either. By agent-deletion is meant the use of syntactic constructions such as: *The text signals that . . .; The text can be read as representing,* or *The semantic patterning here reinforces.* The agent performing the reading, that is *the reader,* is deleted here so that it appears the text is reading itself. The reader needs to be reinstated. It is even more important not to forget that any reader will be located in a particular social, political, and historical environment.

The study of the reader and the reading process is now in the forefront of research in a number of disciplines.[6] But a number of unanswered questions do need to be highlighted. For example: to what extent do all readers perform the same kinds of operation when they read? do they read more intensively at particular times? to what extent might the kind of attention readers bring to a text depend on how they are *taught* to read? In this latter respect, the role of institutions such as colleges and schools can be especially powerful. The French structuralist literary theorist Roland Barthes remarked that 'Literature is what gets taught'. By this he means that literature is whatever is taught as literature in educational contexts; by the same token, learning to read literary texts is being taught to read pre-selected texts in a particular way. It is important to recognize that one of our interests in this book is in helping students of English style to read texts intensively and to use analysis of language as a basis for interpreting these texts and for understanding, and, if necessary, resisting their underlying ideologies. Other analysts of texts will have other interests and priorities.

The fact that the attention brought to bear on a text depends on the reader's own interests can be further illustrated by the kind of interpreting activity which 'readers' engage in when reading texts in particular circumstances. For example, consider how carefully suicide notes are read in order to extract every possible ounce of information or implication. Or consider how in elections or at times of crisis statements by politicians are subjected to especial scrutiny. Even the statement 'no comment' can be read as meaning more than it says. The point to underline here is that readers are interested parties willing in certain sociolinguistic contexts to do interpretive work on all kinds of texts if it is necessary or appropriate for them to do so. Readers may not be so powerful as writers who, as we have seen, have the means to register certain meanings while suppressing others; readers may be bracketed out of discussions of the reading process; but readers are not entirely passive and they always have a choice of resisting texts, particularly if they learn ways of seeing through language.

2.6 CONCLUSIONS

The points covered in this chapter lead us to conclude:

1 That literary language is not special or different in that any formal feature termed 'literary' can be found in other discourses. (See also: Fish, 1980: 97–111; Fowler, 1981; Halliday, 1983.) The 'literary' does not exist without the 'non-literary' and draws constantly on 'non-literary' sources of supply by means of a process of re-registration.

2 That literary language *is* different from other language uses in that it functions differently. some of the differences can be demarcated with reference to criteria such as: medium dependence; re-registration; semantic density produced by interaction of linguistic levels; displaced interaction; polysemy; discourse patterning. What is prototypically literary will be a text which meets most of the above criteria; a less literary text will only meet some of the above criteria; an unequivocally non-literary text will be likely to meet none of these criteria; that is, it will be monosemic and medium-dependent, will project a direct interaction, contain no re-registrations and so on.

3 That the worst excesses of paradox and the essentialist dichotomies of an absolute division into literary/non-literary or fictional/non-fictional can be avoided by positioning a *cline* of literariness along which texts can be arranged.

4 That the terms *literary* and *non-literary* might be best replaced by the more neutral term *textual*.

5 That the sociolinguistic and socio-cultural context of the text as well as the ideological 'position' of the reader are important and cannot be 'bracketed out' by a focus on text-intrinsic linguistic properties.

6 That all texts, whatever degrees of literariness might be read into them, occupy a position in relation to the ideology of the society in which they are produced. Ideology is encoded in the linguistic organization of the text.

7 Far from demeaning 'literature' and reducing appreciation of literary language use, examination of literariness in language leads to greater respect for the richness of 'ordinary' language in all its multiple contexts.

Finally, it is important to return to a paragraph in our introduction in which we pointed out how the term 'literature' has changed its meaning at different stages in the process of history (See 2.1, p. 30). Our explorations of literariness in language here are also conditioned by historical circumstances, and the clines which run from non-literary to literary will inevitably change causing future attempts to define literariness to array texts differently on the cline or to construct an altogether different cline. To propose that our exploration of literariness is anything other than relative to social, cultural and historical contexts would be to return to the paradoxes of essentialism which were rejected earlier in the chapter. However, in saying this we are also not accepting the strong sociological or socio-historical definitions of literature without question. We believe it is over-simplistic to argue that literature is whatever powerful groups decide to read as literature. We have tried to examine the linguistic consti-tuents of literariness: it is only part of the story but it is an important one.[7] If certain groups of readers decide to value certain texts in certain ways then we believe there is a responsibility to try to explain some of the factors that may underlie such acts of reading. This chapter has attempted to lay a basis for such an explanation.

NOTES

1. Names of the early Russian and Czech Formalist critics were Victor Shklovsky, Jan Mukařovsky, Boris Eichenbaum and Roman Jakobson. A useful book charting developments in this area is Victor Ehrlich, *Russian Formalism: History, Doctrine* (3rd edn, Yale University Press, New Haven and London, 1981).

2. Widdowson (1975: ch. II) makes a distinction between reference and representation. Literary texts do not contain direct reference to the real

world; instead it is indirectly represented through particular choices of words which are taken to symbolize the content to which they refer.

3. For further discussion of Jakobsonian theories of the linguistic organization of literary discourse, see Waugh, 1980; Werth, 1976.

4. Indeed, as Leitch (1983) has also argued, the distinction between fiction and non-fiction is not an absolute one since truth itself is a convention determined institutionally and to which commitments differ in different contexts. Work by Hayden White (e.g. 1981) in the field of historiography also raises the intriguing possibility that the writing of history is a kind of narrative in which our interpretation of the past, indeed the facilitating of historical thought, is often made by means of 'literary' tropes. Work on metaphor by Lakoff and Johnson (1980) and others shows how so-called 'literary features' of language routinely occur outside what are commonly called literary texts. And Moeran (1984) (and 1.3 above) has demonstrated the existence in advertisements of such literary-linguistic elements as allusiveness, intertextuality, phonetic symbolism, ambiguity, represented language and so on.

5 Our reference on p.35 to a standard average Western European conception of literary language is apposite. Marxist aesthetics of, say, a Soviet Russian or Cuban variety may consider the absence of incitement to political or moral action to be notably decadent, the preserve of a bourgeois aesthetics concerned only with deflecting interest from social realities.

6 For a useful introduction to this domain see R. Holub, *Reception Theory* (Methuen, London, 1984).

7 This conclusion leads to the much-debated area of the ways in which 'literature' and its interpretation exists ideologically, as it were, by courtesy of communities of socio-culturally and sociolinguistically situated readers with common interests (see Bennett, 1983; Eagleton, 1983; Fish, 1980; Carter, 1985), and to the question of the extent to which Barthes' statement that 'Literature is what gets taught' (and, by extension, that literary language is what gets taught as literary language) is appropriate or not. It certainly requires recognition of the ideology of the writers of this book as middle-class, middle-aged, white, West European, Anglo-Saxon, male, tenured University teachers writing in the 1980s but taught within the institutional boundaries of English studies in the 1940s and 1960s. Differently positioned readers may well frame different answers to questions concerning the nature of literary language. For further discussion with particular reference to contemporary literary theory see Attridge (1988) and Tambling (1988).

3

Sample Cases

Our belief in the value of text and commentary presents us with the problem of selection. Clearly we cannot hope to demonstrate as intensively and comprehensively as we might wish; we must limit ourselves to sample cases. This chapter begins (3.1 to 3.2.2) with some readings in what must qualify as the most familiar, albeit ephemeral, types of written discourse: the language of newspapers and the language of advertising. These are essentially studies in discursive strategy, involving the designs and dispositions of producers and consumers. A sense of *interaction* figures large in our examination of these popular styles of address.

3.1 NEWSPAPER STYLES

3.1.1 Front Pages

In this section we examine the kinds of words used in media reports. We are particularly interested in the language of newspapers and in the degrees of neutrality or bias which are inscribed in the choice of words which reporters make. The examination is continued in section 3.5.1 where the discussion of political rhetorics includes reference to syntactic choices as well. In fact, most recent work on the relationship between language and ideology (see above, p. 20) has concentrated on the employment of particular syntactic patterns which have marked but not always easily noticeable designs on readers. For example, two sentences reporting the same event:

The Prime Minister explained that the budget measures were necessary

The Leader of the Opposition claimed that the budget measures were unnecessary illustrate how the factive verb 'explained' in the first sentence indicates the truth of the proposition where 'claimed' does not. News reports can thus ideologically encode varying degrees of access to the truth of things. Fowler *et al.* (1979) and Hodge and Kress (1981) have gone further and analysed such linguistic phenomena as the uses of passives to invert the order of who is the agent and who the affected party in an event, the uses of nominalizations to 'simplify' or, at least, mask the complexity of causal relations and the ways in which agents and processes can be lexicalized to distort or direct emphasis away from real-world events and towards expression of a particular ideology. (See 1.4.1 above).

The issue of bias in media reporting has remained an area of topical interest in the year of writing (1986) when the chairman of the British Conservative Party accused the British Broadcasting Corporation of bias in the reporting of the American bombing of Libya in April, 1986. A focus of analysis here was the headlines used by the BBC which were compared with those of independent television ITN. Discussion involved comparison of headlines such as:

a   Children are casualties – three from Gadaffi's own family (BBC)

b   Bombs meant for terrorists kill Gadaffi's daughter (ITN)

c   Worldwide condemnation of the American air strike (BBC)

d   Mr Gorbachev tells Mr Reagan 'Our Foreign Ministers can't meet now' (ITN)

For example, the comparison between (a) and (b) enabled some opponents of BBC bias to argue that ITN's reference to *terrorists* and corresponding assignment of intention is more 'neutral'. Similarly, the use of 'worldwide condemnation' in (c) is more emotive than (d) in which a factual statement is reported. (Gadaffi is Colonel Gadaffi, the Libyan leader.)

It is clear here that the *vocabulary* of reporting is not without significance. Lexical choices are as significant as syntactic patterns and, indeed, tend to be the items which attract most attention. Yet stylistic examination of vocabulary has tended to be relatively unsystematic. In part, this is due to the inherent slipperiness of lexical words; in part, it has been due to the focusing of interest by descriptive linguists on phonology, grammar, and more recently, on discourse. The following descriptive scheme for the recognition of *core* vocabulary is no more than a small step towards fuller examination of lexical structure and of the role of lexical items in discourse; but it can allow

us to discuss vocabulary in a more principled way, and can provide a basis for examining 'bias' in the lexis of reporting, and in a more general way, for exploring the relationship between lexis and ideology.

The term *core* vocabulary is used to describe those elements in the lexical network of a language which are unmarked. That is, they usually constitute the most normal, basic and simple words available to a language user. There are many ways in which such words might be isolated. Psycholinguists would probably argue that core words are those which are most perceptually salient; that is, they mark dominant areas of core sensory perception such as size (large/small), weight (heavy/light), colour (red/green) (but not mauve or scarlet or fawn). And so on. Sociolinguistically, they might be isolated as the items to which we have most natural and regular recourse in contexts such as talking to foreigners, or to young children. The following 'tests' (developed more extensively in Carter, 1987) are linguistic tests, designed to isolate the main structural and functional features of core vocabulary.

1   Core words often have clear antonym. Thus, the antonym of *hot* is *cold*, the antonym of *laugh* is *cry*, the antonym of *fat* is *thin*. It is more difficult to locate antonyms for non-core words such as *corpulent* or *skinny* or *emaciated*.

2   Core vocabulary is generally characterized by collocational frequency. A core word such as *fat* has a wide collocational span which includes *fat* man, *fat* salary, *fat* cheque. Words from the same lexical set such as *corpulent* or *chubby* have a more more restricted range; for example, one does not say 'corpulent cheque', 'chubby salary'.

3   In any lexical set there will be a more neutral or unmarked word which can be pressed into service to define the meanings of the related words. For example, in the set *snigger, grin, smirk, beam, smile*, all the words except *smile* can be defined by *smile* (the core item) plus an adverb. For example, *beam* = smile happily; *smirk* = smile knowingly. And so on. *Smile* itself, on the other hand, has to be defined by reference to basic semantic components and cannot be defined using any of the other words in the set.

4   Core vocabulary items are those which do not carry especially marked connotations or associations. Thus in the set of words surrounding a core item such as *thin*, lexical items such as *skinny* or *slim* carry marked negative and positive associations respectively. Similarly, items such as *emaciated* or *scraggy* carry marked associations of, respectively, formal and informal contexts of use. By contrast, *thin* is a relatively unmarked or core word.

5   Core words do not normally allow us to identify from which field of discourse they have been taken. Thus, the words *galley, port, starboard, fore* and *aft* and *knots* per hour immediately recall nautical or aeronautical fields. Corresponding items such as *kitchen, left* and *right, miles* per hour, etc., are unmarked, more neutral in subject matter and thus more *core*.

6   Core words are often superordinates. Thus, in the set of words *rose, tulip, peony, dahlia, carnation*, the superordinate item *flower* can regularly do service and stand in for the other items in a number of contexts.

These tests are not intended to be in any way either final or absolute. More work needs to be done in their refinement. And it is clear that it is preferable to refer to *degrees of coreness* in lexical items, since there can be no clear yes/no divisions among words into core and non-core categories. But recognition of coreness in vocabulary can, at least, enable us to begin to identify degrees of expressivity in vocabulary, and to begin to isolate the kinds of non-neutral expressive vocabulary which will be marked for bias or for 'ideological' connotations. It is particularly rewarding to explore such connotations in newspaper reports of new items. After all, newspaper reports should ideally report the facts in as *core* a vocabulary as possible.[2]

The report reproduced as Example 3.1, from the *Daily Mail*, 8 October 1983, provides a good example of a report which offers no pretence to neutrality or objectivity. Two elements strike the attention first: the huge headline CANUTE KINNOCK (taking up more than one-third of the front page space given to this item), and the photograph.* The headline 'Canute Kinnock' is an ingenious piece of logical and rhetorical sophistry. The two words are linked by similarity of sound and stress pattern, the latter feature of which might subliminally lead us (perhaps fancifully) to imagine something being set up and knocked down. The other similarity, which is later made explicit, is between Canute's and Kinnock's attempts to stop the tide. Though most readers are unlikely to know the 'real' story of Canute (whose failure to prevent the tide coming in was designed deliberately to expose the folly of his followers), they probably know he was a king, and this establishes a mock-heroic tone, a comic dissimilitude which serves to underline Kinnock's alleged predicament. Visually, the photograph reinforces the piece's combination of pseudo-sympathy with the proclaimed ineptitude of Kinnock: *he* looks upwards in an

---

* The photograph, not reproduced here, shows Mr Kinnock in stumbling retreat from the incoming tide as he and his wife walk on the beach.

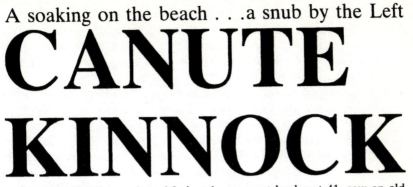

A soaking on the beach . . .a snub by the Left

CANUTE
KINNOCK

NEIL KINNOCK just elected Labour's youngest leader at 41, saw an old party tide threaten to swamp his new beginning last night.

Once again, the nightmare question came up: How far are you going to dismantle Britain's nuclear defence shield?

The answer helped Michael Foot lose the last election and from the way the argument was boiling at Brighton, it clearly threatened to help Mr Kinnock lose the next one.

His induction to the mantle of leadership began with a soaking on Brighton beach as he stumbled and fell at the sea's edge while posing for photographers. But the embarrassment of that Canute-like ducking was nothing to the problem of a backroom row between Labour's Left and Right over the rising tide of pacifism and one-sided nuclear disarmament in the party.

Suicide

An angry session of the National Executive provided a curtain-raiser to a debate on Wednesday which may nail young Mr Kinnock more firmly than ever to getting rid of all nuclear weapons.

It saw the novice leader frantically buttonholing colleagues in an attempt to avert what he sees as political suicide. It also

Toe the line 'or we'll have you'

saw Denis Healey angrily pounding the table and warnings from Anthony Wedgwood Benn and Ken Livingston that Mr Kinnock could blow it in the next year if he does not stick to Left-Wing policies.

And there was a blunt message to Mr Kinnock from veteran Left Winger Joan Maynard at a fringe meeting: 'If you don't walk your shoes straight we'll have you next year.'

But for a few moments the trendy new leader enjoyed the razzmatazz of an election night with an overwhelming victory for the 'dream ticket' — Mr Kinnock plus Roy Hattersley as his deputy.

The result of the leadership ballot with Mr Kinnock streets ahead of his nearest rival Mr Hattersley and Peter Shore and Eric Heffer nowhere, produced an explosion of cheers.

Mr Kinnock clenched his hands above his head boxer-style and gave his wife—and inspiration—Glenys a hearty kiss.

Mr Hattersley's subsequent election as deputy produced more . . .

Example 3.1

---

effort to make light of it; *she* (Mrs Kinnock) looks downward in apparent embarrassment.

The third element to strike our attention is the 'summary' positioned above the main headline: 'A soaking on the beach . . . a snub by the Left'. It represents a further parallelism – both phrases have the same syntactic and rhythmical structure of indefinite article, noun plus prepositional phrase. The parallel phrases serve to link the embarrassment of the fall in the sea with the increasingly embarrassed position into which Kinnock was being put by the left wing of his party, and function to drum home the mock-sympathetic stance towards the inept, ill-fated Kinnock.

The report proper begins with a standard narration of the facts. Inappropriately, however, this statement is rhetorically marked by numerous metaphoric devices and figures which contrast with and contravene expectations of a plain style. Facts such as Kinnock's age

and that he is Labour's youngest leader are overlaid by metaphors of
tide and swamping, and by patterns of semantic contrast working to
prevent any positive connotations remaining. Thus, '*young*est leader' is
placed in disharmony with '*old* party tide'; and '*new* beginning' is then
by contrast with *old* and by extension with *young* given a distinctly
negative and pejorative colouring.

The next short paragraph seems to be a summary statement of the
line to be taken, or of the point at issue, and is generically more
appropriate to the discourse convention of an editorial than to that of a
newspaper report. However, the posing of the question is logically and
rhetorically skilful. We might ask ourselves just *who* experiences the
'question' enforced by this 'tide' as a 'nightmare'? It is a question
designed to arouse fear and insecurity in the reader over the prospect
of a unilateralist Labour government, rather than to be a question to
which an answer might be given, either by Kinnock or by anyone else.
It is, in fact, logically question-begging since Kinnock is presented as
being unwilling to admit how far he is going to be pushed and, in the
following paragraph, as being unlikely to be in a position to do any
'dismantling'. More insidiously still, there is a morphological root
repetition of *mantle* of leadership (which is what Kinnock is described
as assuming in the fourth paragraph), and *dismantle* in this paragraph.
The words echo across the paragraphs to produce an even more subtle
underlining of irresponsibility, especially when framed by the above
question:

> How far are you going to dismantle Britain's nuclear
> defence shield?

The following paragraph provides the 'answer' (rhetorically balancing, in the form of relative opposition, the 'question' of the previous
paragraph), which the new leader is unwilling to face, and which
ironically 'helped' the old leader to his failure in a General Election (we
should note the further disabling contrasts between *old* and *new/young*).
In keeping with a partisan piece of writing which assumes the
undemocratic instability and erroneousness of socialism, the writer
does not pause to consider possible counter-arguments, but is concerned to refute for the newspaper's readers any suggestion that
socialism might ever again become plausible enough to attract a
majority vote. Thus, the piece presses on with metaphors of liquidity –
things effervescing threateningly from above and welling up menac-
ingly from below. 'Boil' adds a note of hot bad temper to the cold and
panic-inducing note of 'tide'; and the encirclement of 'Canute Kin-

nock' is sealed by the relative opposites of 'last' and 'next', bracketing him with inevitable failure.

The next paragraph contains an extension of the mock-heroic tone noted above. This is achieved by the suggestion of decorous ceremony supplied by 'His induction to the mantle of leadership' which is then sharply undercut by the reference both to an unseemly and intractable 'row', and to the 'Canute-like ducking'. The mock-heroic effect is modulated lexically by non-core lexical items, in particular the switch in formality levels from 'mantle of leadership' to 'row', and 'ducking'. Here, the transition fromn formal to informal lexis parallels, in an almost comic burlesque, the action of Kinnock's momentary loss of dignity, but it also deliberately undercuts any serious claim to leadership on the part of Kinnock.

The second phase of this 'report' begins with a sub-heading – SUICIDE – which is as unembarrassingly one-sided as the syntactic tricks which follow in the next paragraph. Here, the 'session' emerges as a conscious entity capable of 'seeing'. The deletion of any agent or witness to the session serves to impart evidence which cannot be authenticated, but which is unlikely to be questioned by many readers. Metaphoric processes are at work again here, together with distinctly non-core evaluative vocabulary, serving, for example, to reduce him to a frantically fluttering flag on the mast to which his colleagues (whose views we are assumed to know and disapprove of), inexorably nail him. The metaphors continue in the next paragraph with warnings that he might 'blow it in the next year' (like an over-inflated balloon or over-worked engine gasket), and that he must 'walk straight' down the Party Line. The accompanying colloquial lexis serves only to reinforce the deflationary effects.

Finally, however, a few moments are spared for reporting the victory celebration. But they are marred by the dissociating quotation marks framing 'dream ticket' and the re-surfacing of non-core evaluative lexical items such as 'trendy' and 'razzmatazz' which return us through the word *novice* to the youthful irresponsibility and general unfittedness to resist the tide which marked the description of Kinnock at the beginning of the report.

This text is a good example of the way in which linguistic devices at several levels interpenetrate to produce some especially dense and subtle effects, even though we must recognize that their interpretation depends on the particular interests of the reader, and that not all readers will be, or will want to be, in a position to interpret in this way the language of a newspaper report. Vocabulary has here, however, a part to play in establishing such effects, at least, for these readers. And the categories of *core* and *non-core* vocabulary, and the clines of relative coreness which run between these categories, do help in establishing some of the more marked and expressive lexical effects. Among the non-core words in the report are: ·

  snub
  ducking
  row
  buttonholing
  blow (it)
  posing
  trendy
  razzmatazz
  boiling (argument)
  induction (to the mantle)

These items are non-core by being either markedly formal or informal or by carrying recognizably evaluative (usually negative) associations. And even a normally core word such as *young* (to which in our culture positive associations are commonly attached) is negotiated by subtle structural semantic contrasts into acquiring disapprobatory connotations. It is the presence of such non-core lexical items in the context of a newspaper report, a context which generates expectations of 'neutral' and dispassionate presentation, that gives grounds for arguing that this piece of text is in a curiously mixed mode. The writer, who at least does not attempt to conceal that he is a political editor, manages to merge 'political' report with editorial commentary. There may be some (possibly deliberate?) confusion about discourse conventions, but he knows where he is going, and for the most part, assumes his readers will go with him.

3.1.2 Problem Pages

Many newspapers and magazines present readers with problems. Problems make news and readers like reading about problems. Different problems require different solutions and newspapers and journals reveal much by the way in which solutions are proposed within their pages. In some cases such as the front page report discussed above (Canute Kinnock) the problems are presented as simply unresolvable. Mr Kinnock is shown to have to face problems of internal division in his own party and to be defenceless against the rising tide of events. No solutions are proposed and any success is only temporary; in fact, there are permanent problems, notably Mr Kinnock's youth and inexperience, which, readers are invited to conclude, make the situation appear not just problematic but irredeemable. As we have seen the lexical organization of the whole report serves only to reinforce this evaluation of things.

Some of the terms used in the above paragraph are arguably important for our understanding of how problems are presented. The *situation* of Mr Kinnock is presented as a *problem* and yet there is no *solution* available and therefore the *evaluation* we make of the whole situation is a negative one. Work by Winter and Hoey on what they term 'clause relations' goes some way towards providing a description of text organization and a framework within which different kinds of journalistic problems and solutions can be analysed. Clause relations have been defined as follows:

> A clause relation is the cognitive process whereby the reader interprets the meaning of a clause, sentence, or groups of sentences in the context of one or more preceding clauses, sentences, or groups of sentences in the same text. (Winter, 1977)

Clause relations establish recognizable patterns in a text. They are *macro* rather than *micro* patterns. The relations established between core vocabulary items are micro-relations, that is, they involve single lexical items, small units of language in combination with one another. Clause relations involve larger units of language organization such as sentences or groups of sentences. One of the most common of these macro-organizational patterns is what Hoey (1983) refers to as *Problem–Solution* structures.

Problem–Solution structures are present in all kinds of texts but especially so in expository texts. They are used frequently in advertising texts; for example:

> 'Funny isn't it; how your favourite TV programmes always seem to coincide with dinner time? Which tends to mean that as the emotions flow across the screen . . . gravy trickles onto your lap! Now help is at hand, in the stylish shape of Scotcade's TV Tables.'

In the first sentence a *situation* is introduced. The second sentence describes a *problem* which is connected with the situation. The third sentence suggests a *solution* to the problem. In fact, as readers and hearers we know from experience that as soon as a problem is identified in an advertising text the solution will be provided by the product being advertised. Here is another example:

THE FOUR O'CLOCK FEELING
AND HOW TO OVERCOME IT

(1)   We all suffer from tiredness sometimes.

(2)   A couple of cups of strong black coffee will usually do the trick, but of course it's not always convenient to drink coffee – in a meeting for instance or if you're out shopping.

(3)   Pro-Plus is the handy way to keep a pick-me-up with you.

(4)   A couple of Pro-Plus soon overcome tiredness and let you get on with enjoying life.

PRO-PLUS FIGHTS FATIGUE

This advertisement is a little more structurally complex than the previous text. Here the headline or title for the text states the problem ('the four o'clock feeling') and that it will be solved ('and how to overcome it'), serving almost as a kind of abstract or summary of the whole text. The specific problem is presented in the first sentence and is reinforced by the lexical items *suffer from*. However, the proposed response to the problem ('strong black coffee') is not an entirely appropriate solution (i.e. it 'will usually do the trick' but it is 'not always convenient'). The second sentence thus receives a negative evaluation and the search for a solution continues. This is provided in the third sentence in the form of the advertised product, the effectiveness of which is then in turn positively evaluated in the fourth sentence. The initial response 'strong black coffee' is a deferred solution thus making the product appear an even more appropriate answer.

Problems sometimes appear in the form of questions to which answers provide solutions. An example of this is the advertisement for the Maxi car discussed above in Chapter 2 (pp. 46–7). Here the advertisement works to establish a dialogue which the reader is invited to complete by answering the questions posed:

Have you had the Sunday car washing ritual?   (Yes)

Have you got better things to do with a
car than run round it with a rag?   (Yes)

Then the Maxi is for you.   (Oh, why?)

Because the Maxi is made for doing things.   (What things?)

One of the effects of this text is to manipulate the reader into a series of two-part exchanges and into the role of a respondent who is allowed little more conversational space than one-word replies. The compliance of the reader is dependent on how far he or she accepts or resists the role which is contrived for them. In this other factors than language have an important part to play, but the dialogic structure is designed to try to secure the reader's willing but passive role in this problem-solving routine.

Although the structure of question/answer is an essentially interactive structure it is difficult for texts to build in text conventions which are formally or overtly dialogic. Interactive and participatory modes can be implicit and it can indeed be argued that all effective written communication presupposes a reader and attempts to anticipate and accommodate a reader's expectations in reading a particular text. In the context of newspapers and magazines there are, however, spaces where a measure of more overt interaction can take place. The agony or advice column is one such opportunity, and this is examined in greater detail below. The other context in which readers can imagine that they are more than merely passive consumers of reports, features and editorials and can insert their own texts is provided by the format of a letter. Such a format is an institutionalized one, appears in several newspapers and journals and is often explicitly signalled as *Letters to the Editor* or *Correspondence*. It is also a further example of problems and solutions being addressed.

In the case of such correspondence the starting point is usually recognition or statement of a problem together with a response of some kind; but, conventionally, the response is not directly solicited in that the problem is one defined by the newspaper and the correspondent writes 'in reply' to the newspaper. (The contrived character of the interaction is further enforced by the fact that only letters which are selected by the editor are actually printed.) The Problem–Solution structure here is also different in that the problem is usually perceived to be one where the original statements or solutions proposed are incorrect and require modification. This leads to letters in which statements are presented as untrue and then corrected by the correspondent's own proper and true version. Winter has commented on these particular text conventions in relation to his categories for macro-structural text analysis:

> The letters . . . have in common the *argumentative function* in communication. The fundamentals are a *fact*, a *statement*, or *situation* (normally presented first) which is opposed by a contrary or different *fact*, statement, or situation (normally presented second). *Evaluation* is a comparison and assessment of the *situations* which may include a *conclusion*. (Winter, 1977).

Here are two representative examples:

> Sir, – David Jenkins is incorrect in his assertion that the National Union of Teachers has studiously taken care to avoid the case of Mrs Beryl

Smith. Indeed, the NUT has consistently sought to help Beryl Smith. On several occasions, twice recently, we have offered her our assistance to seek a reconciliation between the two parties concerned and thus to secure her future at Merivale School. Our offer still stands. Yours faithfully,

Sir, – Myra Wilson attributes (May 12) some views to me that are less than accurate.

I have not argued that Orange Order candidates should be supported against Conservatives; I have said I think it desirable that they should remain within the law in their opposition to Hillsborough rather than provoke riots in the streets by their intemperate words. Yours faithfully,

(Concocted texts based on letters to the editor in the *Guardian*, *Observer* and *Daily Telegraph* newspapers during 1984)

There are particular markers in the use of vocabulary in the letters which indicate the letter writer's design in correcting false statements (e.g. . . . 'is incorrect in his assertion'; 'views that are less than accurate'). Predictably, items which do not have any purchase on fact or truth will serve as especially appropriate lexical signals in the 'hypothetical' section of the letter. Such lexical items are: *hypothesis, claim, belief, assertion, idea, proposition, argument, assumption, theory, suggestion* and, of course a set of related verbs. The hypothetical structure then gets replaced by a corrective or 'real' account of things in which the views of the letter writer, whether or not corroborated by ascertainable facts, are presented. Here, again, predictably, lexical items such as *truth, fact, evidence, correct, accurate* will figure prominently. Syntactically, the countering move will be marked by a negative sentence in response to a preceding positive (but fallacious) statement, or a positive sentence(s) in response to a preceding negativized statement. For example:

David Jenkins is *incorrect* . . .
The NUT has studiously taken care . . .
Myra Wilson attributes some view to me/
I have *not* argued.

In these two examples the problem is unambiguously with the journalists' view of things and the proposed solution is a necessary correction of those views. However, not all letters to the editor divide so neatly into Problem–Solution structures. Here is a further example; for ease of reference the sentences have been numbered.

I   (1)   MY ATTEMPTS to secure full-time employment resemble those of Hamish Reid (Letters). (2) I, too, am a graduate, but over 50. I have accordingly considerable experience of working with people in a variety of situations, mainly in industry.

II   (3)   When I became redundant four years ago, I decided to read for a degree in accountancy, intending to use my experience to work with people in industry in a financial capacity.

III   (4)   At a recent interview I was asked what a B.A. in accountancy meant and why I had bothered to read for a degree. (5) The interviewer then told me proudly that he had no qualifications.

IV   (6)   Hamish Reid says employers are unwilling to train young people. (7) But it is worse than that – they are unwilling to train *everybody*, even though the candidate may possess relevant experience.

V   (8)   Much is talked about personnel, but not much about people. (9) When those responsible for employing people realize that 'people study' pays dividends, our nation will begin to prosper.

(Concocted text based on two letters to the *Daily Mail* and the *Guardian* in 1979)

This letter is clearly more complex in structure. The description of the writer's own situation in sentences (1) and (2) is also a statement of a problem (the writer's inability to find work, underscored with words such as 'attempts' which imply failure). The letter then moves to an embedded situation in which reference is made to past events: (3), (4) and (5), and a rhetorical contrast is set up between present and past situations. In this embedded backwards-reference the situation described again contains signals of problem and difficulty (e.g. 'became redundant') but also indicates a strategy for solution (e.g. '*I decided* to read for a degree' . . . 'use my experience' etc.). It is not until sentence (6) that there is a reference to a problem located in the assertions of others. The writer refers not to a journalistic contribution to the newspaper but to a preceeding letter from Hamish Reid. Here it is not so much a revision to a false hypothesis which is proposed; rather, the writer posits the need to intensify and amplify the nature of the main problem of unemployment. The proposed correction (sentence 7) implies an evaluation of Hamish Reid's statement signalled in lexical items such as 'unwilling' and 'worse'. As is the case with the two letters above the replacement of one view with another involves an evaluation, whether implicitly or explicitly presented, of the preceding view. The letter ends with a solution to the problem (8 and 9) and returns us to the beginning of the letter and the original problem, though in fact the problem has in varying degrees permeated the letter since the opening lines.

The above discussion illustrates that, although Problem–Solution patterns do seem to be fundamental underlying structures in texts, it is no simple task to categorize them. They are not always discrete in the organization of a text. And situation and evaluation are also relevant categories even though they are relatively more optional and open to embedding. We shall return to these broader issues of recognition and functional interrelation at the end of the next section.

Words with the Agony Aunt Another classic instance of Problem–Solution structures in magazines and journals is that of Problem Pages. Interestingly, they occur with greatest density in magazines aimed at a female readership. The problems are mainly concerned with relationships with the opposite sex and the whole genre of problem pages establishes a gender-specific correspondence. What is constructed are texts which underscore ideological presuppositions: that it is mainly women who have problems with relationships and who require advice (usually from another woman); that it is mainly women who can be seen to give a public airing to their difficulties. In this dialogue about problems the text convention is for a letter to be written to the 'Agony Aunt' who then writes a reply. The letter states the problem; the reply proffers a solution. Here is a fairly representative example:

I've recently transferred to a new office and I've fallen for my boss. He has not actually revealed his feelings but a mutual friend has told me he likes me and would like the relationship to go further. We're both married and I'm not sure if he wants an affair. Should I tell him how I feel or just carry on pretending that nothing is happening? My marriage is OK but I really feel I need this man.

So far there's no evidence that there's anything between you and your boss – except on your side. A mutual friend surely isn't his mouthpiece? And if you fell for this man as soon as you started working for him, isn't that a sure sign that you're looking for romance or sex from anyone? So your husband could fit the bill just as well. See what you can do to make your marriage more than just OK – it's a safer, happier route than starting an affair.

(Concocted text based on four separate problem page letters in magazines for women published in 1986–8)

In this sequence the language is not quite as explicit in formally signalling the existence of problems as it is in previous examples in this section. There are no lexical items such as *problem, snag, difficulty, dilemma* to point directly to the existence of difficulties; thus a measure of cultural and moral knowledge is assumed in the opening sentence, as well as a set of ideologically enforced norms governing heterosexual relations. This combines with experience and expectations about the genre of problem pages to secure a reading of 'I've fallen for my boss' as a problem requiring a solution. As the 'letter' develops the problem is inscribed with uncertainties ('I'm not sure'; 'carry on pretending') and with a modality of doubt about obligations ('Should I . . .?')

The reply from the Agony Aunt has an overall global purpose of smoothing over the difficulties and of seeking out a 'safer, happier route' to solutions. The textual tactic is one of strategic admonishment; the modality is one of certainty and conviction and is written from a position of authority and secure values. Linguistically, this manifests itself in theoretical questions (to which no reply is expected) (e.g. 'Isn't that a sure sign?'); declarative assertions ('so your husband could fit the bill just as well'; 'So far there's no evidence'; 'A mutual friend surely isn't his mouthpiece?'); modal adverbs of certainty ('surely'; 'so') and imperative exhortations ('see what you can do to make your marriage more than just OK').

It is not for the first time in this book that analysis of surface linguistic features leads to a recognition that those same features are connected with, and to some cconsiderable extent determined by, ideologies which regulate behaviour within the broader social semiotic of which the text is part. In this problem page sequence, for example, the Agony Aunt addresses problems only in so far as they must be made to go away, if not by sympathetic consideration then by an imperative injunction. If the truth of things cannot be seen to have the obvious, self-revealing evidentiality of the Agony Aunt's discourse then the position of the correspondent is implicitly evaluated as one without real recourse to a solution. The only proper solution is one of acceptance of existing relationships and is in the interests of stability. It is an essentially maintaining position in which existing obligations have to be honoured. The reply reinforces a view of a world in which differences should be reconciled and feelings and needs subjugated to a posited 'moral' of conjugal fidelities. To a question which tentatively opens up difficulties, the reply seeks an almost immediate closure. It is a closure which is patterned into the structure of problem page text conventions since no further questions can follow and the Agony Aunt has the last word.

The infiltration of ideologies into these texts is pervasive. First, as we have noted, the problem is signalled as a woman's problem and no encouragement is given to explore or challenge the man's position. A further signal is that women have emotional problems which require 'solutions'. The male does not have a problem; the woman has a problem only in relation to the otherwise paradoxically marginalized males. For example, it is not questioned why the husband is not fulfilling the needs of his wife; nor is the husband expected to do anything to provide a solution. Both the text convention and the expectation of the reader prescribe a norm in which the woman presents herself as vulnerable and powerless, regulated, as it were, by the confessional mode. However, the Agony Aunt constructs a set of normative social behaviours and shows little interest in the feelings and needs which are confessed. In this context the Agony Aunt does not simply produce a closure of the problems; there is throughout a pervasively implicit evaluation of behaviour which, in the guise of guidance, serves only to reveal the extent of her own beliefs and their supporting ideologies. As far as the position of women is inscribed in this Question/Answer (Problem/Solution) sequence, the final word is normative, conservative, and serves only to reproduce existing ideologies. As with letters to the editor, the letter writer is *controlled* by a convention that the dialogue goes no further.

As far as the main macro-structural categories are concerned we can conclude that the units of *Situation, Problem, Solution* and *Evaluation* are useful descriptive bases for understanding the organization of texts and the kinds of functions they can be made to fulfil. It is important to note the following, however:

1　that evaluative elements are structurally pervasive. Evaluation is regularly embedded in other categories. Readers may like to re-read the Canute Kinnock passage to test this claim (pp. 00–0 above).

2　in some texts situations and problem are indistinguishable since the description of the situation can operate to imply the problem(s).

3　problem and solution are more fundamental categories; situation and evaluation are optional rather than obligatory categories.

4　the notion of a preferred sequence to the categories is an important one. A preferred sequence is S (situation), P (problem), S (solution), E (evaluation). But this sequence can be rearranged for particular effects and the situation and evaluation categories can be removed entirely.

5 there can be an overlap of categories. More detailed linguistic analysis may well establish clearer recognition analysis may well establish clearer recognition criteria for identifying particular units. But the account we have given so far is, we hope, sufficient to allow greater general awareness of the role and function of language in such larger units of text organization.

3.2 ADVERTISING TALK

The making, apprehending and storing of narratives are among the most fundamental of human activities. Narratives shape our lives (which are themselves complex narratives) as well as our understanding of our lives. We use narratives to help us make sense of things and to come to terms with experience or to explain and represent it to others. Narratives are used for a host of different speech acts as Toolan (1988: xiv) points out:

> Just how pervasive and important oral and written narratives are to our lives becomes startlingly clear if we stop to think of the forms of narrative we depend on as props and inspirations: biographies and autobiographies; historical texts; news stories and features in whatever medium; personal letters and diaries; novels; thrillers and romances; medical case histories; school records; curriculum vitae; police reports of incidents; annual performance reviews.

One reason narratives can perform so variously is that all narratives are constructed with varying degrees of directness and indirectness. Narrators have a choice of making quite clear the point of what they are saying or they can leave it to be inferred or interpreted by their readers and hearers.

Narratives are being increasingly employed by advertisers to assist them to sell their products. Here it is especially important that those who read or hear them get the message; but the message should not always be so direct that we do not sometimes discover or work out for ourselves how much we want a product or want to believe the things we are being told stories about. It is the case with all narratives that the balance between truth and fiction is a delicate one.

Recent analysis of narratives suggest strongly that narratives are universal not only in their provenance and ubiquity but in the ways in which they are organized. The components of narrative structure can be said to be more or less the same at least for the cultures in which narratives have been studied. However, the 'universal' properties of narrative organization should not prevent consideration of the 'local' uses to which narrative can be put.

3.2.1 Titles

One of the permanent structural components of written narratives (though rarely of oral narratives) is that of a title. The titles usually serve to tell us what the story is going to be about. Some titles are more explicit and direct than others; for example, several nineteenth-century novels in English point in their title to the essential concerns of the narrative, located as they usually are in particular places or in a projected assessment of particular human qualities:

Pride and Prejudice
Barchester Towers
Mansfield Park
The Mill on the Floss

Twentieth-century novels, however, often have titles which are more oblique, carrying mythic or symbolic resonances which serve to activate the greater interpretive involvement of the reader, for example:

The Waves
Ulysses
The Rainbow

Some advertisements rely for their effect on titles which serve as a kind of caption, as one-liners designed to be easily memorizable and to play with language entertainingly; often they take the form of a direct injunction of a declarative assertion. For example:

Put a tiger in your tank (Esso petrol)
Heineken refreshes the parts other beers cannot reach (beer)
Top people take *The Times* (a British newspaper)
Join the Professionals (British Army recruitment)
Guinness is good for you (beer)

Not all such 'titles' work so directly. Some are more metaphoric and linguistically emblematic, yoking together areas of experience to effect a 'natural' association. Cars and cosmetics are linked in:

Life in the fast lane (Turbo After Shave)

Holidays and food are linked in:

Summer is now being served (Greek National Tourist Board)
Feast on a great American special (Thomas Cook)

Sometimes this play with language is extended into a series of slogans which are best understood in relation to one another. The following additionally all draw phonological patterns and are used to advertise the routes of an American airline:

Seattle with the hassle
San Antonio, sans delay
Phoenix phast

On the other hand, some 'titles' require considerable interpretive working out and are in themselves a minor narrative, drawing attention, as here, to a progression of places and combinign with cultural allusion to television programmes (*Dallas*) and to Hollywood (a place in *Los Angeles* and the centre of the international film industry) (as well as punning on 'appearance'):

How to get to Hollywood via a brief
appearance in Dallas.

And some are again quite explicitly modelled on the standard *form* of a title:

The Wizard of Oz (Australian lager)
The French Connection (Pirelli tyres)

where allusions are made to well-known existing titles of books and films or, as is the case here, to a universally known slogan from *The Communist Manifesto*:

Sports Fans of the World, Unite (N.E.C.)

This is not unlike the ways in which the titles of canonical texts allude to existing titles of other books or texts and creatively play off or against them:

Ulysses (novel by James Joyce/Greek epic narrative)
Decline and Fall (novel by Evelyn Waugh/a history of the Roman Empire by Edward Gibbon)
The Wanderer (poem by Auden/Anglo-Saxon poem)

Two further points about titles can be underlined: one obvious, the other possibly less so. First, newspaper captions bear a close similarity to titles of narrative texts. This is unsurprising since in the act of reporting newspapers engage in varying degrees of story-making. Secondly, newspaper headlines also regularly play with language for purposes of impact or memorability in the process of seeking to summarize the main points of the events which will be narrated. The captions they create also work more directly or more indirectly depending on the degree of interpretive work judged appropriate to the content of the story, to the context and to the attitudes towards content taken by the journalist or editor of the newspaper. For example,

Pound Knocked Centless (on the fall of the pound against the dollar in 1984)
All Disquiet on the Southern Front (on US problems in South America)

– the latter of which alludes directly to a famous novel of the First World War Period (*All Quiet on the Western Front*).

3.2.2 Advertising Narratives

The relationship between narrative and advertising discourse is not confined to titles or captions. It also extends to the construction of complete narrative texts. Here is the opening to such a narrative.

The Cameraman's Day
It's 3.04 a.m. and they have just finished shooting the final scene in the boxing ring.
Tom Becker, the cameraman, heaves a sigh of relief.
After all, it has been a long day. He has been on set for sixteen hours.
There have been thirty different camera positions, each needing careful thought and equally careful framing, lighting and focusing.
Followed by take after take after take.

PAINTING WITH THE CAMERA
Right from the start, Tom knew how he wanted the film to look.
He's always admired the hard shadows and dramatic skies he'd seen in
Expressionist paintings.
And he carefully composed each shot, mixing colours, tones, light and
shadow to create an Expressionist 'feel'.
THE MOMENT OF TRUTH
In a few hours' time he'll watch today's rushes.
He'll feel a gentle glow of satisfaction when he's sure that the smoke-
hazed light of the boxing ring came out just the way he planned it.
It's the only reward he wants for all his work. The only relief in the
pressure before another long day's shoot.

Several narrative theorists have proposed rules for the construction of
narrative discourse. Such rules also serve to identify narrative
organization and help to explain why narratives are recognized as
narratives. The rules refer specifically to the existence of particular
units of text in a usual order. Three main macro-structural units are
agreed to be fundamental to narrative organization.[1]

Macro-units	*Micro-units*
Setting:	in which specific linguistic structures mark time, place and other circumstances, including the 'characters' of participants.
Complication and *Resolution:*	in which specific linguistic structures, most markedly *tense*, define the basic episodes in the story and their final 'resolution' or denouement.
Moral:	in which elements crucial to the telling of the tale are encoded. Here linguistic structures determine the 'point' or 'purpose' of the story.

As stated, the sequence Setting → Complication → Resolution →
Moral is a normal or preferred order. This does not mean that these
units cannot be otherwise disposed; in fact, it is not uncommon for
deviations from this norm to occur and for distinct effects to be
produced as a result. For example, some narratives begin *in medias res*;
that is, the action commences without any orientation to places or
persons and a series of complications are enacted before the reader is
given the setting or settings for those complications. Similarly, actions
or events can be evaluated by the author or narrator as the action

proceeds and not necessarily after it has been enacted. In other words, 'moral' macro-units can be embedded elsewhere in the action. We shall now proceed to a discussion of *The Cameraman's Day* by using the above framework for the analysis of its structural organization.

Setting The narrative follows for the most part a conventional patterning in the reader's orientation to time, place and character with a special emphasis on *time* (e.g. 'It's 3.04 a.m.'; 'a long day'; 'for sixteen hours'; 'in a few hours' time'; 'right from the start'; 'another long day's shoot'). *Place* is sketched in (e.g. 'in the boxing ring') but character is the sense of stating particular aspects of Tom Becker's character is less directly revealed. However, indirectly, we can infer from his work as a cameraman that he values precision and takes meticulous care over the actions associated with his work. (In fact, Tom Becker is not separable from his work, at least in so far as he is represented in this sequence.) We learn that his work 'needs':

careful thought
careful framing, lighting and focusing
he *carefully* composed each shot . . .

and that he responds dedicatedly to these demands 'take after take after take', but with a 'feel' for the aesthetics and creativity which inheres in the conscientious 'composition' of each 'Expressionist' shot (the sub-heading *Painting with the Camera* reinforces this).

Complication and Resolution The depiction of action breaks with expected sequences here. Instead of a consistent chronology of events framed by a narrative simple past tense (e.g. Tom *said*; Tom *decided*; Tom *composed*; Tom *completed*), there is a marked switching of tenses:

It's 3.04 a.m.

Tom . . . heaves a sign of relief	(present tense)
They have just finished	(present perfect:
He has been on set for sixteen hours	recording recently completed actions)
	(conventional narrative
He knew how he wanted the film to look	simple past tense)
He had always admired	(past perfect tense)
And he carefully composed each shot	(simple past tense)
In a few hours time he'll watch . . .	(future tense)
He'll feel a gentle glow of satisfaction	(future tense)
It's the only reward he wants	(present tense)

With this almost unsettling shift of tense comes a varying narrative perspective. There is an overall temporal progression but it is almost as if the writer wants to impart narrative outlines to the discourse without *fully* settling into a conventional narrative scheme. It also serves to project the narrator rather more than the character. We learn about Tom, it is true, especially about his particular qualities in relation to his work; but the narrator is projected as one who is closely involved with the action, controlling how we see Tom and disposing us to see him from a particular angle. Especially important is the foregrounding of 'content' which draws attention to the balance between technical control and precision, on the one hand ('careful', 'composed', 'planned'), and a texture, on the other hand ('colour', 'tones', 'light' and 'shadow'; 'smoke-hazed'; 'dramatic') which ensures everything looks right.

The final resolution to this uneven pattern of narrative complication is conventionally positioned at the end of the sequence of actions. It is, however, realized as a predicted rather than an actual resolution. There are no uncertainties, only a narratorial confidence that Tom will feel that he is sure to feel and that he wants for no more than the 'relief and satisfaction' which successful and precise camerawork confers. The reader might rightly infer that Tom Becker has no life independently from the Cameraman's Day (and 'Night', for it is 3.04 a.m. when this work finishes and 'another long day's shoot' is in prospect). There is no moral drawn from the resolution. We are not invited to conclude that Tom may soon be close to a nervous breakdown, nor that he has suffered a personal crisis from which the only available relief is bestowed by work. Thus far, and even allowing for the breaks with conventional narrative organization, it is hard to determine precisely what the point or purpose of this tale might be. The 'moral' is reserved for the final paragraphs:

TISSOT PR 100

Tom Becker's watch is a Tissot PR 100.

He can rely on the precision of its Swiss quartz movement for the accuracy he needs, wherever in the world he's filming.

Its rugged case incorporates a sapphire crystal that shrugs off the everyday knocks and scratches of a cameraman's life on land or sea. (The Tissot PR 100 resists water to a depth of 100 metres.) And it looks as good in front of the camera as it does behind.

The 'moral' of the narrative now materializes in the form of a valued watch, and the perspective of the narrative now displaces Tom Becker from the central focus and inserts the Tissot PR 100 in his place, drawing Tom into focus only in the form of an analogy with his work as a cameraman. The term 'focus' is not, in fact, an ill-chosen one since there is a narrowing of focus by tense selection which has the whole of the final paragraph in a simple present. Rather in the manner of the sentence *Oil floats on water* (where the simple present *floats* operates to make the action not simply present but permanent – a general truth) the paragraph conveys a sense of the watch being a watch for all times, actions and places:

Its rugged case *incorporates* . . .
Shrugs off the everyday knocks
resists water
looks . . . good

The Tissot PR 100 is a permanent and unchanging feature of the working man's land- and seascape.. It is suited for accuracy and action, for longevity and looks. It is the natural culmination of a 'plotting' which has repeatedly pointed to the careful and *compositional* make-up of Tom Becker's character. The caption which encapsulates the 'moral' to which the action has moved is:

A Tissot isn't out of place for a second.

The earlier narrative concern with the co-ordinates of time have now fused with looks and accuracy in an abstract which confirms the watch as the main character in the story.

When they are a part of advertising talk, narratives are a particular form of telling stories. One of the principal aims is to get us to believe the truth of what is being fictionalized. In this sample case, we are not having experience represented to us in order to explain that experience or for us to participate imaginatively in it. The placing of the moral here is crucial since it invites us not so much to evaluate and assess as to act to purchase. It does not do so directly but the movement of the narrative has been to this end and to no other. *The Cameraman's Day* is a title which invites a different mental set towards experience.

The introduction at this juncture of the complete advertisement demonstrates that a discussion which confines itself only to the *language* of narrative is insufficient. The Tissot advertisement loses a part of its claim to literariness by sacrificing its sovereign status as a text; as a piece of narrative it is *medium-dependent* (see above p. 38), relying for its effects on the reinforcing supplements provided by such extras as pictures and typographical layout. It tells a story using more

The Cameraman's Day.

It's 3.04 am and they have just finished shooting the final scene in the boxing ring.

Tom Becker, the cameraman, heaves a sigh of relief.

After all, it has been a long day. He has been on set for sixteen hours.

There have been thirty different camera positions, each needing careful thought and equally careful framing, lighting and focusing.

Followed by take after take after take.

PAINTING WITH THE CAMERA.

Right from the start, Tom knew how he wanted the film to look.

He'd always admired the hard shadows and dramatic skies he'd seen in Expressionist paintings.

And he carefully composed each shot, mixing colours, tones, light and shadow to create an Expressionist 'feel.'

THE MOMENT OF TRUTH.

In a few hours' time he'll watch todays's rushes.

He'll feel a gentle glow of satisfaction when he's sure that the smoke-hazed light of the boxing ring came out just the way he planned it.

It's the only reward he wants for all his work. The only relief in the pressure before another long day's shoot.

TISSOT PR100.

Tom Becker's watch is a Tissot PR 100.

He can rely on the precision of its Swiss quartz movement for the accuracy he needs, wherever in the world he's filming.

Its rugged case incorporates a sapphire crystal that shrugs off the everyday knocks and scratches of a cameraman's life on land or sea. (The Tissot PR 100 resists water to a depth of 100 metres.) And it looks as good in front of camera as it does behind.

A Tissot isn't out of place for a second **TISSOT**

Example 3.2

than words, and places the watch in more senses than one in the centre of the picture. Fictionally as well as literally, *A Tissot isn't out of place for a second.*

In the following sections we turn to the consideration of literary styles, and in doing so transfer our attention from discourse to text, or from the 'extensional' act of writing involving a writer–reader relationship, to the 'intensional' act that concerns the language and structure of the text in itself. Our 'sample cases' in 3.3.1 and 3.3.2 are not intended as general demonstrations of literary dialogue and narrative; they exemplify, respectively, *a* narrative structure and *a* dialogic structure – with the implication that these are themes having many potential variations. We choose, in these instances, to treat the text as 'sovereign' and 'polysemic', and the communicative act as 'displaced' (see 2.2.1). Section 3.3.3 attempts to deal more generally with a popular variety of writing. Although our main attempt here is to isolate features of style that appear to be 'text-intrinsic' (or at least 'variety-intrinsic'), our treatment of this theme may once again raise questions of discourse going beyond texts; it may be instructive to compare this section with what is said about other popular reading materials in 3.1 to 3.2.2.

3.3   PROSE DEVICES

3.3.1 A Narrative Structure

Even a simple story, unaffectedly or perhaps naively told, must follow a pattern of development and exhibit principles of cohesion which, on examination, will often prove to be ingenious and subtle. The listener hears the narrative without being aware that his attention is being guided, his expectations fulfilled or frustrated; the reader obediently follows the text, not fully realizing – though he has the page before his eyes – how the teller steers him through the course of the tale.

Look, for example, at the text on p. 89 (ignoring for the moment the imposed apparatus of square brackets and Roman numerals). It is taken from a book called *Seventy Years a Showman*, by George Sanger, a nineteenth-century circus proprietor. It describes an incident from Sanger's boyhood, at a time when his father, a showman in a small way, took his stall from fair to fair, often by necessity travelling overnight. The text is paragraphed in a way that makes perfectly good narrative sense, but at the same time slightly disguises an inner principle of structure. This is the import of the square brackets, which suggest a division of the narrative procedure into six phases (I–VI), not in exact alignment with the paragraph division.

These narrative phases are primarily connected by repeated allusions, here called 'strands': a 'time strand' and three discernible 'action strands', all regularly marked out in the phasing of the story. Thus each phase is introduced by an expression of time. The anecdote opens with such an expression (*a night in early January*), proceeds to *then* (in line 5), leading to *presently* (line 12), and so to *after travelling*. These expressions represent the 'time strand', and each phase of the narrative, down to phase V, begins with a time-reference. The strand finally homes upon a phase, *this time* (line 20), which introduces a new phase of action, the crisis of the tale. From this point the time-reference lapse, and it is an 'action strand' that we follow through to the end of the story.

Two 'action strands' are important in the first four phases of the narrative. One of them concerns the activity of walking by the horses, the other that of dropping back to observe the wagon from behind. The walking motif turns up in the last sentences of phases I, II and III, in *my father and I walked by the horses, got back to the horses' heads and plodded along with father*, and *plodded on as before*. The 'dropping back' theme is presented in the first sentences of phases II, III and IV. in *then I fell a bit behind, father stopped . . . and the wagon passed him*, and *I let the wagon pass me and fell behind it*. These two strands converge upon the crucial phrase *this time* – which, we may now begin to realize, is not a simple time-reference like *now*, but a combination of the meanings 'now' and 'with the action'. From this point there is a shift in the phasing, and a third action strand emerges, introduced by *I swung myself up to the wagon rail* in the second sentence of V, and assuming the phase-initiating position in the first sentence of VI.

The 'stranding' of the narrative, as described here, is represented in Figure 3.1. The significance of that ordinary phrase *this time* is quite clear. It interrupts the preceding chain of alternating walking/falling back occurrences, *walked . . . fell behind . . . plodded along . . .passed him . . . plodded on . . . fell behind . . .* phase IV does not end with a recurrence of the 'plodding' motif, because *this time* the principal actor will not return to his plod, but will initiate a new action, i.e. will climb up on to the wagon.

The telling of the tale thus demonstrably coheres round these important points, which are not established by stiffly unvarying formulae, but by artfully artless modulations of grammar and lexicon. No two time expressions are quite alike grammatically and semantically. If they are grammatically or formally akin, like *then* and *presently* (single words, adverbs of time), they are semantically different (*then* = time as point, *presently* = time as relationship). If they are semantic equivalents, like *when we had gone, perhaps, another mile*, and *after travelling for some half a mile further*, they are grammatically different (the latter of these is a participle clause).

In the 'action strands' there are obvious variations in the lexicon and in the phrase structure; *walk* yields to *plod, fall behind* alternates

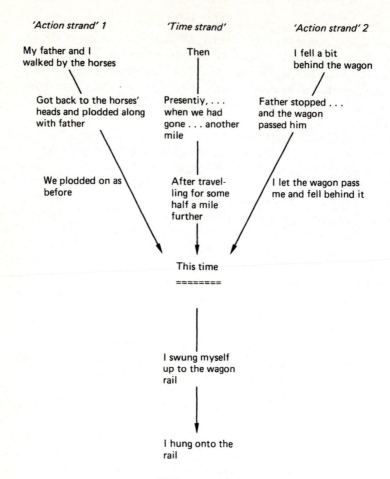

Figure 3.1   The 'stranding' of the narrative

with *pass*, and the constructions in which these words occur repeat a message but revise a wording. Thus '*my father* and I walked', but '*I* plodded along *with father*' and '*we* plodded on as before'. There is even, in these action-references, the suggestion of an orientation to events, in the passivity of what simply happens to the narrator and the activity of what the narrator causes to happen. Thus, *I fell a bit behind the wagon* suggests, in context, a casual, unpremeditated act. The words *in doing so, noticed,* and *a bit* are supportive clues, pointing to the 'incidental' nature of the event. *Father stopped . . . and the wagon passed him* gives no indication of motive, and there is no word in the immediate context that might justify an interpretation of the father's action as 'casual' or 'purposeful'. We infer from what follows that the action is deliberate, but there is nothing on the surface of the text to support the inference. In *I let the wagon pass me and fell behind it*, however, the action is clearly premeditated; *let* tells us as much, and in the ensuing context it appears that *I noticed* has given place to *my eyes once more fixed*. There is a good deal of different between merely 'noticing' and fixing your eyes on something.

The strands of time and action create the underlying fabric of the tale, but there are additional threads of lexical cohesion, words and phrases significantly echoed from phase to narrative phase. The *moonlight*, for example, is a descriptive detail in phase I, at the opening of the story, but an adjunct to the action in phase VI, at the conclusion; the moon is in a dramatic sense the discoverer of the body. There are similar repetitions of plot-sustaining references to other objects or *personae* – to the passengers, to the wagon, to the mysterious 'parcel' (a blatantly misleading word), which becomes a 'bundle' and then a 'sack'. There are repeated references to physical perceptions, i.e. to the processes of seeing, noticing, looking, and to the emotions, specifically that of fear. Furthermore, the riddling element in the narrative, the author's evident concern to prepare a surprise for the reader, is expressed in the deliberate resort to indefinite expressions like *something* and *as though*. The 'something alive' which the boy fancifully perceives in phase II is the 'dead woman' (we note the ironic counterpoise of 'alive' and 'dead') which the moonlight reveals in phase VI.

These coherences of vocabulary and phrasing are set out in Figure 3.2. The density of their occurrence is striking. What at first looks like a very simple piece of story-telling, managed competently but without extraordinary skill, now appears as a feat of remarkable subtlety. There is in the text not a sentence, perhaps not a phrase, that does not have a meaningful and necessary place in the expanding pattern of the narrative. The naive manner, the apparent propensity to literary cliché ('flooding the country with her silver light') are quite deceptive; this story-teller is accomplished and shrewd, with the skill of a spieler, a practised showman.

	[It was a cold, frosty night in early January. The roads were hard	1
	and good and the moon was flooding the country with her silver light,	2
	making everything almost as bright as day.	3
I	My father and I walked by the horses, while our passengers on the	4
	front of the wagon laughed and talked.][Then I fell a bit behind the	5
	wagon and as I did so I noticed the parcel our passengers had put	6

on the back showing out in the strong moonlight. It was a bulky, long,   7
II shapeless sort of bundle contained in a big sack, and it moved in a   8
fashion that made it seem, to my boyish eyes, as though it had   9
something alive in it.   10

However, I did not look closer, but got back to the horses' heads   11
and plodded along with father.][Presently, when we had gone, perhaps,   12
another mile, father stopped by the roadside and the wagon passed him   13
III as it had done in my case. He was some few minutes before he rejoined 14
me and when I looked at his face I was frightened, it was so stern   15
and set. Something had evidently upset him, but he said nothing and   16
we plodded on as before.]   17

[After travelling for some half a mile further, I let the wagon pass me   18
IV and fell behind it, my eyes once more fixed on the mysterious   19
parcel at the back.][This time my curiosity overcame me. I swung myself   20
up to the wagon rail and took a close look at the bundle. I could see   21
V   the neck of the sack was unloosed, as though somebody had recently   22
untied it, and pulling the neck aside, I peeped in.]   23

[I hung onto the rail paralysed with fear. The moonlight shone through   24
VI the loosened sack and I saw a naked human arm and the pale wax-like   25
face of a dead woman.   26

3.3.2 A Dialogic Structure

The dialogues we meet in fiction, no less than the passages of straight narrative, are constructed on discernible cohesive principles. Some of these principles are derived from the 'rules' of naturally occurring conversation; others are founded in a purely literary aesthetic, which stylisticians sometimes appear to discount or neglect. The aesthetic is founded on a single question – what is the function of dialogue in fiction? – to which three answers are relevant:

1   To interrupt the flow of general narration, slow down the movement of the story, and concentrate attention on a particular event, relationship, etc.

2   To bring out character, and relationships between characters; personalities being revealed by what they say, what others say to or about them, and how they respond to what others say.

3   To create the sense of a background by supplying impressions – conveyed through personal interactions – of a society, its manners, its concerns, its material objects.

Any or all of these functions may be realized in a particular sample of fictional dialogue, and the dialogic form will obviously be conditioned by the functional emphasis, or the number of functions that have to be

A. Time links
in early January (I) . . . *Then* (II) . . . *Presently, when we had gone, perhaps, another mile*
(III) . . . *After travelling for some half a mile further* (IV) . . . *This time* (V)

B. Action links
Strand 1: *My father and I walked by the horses* (I, end) . . . *got back to the horses' heads and
plodded along with father* (II, end) . . . *we plodded on as before* (III, end)
Strand 2: *I fell a bit behind the wagon* (II, beginning) . . . *father stopped by the roadside
and the wagon passed him* (III, beginning) . . . *I let the wagon pass me and fell behind it*
(IV, beginning)
Strand 3: *I swung myself up to the wagon rail* (V) . . . *I hung onto the rail* (VI)

C. Setting
the moon was flooding the country with her silver light (I) . . . *showing out in the strong
moonlight (II)* . . . *The moonlight shone through the loosened sack* (VI)

D. Objects, persons, locations
wagon, wagon rail (I, II, III, IV, V, VI)
the parcel (II) . . . *the mysterious parcel* (IV) (NB. only in II and IV)
a bulky, long, shapeless sort of bundle (II) . . . *the bundle* (V)
a big sack (II) . . . *the sack* (V) . . . *the loosened sack* (VI)
our passengers (I, II) (NB. not after II)
on the front (I) . . . *on the back* (II) . . . *at the back* (IV)

E. Perceptions, emotions
I noticed (II) . . . *to my boyish eyes* (II) . . . *I did not look closer* (II) . . . *I looked at his face*
(III) . . . *my eyes once more fixed* (IV) . . . *took a close look* (V) . . . *I could see* (IV) . . .
I peeped in (V) . . . *I saw* (VI)
frightened (III) . . . *paralysed with fear* (VI); NB. also *overcame* in *my curiosity overcame
me* (V) versus *paralysed* in *paralysed with fear* (VI)

F. Hints and inferences
something alive (II) . . . *dead woman* (VI)
as though it had something alive in it (II) . . . *something had evidently upset him* (III) . . . *as
though somebody had recently untied it* (V)

Figure 3.2   Cohesive schemes in the 'Sanger' narrative

realized. Concerning the form of the dialogue, the following questions
may be asked:

a   Do the characters 'interact' in short, fairly simple utterances, or
    do they 'converse' in longer utterances often amounting to set
    speeches?
b   Is it 'bare' dialogue, or is it interpolated with comments,
    references to the characters' appearance and behaviour, allu-
    sions to a context of objects and phenomena?
c   Are the utterances accompanied by expressions reporting the
    style of speech, or indicating the state of mind of the speaker?
d   Are the commentary elements mentioned in (b) above merely

decorative – i.e. setters of a scene – or do they have a profounder relevance, i.e. as indices of character, relationship, state of mind?

e   Is there a predominance of certain types of formulation, e.g. questions, requests, directives, statements? Is the distribution of any of these at all significant? (e.g. does someone use directives all the time? does someone often respond to a question with a question?)

f   Is there an evident discrepancy, suggesting irony, symbolism, or some such undercurrent of meaning, between utterance and ostensible reference?

g   Is typography used to suggest intonations, emphases, or styles of speech? (e.g. 'How *can* you?' she said. 'But my *de-ee-ar*,' he drawled).

In trying to answer these questions we inevitably touch on matters arising from the analysis of 'natural' conversation. But clearly, a literary conversation is unnatural, an artifice; and the essence of its artificiality is the subordination of conversational features, having an immediate pragmatic import, to the larger aesthetic design, the planned plural significances, of a text. Talking is subsumed in a creative texture that involves more than talk.

A specimen text   There is perhaps no single instance of literary dialogue from which all the points suggested above might be illustrated. However, one chapter of Galsworthy's *The Man of Property* opens with an extended passage of 'multifunctional' dialogue – that is, one that halts the impetus of the general narrative, that obliquely illustrates characters and relationships, and that suggests an ambience and a way of life. Furthermore, this dialogue exemplifies several features of dialogic pattern and form – specifically in a controlled brevity of utterance, a significant, near-symbolic use of 'commentary elements', and an adroit use of reporting verbs and tags. Here, then, is the text:

> Dinner began in silence; the women facing one another, and the men.
>   In silence the soup was finished – excellent, if a little thick – and fish was brought. In silence it
> 5   was handed.
>   Bosinney ventured: 'It's the first spring day.'
>   Irene echoed softly: 'Yes – the first spring day.'
>   'Spring!' said June: 'there isn't a breath of air!'
> No one replied.
> 10   The fish was taken away, a fine fresh sole from Dover. And Bilson brought champagne, a bottle swathed around the neck with white.

Soames said: 'You'll find it dry.'

Cutlets were handed, each pink-frilled about the
15 legs. They were refused by June, and silence fell.

Soames said: 'You'd better take a cutlet, June;
there's nothing coming.'

But June again refused, so they were borne away. And
then Irene asked: 'Phil, have you heard my blackbird'?
20 Bosinney answered: 'Rather – he's got a hunting-song.
As I came round I heard him in the square.'

'He's such a darling!'

'Salad, sir?' Spring chicken was removed.

But Soames was speaking: 'The asparagus is very poor.
25 Bosinney, glass of sherry with your sweet? June, you're
drinking nothing!

June said: 'You know I never do. Wine's such horrid
stuff!'

An apple charlotte came upon a silver dish. And
30 smilingly Irene said: 'The azaleas are so wonderful
this year!'

To this Bosinney murmured: 'Wonderful! the scent's
extraordinary!'

June said: 'How *can* you like the scent? Sugar, please,
35 Bilson.'

Sugar was handed her, and Soames remarked: 'This
charlotte's good!'

The charlotte was removed. Long silence followed.
Irene, beckoning, said: 'Take out the azaleas, Bilson.
40 Miss June can't bear the scent.'

'No, let it stay,' said June.

Olives from France, with Russian caviare, were placed
on little plates. And Soames remarked: 'Why can't we
have the Spanish?' But no one answered.
45   The olives were removed. Lifting her tumbler June
demanded: 'Give me some water, please.' Water was
given her. A silver tray was brought, with German
plums. There was a lengthy pause. In perfect harmony
all were eating them.
50   Bosinney counted up the stones: 'This year – next
year – some time –'

Irene finished softly: 'Never. There was such a glorious
sunset. The sky's all ruby still – so beautiful!'

He answered: 'Underneath the dark.'
55   Their eyes had met, and June cried scornfully: 'A
London sunset!'

Egyptian cigarettes were handed in a silver box.
Soames, taking one, remarked: 'What time's your play
begin?'

60   No one replied, and Turkish coffee followed in
        enamelled cups.
            Irene, smiling quietly, said: 'If only –'
            'Only what?' said June.
            'If only it could always be the spring!'
65   Brandy was handed; it was pale and old.
        Soames said: 'Bosinney, better take some brandy.'
        Bosinney took a glass; they all arose.
            'You want a cab?' asked Soames.
        June answered: 'No. My cloak, please, Bilson.' Her
70   cloak was brought.
            Irene from the window, murmured: 'Such a lovely night!
        The stars are coming out!'
            Soames added: 'Well I hope you'll both enjoy
        yourselves.'
75   From the door June answered: 'Thanks. Come, Phil.'
        Bosinney cried: 'I'm coming.'
        Soames smiled a sneering smile, and said: 'I wish
        you luck!'
            And at the door Irene watched them go.
80   Bosinney called: 'Good night!'
            'Good night!' she answered softly . . .

Among the reader's first impressions must be the thought that this is
one of literature's big meals. Here are soup, fish, cutlets, spring
chicken, salad, apple charlotte, olives and caviare, plums; accompanied by champagne, sherry, brandy, coffee and cigarettes; served on
silver, and representing a global tour of gourmet delights – from
Dover, France, Russia, Germany, Egypt and Turkey. What is Galsworthy's objective in describing this bewildering – even ludicrous
succession of courses? Is it simply to portray realistically the customs
of an affluent middle-class household in Victorian England? Clearly it
is that, but so much more than that. The reader must quickly notice
how the comings and goings of the various dishes are a sort of
measure, 'timing', so to speak, the conversation, filling in the communicative gaps, even illustrating interactional roles. Soames, the 'man of
property', talks of little else but the food, its quality, its provenance (he
wishes the olives had come from Spain). Of the twelve sentences
allotted to him eight concern food, and three of these are brief direct
statements about the quality of the meal ('You'll find it dry'; 'The
asparagus is very poor'; 'This charlotte's good!'). Galsworthy ostensibly conspires with his character in confining his own evaluative
comments to the food and avoiding overt judgement on anything or
anyone else. It is the authorial voice that tells us how, for instance, the

soup is 'excellent, if a little thick', or how the brandy is 'pale and old'. A crassness of perception, Soames' own crassness, is thus emphasized; for the real concern is not with the dishes but with the diners, and things are going on under Soames' nose that he apparently fails to see – though it would be a very dull reader indeed who could not infer from this passage that Irene and Bosinney are in love.

Irene is married to Soames and Bosinney is engaged to June – but the table-placing so casually described in the first sentence suggests a realignment of alliances and confrontations. June confronts Irene as an enemy, Soames unwittingly faces Bosinney as a rival, Bosinney adjoins Irene as a conspirator. Intimations of rivalry, collusion, or mere impercipience run through the whole of the dinner-table conversation – if 'conversation' is the right word. Soames, preoccupied with the meal and with his own status as the provider of it, never really enters into conversation with anyone ('Why can't we have the Spanish?' he asks, when the olives are served, and no one answers him). Irene and Bosinney are the real conversationalists, addressing and answering each other in tones of obvious intimacy, detected by June, who is not unnaturally wounded by her own perceptions. Her resentment can only be expressed in one way; she becomes a conversation-stopper, refusing to co-operate in any initiative. Again and again, when a conversational overture is made to June, or when June might easily and conventionally enter into a conversation, she rejects the advance and behaves rudely. Readers with no knowledge of Galsworthy's story, and with only this extract to guide them, would be bound to notice June's uncooperative behaviour, would be bound to seek a reason for it, and would be virtually bound to conclude either that June was a very prickly personality or that she was jealous. For the reader who has read the book up to this point her conversational behaviour is all the more remarkable because she has been established as a 'good' character with strong sociable instincts.

The diners' diverse attitudes and perceptions are clearly indicated in the verbs and additional tags used to report their utterances. (See Figure 3.3.) An overview of these makes it immediately apparent that Bosinney and Irene are a conversational duo. The arrows in the figure indicate that they address and reply to each other; in one instance an exchange actually runs to three utterances (when Bosinney counts the plumstones, is interrupted by Irene, and in his turn replies to her remark). The verbs marking the Bosinney–Irene exchanges are symptomatic of their close relationship. Bosinney 'ventures' or 'calls', Irene 'echoes' and 'answers'. Irene's utterances are frequently reported with some adverbial tag indicating her pleasure in Bosinney's company:

'echoed softly', 'smilingly said', 'smiling quietly, said', 'answered softly' – the adverb *softly* is, indeed, used with exclusive reference to her speeches. Bosinney is never reported as simply *saying* something. Irene's utterances are only three times reported with 'say'; one of those cases is a directive to a servant, and in the other two instances the verb is reinforced adverbially by *smilingly* and *smiling quietly*.

By comparison, the reporting verbs and tags associated with Soames and June are bare and non-committal. The verbs that might be thought to imply some kind of interaction (e.g. *ask, add, demand*) are in fact related to perfunctory social routines (leave-taking) or giving orders to a servant. Soames' speeches are generally reported with 'say' or 'remark' – the latter a significant item indeed, for his 'remarks' invite no reply and do not always get one. (He 'remarks' instead of 'enquiring' when the play begins; and significantly, nobody answers him.) Only once, towards the end of the passage, is one of Soames' utterances adverbially qualified; he wishes Bosinney and June luck 'with a sneering smile' – as though, after all, he *did* know something, though the reader cannot be sure. This is the one moment of particular comment on a character otherwise presented in elaborate nullity. June also has her moment of adverbial distinction, when she is said to 'cry scornfully' – the very moment, it may be noted, when the lovers have just enacted their most intimate coded exchange, in their romantic praise of the sunset. June is well aware that they are not talking about the weather. Apart from this, her reporting tags are as dull as Soames' own; for the most part she 'says' or – responding with the bare minimum of politeness to her host – 'answers'. (Her answers are indeed bald: 'No', she says, and 'Thanks'.) Once, when speaking to a servant, she 'demands', which suggests a less than polite intonation of the courteously formulated 'Give me some water, please'. And once, when 'ask' might be the appropriate index to a genuinely co-operative tone of voice, she appears to challenge rudely with 'say':

> Irene, smiling quietly, said 'If only . . .
> 'Only what?' said June.

Quite as important as these modes of exchange are the frequent silences. (Again see Figure 3.3) This is, after all, a dinner party, a celebration of sorts; but words are few and silences are many as the dishes are brought in and taken out. Twice the silence is protracted. During one of these long pauses there is at least some feeling of unity – because everybody is enjoying the German plums. The food and drink, as we have already noticed, becomes a kind of secondary cast-list, standing in for the bored or embarrassed or tongue-tied principal

Line	Soames	June	Bosinney	Irene	Silence
1					'In silence'
3					'In silence'
4					'In silence'
6			Ventured →		
7				Echoed softly	
8		Said			
9					No one replied
13	Said				
15					Silence fell
16	Said				
19				Asked	
20			Answered →	φ	
22					
24	(Was speaking)				
27		Said			
30				Smilingly said	
32			Murmured		
34		Said			
36	Remarked				
38					Long silence followed
39				Beckoning, said	
41		Said			
43	Remarked				
46		Demanded			
48			Counted up the stones →		48 there was lengthy pause
50					
52				Finished softly	
54			← Answered		
55		Cried scornfully			
58	Remarked				60 no one replied
62				Smiling quietly said	
63		Said			
66	Said				
68	Asked				
69		Answered			
71				Murmured	
73	Added				
75		Answered			
75			Cried		
76					
77	(With a) sneering smile said				
80			Called →		
81				Answered softly	

Figure 3.3 Speeches and silences: the report tags

actors. An apple charlotte comes in upon a silver dish, for all the world like a vaudeville player about to do a turn, and is applauded. This in fact is the only instance in which the food is presented as a kind of agent, the subject of an active verb. Verbs relating to the service of the meal are preponderantly in the passive (see Figure 3.4). Diners and dinner alike figure in an unavailing social ritual. The fish is brought and 'handed' and taken away, the cutlets are handed and borne away, the olives are placed on little plates and then the olives are removed. The apple charlotte makes an impression on Soames, but it too is removed. Only the German plums are an unqualified social success; they are not removed, because 'in perfect harmony all were eating them'.

The account of the meal is not without its comedy, which Galsworthy may or may not have intended; its serious function is to suggest, perhaps more pointedly than any dialogue, the unease and isolation of the diners, the ludicrous rarity of anything like a genuine festive rapport between them.

The text described here constitutes two pages out of a book of over three hundred pages; yet this dialogue contains much of the thematic material that fills the novel. It is more than a 'conversation' in the ordinary sense, for conversations as a rule are transactions with immediate purposes, in which whatever is said is valid for the period of the exchange. As 'conversation' Galsworthy's text is dull and perhaps unconvincing, but it is not uninteresting or unimportant as *dialogue*.

The Meal : Passives

3	The soup was finished
4	Fish was brought
5	It was handed
10	The fish was taken away
14	Cutlets were handed
15	They were refused by June
18	They were borne away
23	Spring chicken was removed
36	Sugar was handed her (June)
38	The charlotte was removed
42	Olives . . . were placed on little plates
45	The olives were removed
46	Water was given her (June)
47	A silver tray was brought
57	Egyptian cigarettes were handed
65	Brandy was handed
69	Her cloak was brought (June)

Figure 3.4   The meal: passives

For the reader, what is represented here will go on being valid and significant after the page is turned. It will be one of many points of reference that accumulate as the text is read – or, to put it more appropriately, it will be one of the many patterns, each complete in itself, that enter into the larger pattern.

3.3.3 Style in Popular Fiction

Most works of popular fiction are characterized by a paradox of realistic unrealism, in many cases so marked as to amount to a game played with the reader. They are often elaborately 'researched', in historical, technical, topographical, institutional and sartorial detail, documenting reality with overwhelming care; at the same time, however, they are doggedly stereotyped, with well-tried and uncomplicated moral recipes, with actors who present conventional appearances (no heroes afflicted with warts, no heroines burdened with unsightly fat), who think and act predictably, who undergo helter-skelter changes of violent fortune but are seldom more than transiently affected by their doings and sufferings. Jack, his arm broken, flies the plane into the sunset; Jill, her heart broken, looks forward (sipping her cocoa) to a bright new tomorrow.

The authors of such fictions spare no effort to engross their readers, making them accept as credible – because the cars, the guns, the cocktails, the hemlines and street-names are so ruthlessly right – narratives which at another level invite scepticism, or at least the privilege of indifference, the right to turn away, withholding comment and commitment. This is indeed a very powerful principle, a convenient game that permits us to enjoy the TV soap-opera, or indulge a taste for lurid paperbacks. The realism game offers us a credible world of fact, but never threatens to modify, with uncomfortable, homecoming reflections, our view of what experience is and what human nature embraces. James Bond is James Bond and his devotees can sleep soundly in their beds, little reckoning that the master is dangling in a snake-pit, or tied to a buzz saw.

These observations are generally applicable to what is, in fact, a rather diverse genre, or complex of genres. Its principal categories are Adventure and Romance (with various sub-species), Crime Fiction, Spy Fiction, and Science Fiction – this last a huge field, ranging from the crude comic strip to writing of great imaginative merit. Even a description as perfunctory as this must suggest that 'popular fiction' is a rather intricate cultural phenomenon, the ramifications of which have yet to be adequately studied. What is intuitively apparent (some would say obvious) is its base in conventional assumptions about maleness and femaleness, and its appeal to these assumptions. The appeal is expressed in the vibrant adjectives of the publisher's blurb or the bookseller's hype. This, for example, from a book-club pamphlet:

> In a story as thrilling, chilling and intricately woven as any he has crafted, Jack Higgins takes his readers and his characters through a pulse-racing series of twists and turns to a heart-stopping climax.

Adventures are 'pulse-racing' and 'heart-stopping'. They may also be 'action-packed', 'spine-tingling', 'fast-moving', and 'tough'. Romantic tales, on the other hand, may be characterized as 'heart-warming', 'emotional', 'delightful', 'tender', and 'human'. There is an implicit supposition that men like their stories to be 'action-packed', whereas women prefer a 'heart-warming' tale. Indeed, these epithets *keynote* a stylistic intention, another game played by crafty writers for the benefit of enthralled readers. Popular fiction at its most popular – that is, at its most successful commercially – makes an adroit combination of the realism game and the keynote game.

Language and the realism game   Now here are some elementary moves in the game of making it all seem so real:
   1   *Naming.* The magic of names is a central device of popular narrative, particularly in the 'masculine' style of the adventure or the spy story: names of people – fictional and factual in free assembly – and of geographical features, of towns, streets, buildings, names of vehicles, ships, machines, weapons, materials, fabrics. In Frederick Forsyth's *The Devil's Alternative* (a book from which many of the examples quoted here have been culled), there is hardly a page on which the naming device is not hard at work, constructing the realistic scene in such detail that the reader is almost distracted by realism. A typical example, from a minor, transitional passage:

> On another track south of the VC-10 a Boeing jumbo jet of British Airways left Heathrow bound for New York. Among its 300-plus passengers it bore Azamat Krim, alias Arthur Crimmins, Canadian citizen, heading west with a back-pocket full of money on a buying mission.
>   Eight hours later the VC-10 landed perfectly at Andrews base in Maryland, ten miles southeast of Washington. As it closed down its engines on the apron, a Pentagon staff car swept up to the foot of the steps and disgorged a two-star general of the USAF.

Apart from its use of personal, topographical and institutional names, this extract exemplifies two further characteristics of the realism game:

the nomenclature of letters and numerals (VC-10, USAF), and a
sedulous concern for counts and measurements ('300-plus passengers',
'ten miles southeast of Washington'). In another extract from the same
novel we find the writer doggedly naming names in order to establish
his credentials as an authority on the intelligence services of America,
Russia and Britain:

> That was the first time Munro had heard the term 'the firm'. Later he
> would learn the terminology. To those in the Anglo-American alliance
> of intelligence services, a strange and guarded, but ultimately vital,
> alliance, the SIS was always called 'the firm'. To its employees those in
> the counter-intelligence arm, the MI5, were 'the colleagues'. The CIA
> at Langley, Virginia, was 'the company' and its staff 'the cousins'. On
> the opposite side worked 'the opposition', whose headquarters was at
> Number 2, Dzerzhinsky Square, Moscow, named after the founder of
> the old Cheka, Feliks Dzerzhinsky, Lenin's secret police boss. This
> building would always be known as 'the centre' and the territory east of
> the Iron Curtain as 'the bloc'.

At no point in the subsequent narrative is this glossary really needed.
The names serve something other than a merely informative purpose;
they tell the reader, in effect, that he may trust this fiction as he might
trust a well-documented narrative of historical fact, because the
author has clearly 'researched' his subject and can be assumed to have
a more than passing acquaintance with the worlds and underworlds
through which his story moves.

  2 *'Dossier' epithets and additions.* Names are often accompanied by
stock modifiers indicating age, military rank, civil title, profession,
social role, or perhaps some idiosyncrasy, biographical detail, or
physical characteristic ('Burly, bearded Captain Andrew "Brainy"
MacBraine, RN . . .'). This is a stylistic mannerism that popular
fiction occasionally shares with tabloid journalism, in which a dustman is not a dustman unless he can be called a 47-year-old refuse
collector and father of two. In magazine fiction, such 'dossier' details,
besides occurring as premodifying noun-epithets (Captain X, Staff
Nurse Y, successful architect N.N.) also commonly take the form of
appositions, parentheses, or 'additioning' clauses. Thus, from a story
synopsis in *Women's Own*:

> Though the groom, Andrew Morton, had only ever treated her as a
> friend – the local doctor's second daughter, who had trained as the
> nurse at a nearby hospital – she loved him.

  3 *Periphrasis.* Periphrases occur as stylistic variants in the naming
game, and are often used in preference to pronominal connectives,

whenever it is apparently judged inconvenient to repeat a name. To illustrate, let us invent a pair of sentences:

Jill looked at Mr Hogan. Mr Hogan was evidently upset.

This minimal narrative could be rewritten in the form:

Jill looked at Mr Hogan. He was evidently upset.

Or, using a relative pronoun to make one sentence:

Jill looked at Mr Hogan, who was evidently upset.

In the periphrastic style, however, the connection might be made thus:

Jill looked at Mr Hogan. The kindly old Irishman/one-legged seadog/pugnacious leprechaun/grizzled freedom fighter . . . etc. was evidently upset.

The periphrasis introduces, or reiterates, dossier information; it also makes a connection between the tricks of realism and those of keynoting, since periphrases commonly include evaluative adjectives and cliché epithets (e.g. *kindly, pugnacious, grizzled*).

   4   *Technical specification.* Here is a prominent stylistic feature of 'adventure' fiction, a form of verbal *machismo*, easily parodied, e.g.:

Her Majesty entered the waiting car. It was a Daimler Benz Mark IV crosshead sedan de ville with the Jinglebacker struts on the rear axle and a Ferlighetti modified supercharger. You don't see many of them nowadays. Suddenly a shot rang out. It came from a snug-nosed Pottinger .307, the kind with the balanced recoil and the filed-down front sight. Hearing it, one of the motor-cycle escort quickly turned his 1500cc twin-cylinder cone-driven Harley Granville Barker . . .

Weapons and automobiles are preferred topics for this kind of stylistic decoration. An actual sample, once more from *The Devil's Alternative:*

What was missing, the proprietor confirmed, was a single hunting rifle, one of his finest, a Finnish-made Sako Hornet .22, a highly accurate precision piece. Also gone were two boxes of shells for the rifle, soft-nosed 45 grain hollow-point Remingtons, capable of high velocity, great penetration, and considerable distortion on impact.

And these, from an author widely read yet not commonly included in the 'popular' category:

Robert Wilson came up then carrying his short, ugly, shockingly big-bored .505 Gibbs and grinning.

... he [i.e. a lion] turned his heavy head and swung away toward the cover of the trees as he heard a cracking crash and felt the slam of a .30-06 220-grain solid bullet that bit his flank and ripped in sudden but scalding nausea through his stomach.

These last examples, taken from *The Short Happy Life of Francis Macomber*, should remind us that the modern *macho* narrator owes many of his stylistic techniques to Hemingway – whose use of such devices, however, is more creative, more poetic, more effectively keyed to his psychological themes.

5 *Measurements, weights, volumes, times, dates, distances.* The illusion of realism sometimes requires the elaboration of statistics. Even in simple cases a number rarely comes amiss; popular fiction abounds in expressions like 'she took two faltering steps forward', 'three inches from his nose was the barrel of a Walther P.38', 'his suitcase contained nine ounces of a new and powerful explosive', '15,000 tons of rock fell into the Pacific', 'at precisely 0827 hrs on the 3rd of May, 1985, a Boeing 347 took off from Heathrow, climbing steeply to an altitude of 28,000 feet'. (The examples are invented but will perhaps be recognized as plausible.) Desmond Bagley provides an extended instance of numerological narrative:

'In 1955 the Scripps expedition fished up a nodule from about – here.' I pointed to the spot. 'It was two feet long, twenty inches thick and weighed a hundred and twenty-five pounds. In the same year a British cable ship was grappling for a broken cable here, in the Philippines Trench. They got the cable up all right, from 17,000 feet, and in a loop of cable they found a nodule four feet long and three feet in diameter. That one weighed 1700 pounds.'

'I begin to see what you're getting at.'

'I'm trying to put it plainly. The orthodox boys have sampled sixty spots in sixty-four million square miles and have the nerve to think they know all about it. I'm banking that there are places where nodules lie fifty pounds to the square foot – and Mark knew of such places, if I read enough of his notes correctly.'

'I think you had a point to make about cobalt, Mike. Come across with it.'

I let my excitement show. 'This is the clincher. The highest assay for cobalt in any nodule has been just over 2 per cent.' I pushed the half-nodule on the table with my finger. 'I assayed this one today. It checked out at ten per cent cobalt – and cobalt, Geordie, is worth more than all the rest put together and the rocket metallurgists can't get enough of it!'

This extract is from Bagley's *Night of Error*. At this point in the narrative, the speaker having 'come across' with his revelation, a sub-chapter ends. The next sub-chapter begins humanely: 'We ate Geordie's stew, and very good it was . . .' The problem of reconciling statistical recitals with the ordinariness of human interaction can produce moments of unintended comedy. Here is another snatch of table talk – again, a sub-chapter ending – this time from *The Devil's Alternative*:

> Larsen was aware that the two biggest tankers in the world were the French Shell tankers *Bellamya* and *Batillus*, both just over 50,000 tons.
>
> 'What will be her deadweight, the *Freya*?' asked Larsen. 'How much crude will she carry?'
>
> 'Ah, yes, I forgot to mention that,' said the old shipowner mischievously. 'She'll be carrying one million tons of crude oil.'
>
> Thor Larsen heard a hiss of indrawn breath from his wife beside him.
>
> 'That's big, he said at last. 'That's very big.'
>
> 'The biggest the world has ever seen,' said Wennerstrom.

One might almost suspect this knowledgeable and precise author of impishly using numbers as erotic substitutes. The extract additionally illustrates the use of names (*Bellamya, Batillus*), of dossier epithets (*French Shell tankers*), and of periphrasis (*the old shipowner*).

Language and the keynote game   The intention of the realism game is to present readers with the material credentials of fantasy; that of the keynote game is to express or stimulate appropriate states of feeling. This is achieved by some fairly simple manipulations of lexicon, syntax and text-structure, as in the following examples.

1   *Verbs*. Many of the verbs in popular fiction are not assignable to the *core vocabulary* (see 3.1.1), but are synonyms denoting energetic action and reaction, or particular and intense states of perception and cognition. Thus, fictional agents may be allowed to *go*, or even *run*, but will preferentially *dash, rush, fly, hurry, scuttle*, etc.; they may *look*, but are just as likely to *stare, glare, gaze, glower*, or *shoot a glance*; their tears can *flow*, but usually *spring* to their eyes before *streaming* or *coursing* down their cheeks. (In extreme cases they *pour*.) In everyday usage the purpose of a 'core' item may be modified or more closely defined through the addition, in tag-fashion, of a 'manner' adverb, eg. *walk slowly, run quickly, look steadily, flow freely*. Pop-fiction style quite frequently assigns manner adverbs to the inherently 'stronger', 'non-core' items: *stroll lazily, dash hastily, stare fixedly, pour uninterruptedly*. Uncritical reliance on these devices is often responsible, in women's

magazine fiction, for some oddly maladjusted turns of phrase. An example, from a story in *Woman and Home*:

She sighed, a great peace creeping over her . . .

Like a lecherous spider, perhaps; one step further down the rocky road from *descend* would have brought us to *crawl*. Or again, from the same story:

Stefan's amber eyes glowed brilliantly.

Eyes conventionally *shine*, or possibly *gleam*; they may conceivably *glow*, if the intention is to convey a benign warmth; but the addition of the manner adverb here makes the description verge on the grotesque.

2 *Adjectives*. There are three stylistically prominent types:

(a) Adjectives of sensory perception, i.e. colour words, participial adjectives expressing intensities of light (*glittering, gleaming, sparkling*) or of sound (*tinkling, booming,*) words descriptive of texture (*rough, smooth, silky*), words indicating tactile sensation (*hard, soft, warm, cool, sharp*), words denoting dimension or bodily shape (*long, round, broad, slim, lean*). Women's magazine fiction makes extensive use of such words, in descriptions of dress and physical appearance, or in the occasional demure venture into the erotic.

(b) Terms denoting the responses and emotional states of the fictional characters, eg. *angry, furious, anxious, loving, affectionate, despairing, quizzical, blazing, cold*. Many of these have corresponding manner adverbs, and either the adjective or the adverb or both may occur in collocation with an emphatic, 'non-core' verb: 'she shot a furious glance at Tom', 'his cold blue eyes transfixed her with an icy stare', 'she shrank miserably into herself', 'his loving face loomed enticingly'.

(c) Terms suggesting an appropriate response from the *reader*. Of these, some are participial compounds – e.g. *heart-warming, gut-wrenching, spine-chilling* – which quite blatantly dictate to readers the feelings they are expected to have ('let your heart, too, be warmed'). Other participial adjectives (*menacing, thrilling, appalling*) work in much the same way. More subtly, there are words that ostensibly denote physical features of shape, colour, and so forth, but which in their context are designed to enlist the reader's emotional support. In romantic fiction, words like *small, pale, young*, are often made to exert a conspiratorial appeal; when the narrator describes 'Jennifer's pale face' or 'Stephen's clear young voice', the reader is invited to feel protectively concerned for Stephen and Jennifer.

3   *Participle clauses*. These play an important part in the keynote game. Semantically, they operate in two ways. They may denote concurrent or overlapping phases of (usually violent) action: 'smashing his fist into the plump face of the astonished KGB man, he plunged into the raging torrent below'. The invented example parodies the style of adventure fiction. In romance, on the other hand, the participle clause usually suggests a concomitant emotion, reflection, state of mind: 'she sighed, remembering their happy holiday in the Alps when Greg, caring nothing for the shameless expense of it, brought her flowers and champagne every evening'. For purposes of narrative economy and neat packaging of sentiment, the construction is often reduced to the bare participle:

> In the foyer of the hotel, Andrew Campbell rose from the bench seat and Claire, shocked, stumbled forward, staring at him, disbelieving.

This is from a story in *Woman and Home*. Note how Claire does not simply *walk* or *step*; she *stumbles* (having quite recently had the awful experience of being kissed by a bounder); she does not *look*, she *stares*; and so – carrying the kit of participial emotions appropriate to stumbling and staring – she is *shocked* and *disbelieving*. This little passage, making a crisis out of a mere encounter, illustrates quite well the technique of emotional keynoting in magazine fiction. Claire's fiancé turns up unexpectedly; the adequate feeling on Claire's part, as she *walks* into the hotel, would be one of surprise and puzzlement ('how lovely – but I thought you were in London?'); instead, the pitch is raised to disbelief and shock.

4   *Inanimate or impersonal agents as clause subjects*. Sentences of the type 'Tears shook her', 'A spasm of irritation ruffled his usually impassive features', 'Her ears warned her of the danger', 'Jealousy fretted at her peace of mind' occur again and again in contexts presenting the 'character as a victim-object of uncontrollable forces. When soldier Sam is in a spot, his stomach tightens; when nurse Nancy is alone in the fogbound clinic, fear grips her with an icy claw, and cold scalpels of apprehension threaten to cut incisively into her firm resolve. The following examples are from stories in *Annabel* and *Woman and Home*:

> A torpedo of anxiety shot through her system.
> Hot anger trembled through her body . . .
> She sat on the edge of a hotel bed, tears tightening her throat.
> Claire turned abruptly, going back into the house, remorse burning her as hotly as the sun had done.
> His hand was on her bare shoulder, and it slid beneath the shoulder

strap, savouring her bare skin as though his fingers had tongues. A clamour of desire rose in her, destroying her cool control.

These sentences illustrate, startlingly in some cases, the myth of agency that pervades magazine fiction, in which heroines do not *act*, but are *acted upon*.

5 *Figurative language*. Popular fiction rarely, if ever, cultivates the resources of symbolism, the possibilities of extended metaphor or patterns of imagery that gradually inform a whole narrative, creating different planes of interpretation. Instead, it makes persistent use of a kind of metaphoric cliché, repeatedly parading a few figurative devices with the aim of infusing energy, excitement, interest, into practically every sentence. Packing the verb with metaphoric vitality (as when a hand 'savours' bare skin) is one favourite tactic. The use of the sizzling simile (some examples are given below) is another. A recurrent syntactic symptom of figurative processes in pop style is the phraseology of *as if* and *as though*. These expressions, which are ordinarily used to introduce an elucidation or reformulation ('He felt tongue-tied, as though he had forgotten every word of English he ever knew'), are also the operators that pile the improbable on the unlikely. Struggling to consciousness in the terrorists' cellar, the hero feels as though a horse had stepped on him in the night; embroiled in the tangles of office intrigue, the heroine feels as if she were helpless in the grip of an octopus. Emphasis, not insight, is the role of *as if* in popular fiction; and so it is with all its metaphoric forms, as the following examples may suggest:

> But it was as if the last few days had soaked her will in a lassitude that weighed down her ability to make any decision at all.

This does not explain her inability to make decisions, or provide an analogy that might help the reader to understand her mental state; it tells us that her will was not simply weak, or inert, or sluggish, but soaked in lassitude. Another example, involving the same heroine:

> Time only to cry 'No Stefan, no!' before his mouth silenced her, and the strong, impenetrable armour of the past three years melted like molten steel.

The meaning is that she stopped resisting him, but the emphasizing metaphor gets lost somewhere between the castle and the crucible, and drifts into nonsense. Things molten have already melted. However, pop style readily allows the semantic stammer, for example:

> It was November before Derek Trehone entered Lorna's life again, storming into the department like a tornado.

In other words, he stormed in stormily; or breezed in breezily; or blew in gustily – but not, of course, spinning and sucking up papers and loose objects into the vortex of his transit. Metaphor may, as in this instance, pitch its claims excessively high; or, as in the following, may lower them towards banality:

> It was a monstrous wave, roaring mast-high, creamed with dirty grey spume and coming with the speed of an express train.

The intention is clearly to make sensation ever more sensational, but the effect is deflationary.

At its most ambitious, the pop-fictional metaphor is an attempt to link the emotional tenor of the narrative with its pretensions to realism. The point is illustrated by yet another passage from *The Devil's Alternative*:

> Thor Larsen came at him down the length of the table with all the pent-up rage of the past fifty hours unleashed in the violence of a maddened bear.
>
> The partisan recoiled, reached for his gun, had it in his hand and was about to fire. A fist like a log of spruce caught him on the left temple, flung him out of his chair and backwards across the cabin floor.

We note the 'action' verbs (*recoiled, flung*), the device of alternating personal name and periphrasis (*Thor Larsen* vs. *the partisan*), the specious precision (*the past fifty hours; the left temple* – which indicates, for devotees of boxing, that Thor Larsen must have thrown a right hook). But the most striking feature of the passage is its figurative endeavour. Why the simile 'a fist like a log of spruce'? Because Larsen (or rather, *Thor Larsen* – the name is frequently cited in full) is a Scandinavian, and spruce is a Scandinavian timber; had he been a Canadian his fist might have been made of maple, in the interests of realistic decorum. The image of the bear is also a decorous one; it is in keeping with the descriptive formulae applied to this character elsewhere in the narrative. He is large, hirsute, and full of animal vigour. See him meeting his wife at the airport:

> When Lisa Larsen arrived on the concourse with her overnight bag, he greeted her with the delicacy of an excited St Bernard, swinging her off her feet like a girl.

Thus on p. 97 Thor Larsen has *the delicacy of an excited St Bernard*, and on

p. 418 *the violence of a maddened bear*. That he has not the delicacy of an excited gorilla, or the violence of a maddened rhinoceros must depend at least to some extent on the fact that gorillas and rhinoceroses are not denizens of the snow-swept northern wilderness which is Thor Larsen's native habitat. The comparisons have to fit the dossier.

6   *'Topic skipping (vs. 'topic holding')*. This refers to a technique of structure in passages of narrative or description; a technique which, however, is also implicated in the keynote game. Two brief inventions may serve to capture a thesis:

> A.   His room was at the end of the corridor. It was bare and gloomy, badly lit by a single window under which he had placed his desk. This was always littered with papers, in such disorder that he could never lay hand immediately on any document, or find without much searching a pen, a ruler, a pair of scissors. These were only some of the objects that lay hidden somewhere on the desk. There was in fact a specimen of every office accessory apart from an ash-tray. He did not smoke.

> B   His room was at the end of the corridor. Students trooped up and down outside, in chattering groups. Charlie used to call the place the command post. It really did look like something out of the Waffen SS – except for the untidy pile of papers on the desk. Jack wouldn't have got any marks for neatness. He was, as they say, easy-going. The only thing he wouldn't tolerate was smoking. I always left my cigarettes behind when I went to see him in his room.

The first of these passages pursues its topic dutifully and coherently, following a logic of construction that assigns each sentence to its place in the developing narrative. There is an effect a single topic, or strand of exposition, taking up subordinate strands, perhaps, but never breaking off. The cohesion of the piece is simply but firmly marked by successive anaphoric pronouns (*it . . . this . . .these*), or, in the penultimate sentence, a disjunct (*in fact*). Such a technique of construction might be called 'topic holding'.

Passage B, by contrast, is full of breaks and shifts, with no obvious central strand, and with weaker marks of sequence and cohesion. With minor adjustments of wording it would be quite possible to work changes of order in the sequence of sentences without affecting the supposed exposition. For instance:

> Jack was, as they say, easy-going. He wouldn't have got any marks for neatness. His room was at the end of the corridor. Charlie used to call the place the command post. Students trooped up and down outside in chattering groups. It really did look like something out of the Waffen SS – except for the untidy pile of papers on the desk. I always left my

cigarettes behind when I went to see Jack in his room. The only thing he wouldn't tolerate was smoking.

This flexibility of order is a symptom of 'topic skipping'. What is the central theme of the passage? Is it Jack's desk? Jack's character? Jack's relationships with his friends (*I, Charlie*)? The resemblance of Jack's room to some sort of institutional HQ?

Topic skipping occurs with some frequency in passages of transition, scene-setting, or re-setting, when the author wants to maintain the pressure of an 'action-packed' yarn; this technique underlies many brisk descriptions of street-scenes, bars, airports, railway stations, workplaces. An example is discussed below.

Comparing styles 'pop fiction' and 'art fiction'   There is a certain danger in isolating popular fiction from other species of narrative; the danger of implying that 'pop fiction' has a polar counterpart in 'art fiction', a mode of writing that has no commerce with such tricks of rhetoric as those we have been discussing. Indeed art fiction does not shun and cannot wholly avoid these devices; nor would it be very difficult to turn up an extract from a recognized 'literary' author exhibiting one or other of them. They are part of the stock – sometimes a little soiled and shopworn – of the tradesman in story-telling. However, striking contrasts of procedure between art fiction and pop fiction become apparent when we examine how authors deal with necessary operations in the construction of a story – describing a character, setting a scene, summarizing a state of affairs, presenting a relationship or an interaction. Here are two passages offering some instructive comparisons:

A.   Ever since the sun rose I had been looking ahead. The ship glided gently in smooth water. After sixty days' passage I was anxious to make my landfall, a fertile and beautiful island of the tropics. The more enthusiastic of its inhabitants delight in describing it as the 'Pearl of the Ocean'. Well, let us call it the 'Pearl'. It's a good name. A pearl distilling much sweetness upon the world.

This is only a way of telling you that first-rate sugar cane is grown there. All the population of the Pearl lives for it and by it. sugar is their daily bread, as it were. And I was coming to them for a cargo of sugar in the hope of the crop having been good and the freights being high.

Mr Burns, my chief mate, made out the land first; and very soon I became entranced by this blue, pinnacled apparition, almost transparent against the light of the sky, a mere emanation, the astral body of an island risen to greet me from afar. It is a rare phenomenon, such a sight of the Pearl sixty miles off. And I wondered half seriously whether it was a good omen, whether what would meet me in that island would be as luckily exceptional as this beautiful, dreamlike vision so very few seamen have been privileged to behold.

B.   As *Esmerelda* drew nearer to Tahita the sea gave place to mountains, hazy green, and then we began to see the surf breaking on the beaches as we sailed along the coast. We all turned our thoughts to cold beer ashore.

Papeete, the Pearl of the Pacific, is a pleasant town with all the usual offices – banks, a hospital, shops and so forth, but it is also a collection of tin huts set down on a tropical island and therefore a trifle squalid; but the setting is magnificent. Arriving there we tied up almost in the main street and there are not many ports in the world where you can do that. Looking over the harbour you can see the island of Moorea nine miles away, a volcano which exploded in the far past leaving a jumble of spires and peaks leaning at impossible angles, one of the most splendid sights in the world, and one which must go a long way to compensate for any inconveniences occasioned by living in Papeete.

I looked round the harbour for the *Eastern Star* but there was no sign of her, so I tried to relax as we waited for customs clearance. Campbell was fretful, anxious to go ashore and see if there was anything for him at the post office. He was too much in the dark concerning the Suarez-Navarro expedition. I wasn't any too patient myself. I had questions to ask and I wanted to try and see the Governor. I believe in starting at the top.

Passage A is the opening of Joseph Conrad's story, *A Smile of Fortune;* Passage B is from Desmond Bagley's *Night of Error.* In content they bear some striking resemblances to each other. Each sets a scene; each describes a ship approaching its destination – and oddly enough the destinations in the two extracts have the same nickname; in each the narrator is a character in the story; in each, the narrator is impatient to go ashore. They invite stylistic comparisons which might be misdirected in one respect only: Passage A is the opening of a story, whereas extract B represents Mr Bagley and his hero in mid-narrative.

Perhaps the reader's first intuitive impression of the two passages will be of a certain leisureliness and deliberation in the Conrad, an unforced pacing from sentence to sentence, somewhat in contrast with the brisk and bustling air of Desmond Bagley's description. Such a response to the style of the two pieces can be related to perceptions of 'topic holding' and 'topic skipping', as described in the preceding section. The order of the first two sentences in Conrad's narrative exordium might be reversed; thereafter, however, there is no sentence that can be convincingly shifted from its position, and the reader who cares to examine the syntax closely will see how the text is held in a tight cohesive harness. The topic is consistently and consequentially developed. At the beginning of the passage, Conrad's narrator is looking for his island; then he tells his audience why he is going there; then he sees it, and finds it beautiful; then he wonders what fortune it will bring him. The theme is unfolded without distractions. We are not tempted to turn our attention to the briefly intrusive figure of Mr Burns, and the artful colloquial hesitancies – 'Well . . . as it were . . . this is only a way of telling you . . .' – are not allowed to blur the determined narrative line.

Passage B, by comparison, is a fine example of topic skipping. One sentence in particular ('We all turned our thoughts to cold beer ashore') could be located at several different points in the passage with no change of sense. The sentences in the second paragraph, the descriptive middle of the extract, coming, as it were, after 'we arrived' and before 'we got on with the plot', can be variously shuffled without damage to the integrity of the narrative, for example:

> Arriving there we tied up almost in the main street and there are not many ports in the world where you can do that. Papeete, the Pearl of the Pacific, is a pleasant town with all the usual offices – banks, a hospital, shops and so forth, but it is also a collection of tin huts set down on a tropical island and therefore a trifle squalid; but the setting is magnificent. Looking over the harbour you can see the island of Moorea nine miles away, a volcano which exploded in the far past leaving a jumble of spires and peaks leaning at impossible angles, one of the most splendid sights in the world, and one which must go a long way to compensate for any inconveniences occasioned by living in Papeete.

This rewriting shuffles the original's three sentences into the order 2–1–3; 3–1–2 would be equally intelligible, and also 3–2–1; and any of these orderings admits the free interpolation of wishes for cold beer. ('Arriving there we tied up almost in the main street, and there are not many ports in the world where you can do that. We also turned our thoughts to cold beer ashore. Papeete, the Pearl of the Pacific, is a pleasant town . . .' etc.) In the whole paragraph there is one rather vague connective, the word *there* in 'Arriving there . . .'. This apparently has anaphoric reference (in the original text) to *Papeete*, but the deictic scope is so broad that in a reordering the word can as convincingly refer to *ashore* or *the harbour*; and the name *Papeete* itself conveniently occurs more than once.

Unlike Conrad's text, which is truly *com*posed, Bagley's descriptive observations are *dis*posed on the page, if not randomly then at least in a rather free procedure. There is clearly an affective, 'keynoting' purpose in this: the author is intent on producing a 'fast-moving' story.

He is in something of a hurry; his descriptions are here and there peremptory (*hazy green* will do for the mountains) or casual ('the usual offices – banks, a hospital, shops and so forth') or inclined to make do with catch-all phrases ('peaks leaning at impossible angles'). His jotterbook haste has him at one point tripping over his conjunctions ('but it is also a collection of tin huts . . . but the setting is magnificent' – a conjunct such as *however* or *in spite of which* would have been stylistically preferable to the second *but*); and at another point he hurries paradoxically into a needlessly sprawling construction ('One of the most splendid sights in the world, and one which might go a long way to compensate for any inconveniences occasioned by living in Papeete').

The two passages invite comparison in another important respect. Desmond Bagley plays the realism game. He knows, and passes the knowledge on to his readers, that Papeete is called the Pearl of the Pacific, that it is nine miles distant from a volcanic island called Moorea, and that the quay where ships moor is very close to the town's main street; to complete this factual account he adds a short guidebook note on the town's facilities, failing only to indicate population figures and early closing day. This is the real, everyday world, in which a man thinks about cold beer, frets about the Suarez-Navarro expedition, and makes up his mind to go and see the Governor.

It may seem at first glance that Conrad, too, is attempting documentary realism with those numbers: 'sixty days at sea', 'sixty miles off'. But he makes no attempt to disguise this as anything other than an imaginary statistic. Had he been writing in the full spirit of the realism game, he would have untidied his numbers a little – 'fifty-seven days at sea', 'sixty-one miles off'. By 'sixty days' and 'sixty miles' Conrad probably wishes to convey to his readers no more than 'a long time at sea' (or as his narrator might have said, 'a long fetch'), and 'a long way off'.

The most interesting point of comparison is raised by the use, in both passages, of the sobriquet 'the Pearl'. In Bagley's account it functions simply as a dossier detail, a device of realism. In Conrad – though we may not at first perceive this – it is anything but realistic in the crude factual-documentary sense. The narrator's introduction of the name is diffident, almost embarrassed: this is what 'the more enthusiastic of its inhabitants like to call the island (the 'real' name of which is never given). Then the story-teller, with an artless shrug, decides that this name will do as well as any other – not for realistic, but for figurative purposes. The Pearl, he tells us, mixing a curious metaphor, distils much sweetness; then, again ostensibly embarrassed by the extravagance of figurative language, he explains that the principle product of 'the Pearl' is sugar. Call it the Pearl, because pearls are precious as sugar is sweet.

From the point of view of the narrator-within-the-story, then, 'the Pearl' is an adventitiously figurative, not a realistic name. But this is at the beginning of the story; as readers proceed, hindsight tells them that the narrator-outside-the-story – the author, Joseph Conrad – has good reasons for planting this name in the first paragraph, drawing attention to it through his narrator's fumbling attempt at a figure of speech. The words *pearl, sugar, sweetness*, together with the nouns *smile, fortune* in the story's title, together create semantic suppositions which the story ironically frustrates. For the narrator, the island has something less than the perfection of a pearl; his experiences there are tart, if not downright sour; fortune's single smile is a wry one; he has the casual luck to pick up a profitable cargo, not of sugar but of potatoes – which stink. Towards the end of the story, the captain bitterly describes his 'bargain':

> Everlastingly, there was a tackle over the after-hatch and everlastingly the watch on the deck were pulling up, spreading out, picking over, rebagging, and lowering down again, some of that lot of potatoes. My bargain with all its remotest associations, mental and visual . . . was everlastingly dangled before my eyes, for thousands of miles along the open sea. And as if by a satanic refinement of irony it was accompanied by the most awful smell. Whiffs from decaying potatoes pursued me on the poop, they mingled with my thoughts, with my food, poisoned my very dreams. They made an atmosphere of corruption for the ship.

'My bargain with all its remotest associations' must remind us of the beginning of the story, with its distant prospect of the Pearl, and its expression of the young captain's hope for a 'luckily exceptional' transaction there. It is indeed a 'satanic refinement of irony' that the 'much sweetness' of the first paragraph becomes the 'most awful smell' of the closing pages. The reader understands that the 'sweetness' connotes a youthful idealism and the 'smell' expresses a sense of moral contamination – understands, in short, that this talk of sugar and potatoes is not simply a matter of verisimilitude, but that the very theme of the story is contained in its lexicon, and that the power of the lexicon to carry the theme is carefully controlled from first to last. Such meticulous design is rare in 'pop fiction', whose writers, aiming simply to distract and entertain us (though the task may not always be so simple), court our attention page by page, from event to event, so that at any moment we may easily put the book aside and go about our business, or turn over and go to sleep.

(For further exploration of language, style and popular fiction, see Nash, 1990.)

3.4   POETIC STRUCTURES

3.4.1 Lexis and Syntax

In the next two sections we examine some stylistic features of two poems by two widely studied, canonical nineteenth-century poets. Poems are interesting sample cases of styles of writing because poets usually pattern language to produce specific sound effects; in the analysis of Robert Browning's 'Meeting at Night' we demonstrate an introductory method for analysis which enables us to discuss the basic phonaesthetic contouring of patterns of sound.

In this chapter we have operated at a descriptive level which has taken in progressively larger units of language – from vocabulary, through sentences, clause relations and problem solution structures to components of narrative organization. Although grammatical effects have been examined, it may be useful to remind ourselves how crucial to the organization and patterning of a text some very basic features of syntax can be. Such key features as tense, pronouns and modality have been drawn attention to on several occasions in the book. We return to such features here to demonstrate how significant they can be in the creation of text-intensive poetic meanings. In keeping with one of our main global aims for the book we also hope to underline that by *seeing through* such features of language we can come more confidently to understand and to perceive how and why such meanings may be made. It is not our intention, in undertaking such an exercise (we claim no more for it than that), to imply entry into the general field of poetics or to define the parameters of poetic communication.

In the first section an analysis of the grammar of a poem by Thomas Hardy is undertaken. We do not pretend to say everything about the poem's language or even everything about its grammar, but we hope to show that it is possible to get quite a long way towards an interpretation by drawing on an awareness of grammar in use. We also do not pretend to be able to unlock the meaning of the poem; instead we have the (hopefully) more realistic goal or accounting for our own intuitions and of attempting to persuade readers that such an account is a reasonable one. We begin with those intuitions:

The Oxen

Christmas Eve, and twelve of the clock,
  'Now they are all on their knees,'
An elder said as we sat in a flock
  By the embers in hearthside ease.

We pictured the meek mild creatures where
  They dwelt in their strawy pen,
Nor did it occur to one of us there
  To doubt they were kneeling then.

So fair a fancy few would weave
  In these years! Yet, I feel,
If someone said on Christmas Eve,
  'Come; see the oxen kneel

In the lonely barton by yonder coomb
  Our childhood used to know,'
I should go with him in the gloom,
  Hoping it might be so.

The speaker in this poem is looking back to a point in time ('then') when patterns of life appeared to be less complex, when religious belief was less likely to be displaced by rational scepticism and the ritual supports of a community of people were more likely to be permanently in place. By contrast, the present time ('in these years') is characterized by self-doubt and a certain spiritual vacillation as well as by an isolation from that past world in which values and beliefs were more secure. What is particularly interesting about this poem is the way in which language is patterned to provide stylistic contrasts which can be read as reinforcing this division between a past and present world. The contrasts exist primarily at the level of grammar but there are also interesting lexical and phonological effects which contribute to a densely woven network of language.

Tense In this respect the division in the poem is especially neat: the first two stanzas contain patterns which are contrastively displaced in the second two stanzas. For example, there is a marked contrast between past and present tenses. With the exception of l.1 (which lacks a main verb, in part at least in order to provide a linguistically economic frame for the action) and l.2 which is spoken, the remaining clauses are all in the past tense (*said, pictured, dwelt, did occur, were kneeling*). The tense in which the main clause operates in the second half of the poem is the present tense. Here *I feel* (l.10) carries the main burden of response to the present situation brought about by the speaker's retrospection.

Pronouns A similarly prominent contrastive pattern is displayed by the pronouns employed across the poem. In the first two stanzas the pronoun *we* is used: in the last two stanzas it is replaced by *I*. The contrast provides a stylistic corollary for the move from community to isolated individuality which is in part a consequence of the speaker's habitation of the uncertain present of 'these years'.

Modality Another contrast which serves rather more to underline an expression of greater uncertainty is one between degrees of modality in the poem. Modal verbs are a limited sub-set of verbs in a language which generally signal a subjective orientation towards events, processes or conditions. (Modality can also be conveyed by other parts of speech such as adverbs.) The modal verbs include: *must, should, can, might, ought to, will,* etc. In 'The Oxen' there are no modal verbs in the first half of the poem while in the second half there are three (*would, should, might*). Their presence can be equated with the more subjective alignment to events adopted by the speaker, who in this more complex time expresses a somewhat less clear-cut view of a world in which oxen, moved by a supernatural force, might kneel at Christmas and thus re-enact the kneeling of animals in the stable at the birth of Jesus Christ. The increased modality mediates both this increased subjectivity and a perceptible vacillation which provide a further contrast with the greater certainties and securities of the communal past.

Clause Structure There is in this poem a clear opposition between how things are *now* and how they *were*. Contrasts between the two 'halves' of the poem can continue to be categorized; one syntactic contrast in particular repays further exploration. This contrast is patterned in the clause structures in the poem and resides in very general terms in a shift from simple to more complex structures during the course of the poem. An analysis of this contrast can begin by tracing the organization of the final clause in the poem. The sentence is inscribed over six lines (ll.10–16) and also contributes to the only run-on lines in the whole poem (those linking the third and fourth stanzas). The sentence is marked by the following features:

1 The main clause which begins the sentence is 'interrupted' by a conditional clause (l.11) and this in turn contains reported clauses which are embedded within it (ll.12–14).
2 L.14 is a clause known as a defining relative clause. It imparts a more precise definition to the coomb but it also adds to the greater clausal complexity.
3 The main clause continues over five lines of the poem to l.15 but

is then extended by another clause – here a participial clause
(l.16).

This patterning is in marked opposition to the sentence structures
which occur within the first two stanzas.

The first two stanzas are characterized by a greater simplicity. The
predominant sentence structure is one of main clause followed by a
subordinate clause with the latter clause indicating either the time or
the manner or the place of the action. Also no single sentence is longer
than two lines of the poem. For example:

```
    An elder said        as we sat in a flock
←[main clause]→       ←——[subordinate
        By the embers in hearthside ease
        ←——————— clause] ————→
```

The effect of these structures is to highlight the six-line sentence of the
third and fourth stanzas with its contrasting structural interruptions
and extensions. While recognizing the dangers of suggesting too
isomorphic a fit between language structure and particular meanings,
it is not unreasonable to suggest that the contrasting clause patternings underline differences between a more certain experience and one
which is more affected by wavering doubt and a measure of vacillation. By the end of the poem the speaker seems to look back at a
disappearing word with some mixed feelings and in a kind of
suspension between belief and disbelief, between knowing and
unknowing. Mingled with this is a scepticism about the possibility of
knowing anything. Stylistic patterning plays its part in establishing
this sense of balance or suspension.

The main stylistic contrasts across the poem can be summarized as
follows:

Stanzas 1–2	*Stanzas 3–4*
pronoun 'we'	pronoun 'I'
tense *past*	tense *present*
no modal verbs	modal verbs
simple clause structure	more complex clause structure

This is not to suggest, of course, that there are no other significant
patterns or that they do not have a part to play. For example, the
'points of reference' are not as clear in the latter half of the poem. That
is, in stanza 1 it is *an elder said*; in stanza 3 what is said is spoken by a

more indefinite *someone*. In stanza 4 the coomb is simply *yonder* and it is 'known' not by a specific individual but by the rather vaguer *our childhood*. The greater indefiniteness is compounded too by the lexical item *gloom* which itself echoes the dying light of the embers of l.4 but which contains, almost incrementally, further associations of pessimism and lack of real hope. There are contrasts, too, between *interior* and *exterior* in the verbs. The directness of *said*, accompanied by actual citation, compares with the main verb *feel* which frames a projected and provisional speech which is indirect and interiorized.

What we do find from a relatively preliminary analysis of 'The Oxen' is that a skilful and careful modulation of grammatical patterns is a key contributory factor in a recognition of divisions and oppositions in the poem, and that an analysis of the poem's grammar is a necessary prerequisite for further exploration and interpretation.

3.4.2 Sounds and Meanings: Browning's 'Meeting at Night'

In any composition of a literary kind, we assume the presence of the spoken word in the written. Our attempts to achieve a personal style reinforce this assumption; when we ask of our own writings whether they 'read well', we do not mean 'Does the eye agreeably take in this sequence of written signs?' but something like 'Does this text enable a reader to imagine a fluent sequence of *sounds*?' — often with the implication that well-sounding discourse enhances a well-conducted argument. No one would dispute that in written style there is a phonetic component, the function of which is primarily aesthetic.

The aesthetic attributes of speech sounds are most intensively exploited in poetry. Verse composition may be obviously mellifluous:

> And ever the wind blew, and yellowing leaf
> And gloom and gleam, and shower and shorn plume
> Went down it . . .
> > (Tennyson, 'The Last Tournament')

or just as obviously harsh:

> Frets care the crop-full bird? Irks doubt the
> > maw-crammed beast?
> > (Browning, 'Rabbi Ben Ezra')

In either case, the stylistic effect is explicable in terms of the rules governing the distribution and sequencing of sounds in English. A linguist might say that Browning (the author of the second example) has infringed phonological constraints on consonant clustering; in other words, he has produced bundles of consonants (the /tsk/ of *frets care*, the /ksd/ of *irks doubt*) the formation of which our language ordinarily resists. This is one of the reasons (there are others) why we might deem this line from 'Rabbi Ben Ezra' 'harsh' or 'ungainly'. Adjacent sounds in adjacent words are in awkward collision with each other.

But sounds in verse – or the sounds implied by the verse text – have a more than musical value. While they decorate the poem, they may also help to organize it, acting as more or less emphatic markers of the phrase, the line, the stanza. Rhyme, for example, offers something more than a pleasant variation of sonorous chimes; it is also a kind of acoustic punctuation, a designator of the boundaries and overlaps of verse-form and grammatical form. Alliteration occurs quite commonly as a device which not only picks out the balancing halves of a line, or the matching lines of a distich, but also gives emphasis to the grammatical shape of clause and phrase.

The *p*loughman homeward *p*lods his *w*eary *w*ay.

Gray's verse-line embodies a grammatical clause in which subject and verb are linked by one alliteration, and the phrase-constituents of the direct object by another. There is repetition and there is alternation, and both are essential to a stylistic texture in which change produces pattern and pattern implies significance. Had Gray written 'The *p*loughman homeward *p*lods his *p*atient *p*ath' or 'The *w*orkman homeward *w*ends his *w*eary *w*ay', he would have committed himself to something phonologically as well as semantically inferior. In these versions the alliterative sequences no longer distinctively mark the prosodic and grammatical structure of the line, the turn round the caesura, the movement from subject to predicate.

Clearly, the idea of *patterning* is as important here as in any other field of stylistic description. It is particularly important when discussion turns to the third, most controversial, function of sounds in poetry: that of sound-symbolism, or phonetic imagery. Linguists are often impatient with any suggestion that particular sounds or combinations of sound are especially representative or mimetic of particular experiences. Their position is that 'the linguistic sign is arbitrary', that is, that sounds and words have no immanent meaning, but express only the senses conventionally attributed to them. What the Romans called *equus* the English call *horse*, the Swedes *häst*, the Germans *Pferd*, the French *cheval* – and there never has been any suggestion that one of these is more peculiarly equine or sounds more horsy than another. A horse by any other name would run as fast or pull as big a cart. The nature of the thing is constant, its name is arbitrary.

We need not quarrel with this position, however, if we point to the power of onomatopoeia as a motive in linguistic creativity, and further to a well-established synaesthetic habit that relates the experience of sound to other perceptual experiences such as the sensation of colour, temperature, weight, bulk, distance. There is a known tendency to assign to the contrasting sonorities of vowels distinctive physical correlates, whether of colour, light intensity, weight, temperature or distance. Front vowels are commonly perceived as 'bright', 'thin', 'light', 'cool', back vowels as 'dark', 'full', 'heavy', 'warm'. These 'intersensorial analogies' are familiar to psychologists studying the phenomena of perception.

Consonants, too, have acoustic properties commonly suggestive of certain sensory phenomena. The major articulatory/acoustic contrast between voiced and voiceless sounds is exploited over and over again, in poetic texts, to evoke shifts from sound to silence, sonority to sibilance, loudness to softness.

> Till an unusuall stop of sudden silence
> Gave respit to the drowsie frighted steeds
> That drew the litter of close-curtain'd sleep.
> At last a soft and solemn breathing sound
> Rose like steam of rich distill'd Perfumes,
> And stole upon the Air, that even Silence
> Was took e're she was ware . . .

We can hardly escape the conclusion that in these lines from Milton's *Comus* the voiceless consonants, in particular /s/, are designedly correlated with the interlinking themes of silence and softly penetrating sound. They occur in such density as to force that conclusion upon us. But Milton here perhaps does no more than make capital out of a perceptual commonplace, i.e. the regular link between the phonological feature of voicelessness and some lexical formations representing the perception of etiolated or muted or half-suppressed sounds. Words like *hiss, hush, whisper, titter*, illustrate this. Other words, such as *fizz, sizzle, whimper, snigger*, with their commingling of voiceless and voiced sounds interestingly suggest a vacillating sound-state, half-way towards the full sonorities of *babble, rumble, burble, murmur, buzz*, with their voiced consonants (and their predominantly retracted, sometimes long vowels).

Of course there are countless instances in which the sound of a word makes no arguable match with its meaning; but still the onomatopoeic principle works often enough to be taken seriously. Simply to compare *titter* and *snigger*, or *whisper* and *murmur* or *cackle* and *babble*, or *ping* and *bang*, or *slap* and *slog* is to perceive in 'ordinary' language a primitive mimetic impulse that poets regularly turn to sophisticated use.

The bases of the 'onomatopoeic principle' are the following.

1 Vowels are characterized by potentially mimetic contrasts of sonority, the workings of which are illustrated in everyday language by some playful compounds and turns of phrase, eg. *see-saw, ping-pong, tit for tat, Tom, Dick and Harry,* as well as lexical items such as *screech* and *boom,* which are affective variants on a semantic theme (represented in this case by *shout*). Onomatopoeia is frequently not a discernible feature of the 'central' or 'core' vocabulary item, but enters into the non-central vocabulary. The length of vowels is in some instances a critical feature of the onomatopoeia, for example the short vowels in *whip, clip, slap, cuff, punch, thrash.* Most monosyllabic verbs denoting physical assault have a short vowel in the monosyllable – though there are exceptions, among them the 'core' words *beat* and *strike*. In general, the sensory analogy of the short vowel is with phenomena characterized by sudden onset, rapidity, brief duration, sometimes frequent repetition.

2 Consonants have primarily the distinctive features of voice and voicelessness, and are additionally divisible into types distinguished by the mode of articulation, i.e. *stops, fricatives, nasals, approximants.* These articulatory types correlate readily with perceptions of striking or tapping (e.g. the stops /p/, /b/, /t/, /d/, /k/, /g/), with rubbing, hissing or scratching (e.g. the fricatives and sibilants /f/, /v/, /ʃ/, /ʒ/, /s/, /z/, /θ/, /ð/, /h/, and the affricates /tʃ/ and ∂ʒ/), with flowing, rippling, or humming (e.g. the approximants /l/, /r/, and the nasals /m/, /n/, ŋ/). These correlations can be expressed in a general way as percussiveness, friction, continuity.

3 Vowels and consonants enter into complex combinatory patterns suggesting a complex perception of whatever external event stimulates the onomatopoeia. This is evident in the most commonplace of onomatopoeic inventions. The word *clip-clop,* for example, representing the sound made by horses' hooves on a paved surface, is an intricate phonological response to an intricate stimulus.

4 The process of onomatopoeia is arbitrary as to its linguistic consequences, but consistent and cogent in poetic principle. Once we have invented the word *crunch,* for instance, we are free to use it in any sense we communally choose – we crunch an apple, a stick of celery, a sweet; hear the crunch of boots on gravel, hear the car crunch on the gatepost; wonder what will happen 'when it comes to the crunch', and,

in financial difficulties, know that we shall feel the crunch on quarter-day. The word derives its meaning from its use, and is not tied to a particular meaning through the mystique or mumbo-jumbo of sounds. But onomatopoeic creation does not specify the singular event; it relates to *types* of event in the physical world. The type onomatopoeically expressed by *crunch* involves (i) the abrupt impact of something compact and hard striking on something that yields, (ii) a yielding surface that is also hard, but brittle, and (iii) a harsh or strident sound of brief duration. The word in its entirety is a kind of argument representing these properties by shrewdly matching them with the acoustic properties of certain consonantal and vocalic speech sounds. We can defend *crunch* as an 'onomatopoeic argument', against other possibilities, e.g. 'crinch', 'crunge', which are less convincing.

In poetic discourse there are two kinds of onomatopoeic activity. One, the lesser kind, appears in the relatively frequent occurrence of familiar mimetic items, e.g. such words as *scratch, clash, buzz, moan, howl, yell, growl, roar, thud, croon, crunch*. The other, more important, kind consists of a patterning, or texture, or combinative design of sounds presented to the reader in conjunction with a theme or an image. The conjunction is an arbitrary one, but if the poet is successful, if his 'onomatopoeic argument' is well designed, it is compelling. Illusion is accepted as momentary reality. The reader (by implication the listener) is persuaded by means of a *phonetic metaphor* – a term which is arguably more appropriate than 'phonetic symbolism', since 'symbolism' requires a fixed and exclusive correlation between an A (the symbol) and a B (the thing symbolized), whereas metaphoric correspondences are freely constructed and are, so to speak, negotiated in context. No competent reader of Milton's lines quoted on p. 121 above would want to argue that the recurrent voiceless /s/ is in itself 'symbolic' of anything. That argument could be confounded by the very passage in question, where the poet talks first of *silence*, and then of the counter-phenomenon of a *soft and solemn breathing sound*. Which of these, then, is symbolized by the /s/-motif? The answer is, surely, that neither is 'symbolized', but that the 's'-pattern works in a freer, metaphoric way, with a shift of nuance, to connote each in turn. In metaphor, a given vehicle can bear diverse tenors.

Now let us apply some of these ideas to the interpretation of a text, Browning's dramatic lyric called 'Meeting at Night'

> The grey sea and long black land;
> And the yellow half-moon large and low;
> And the startled little waves that leap
> In fiery ringlets from their sleep,

> As I gain the cove with pushing prow,
> And quench its speed i' the slushy sand.
>
> Then a mile of warm sea-scented beach;
> Three fields to cross till a farm appears;
> A tap at the pane, the quick sharp scratch
> And blue spurt of a lighted match,
> And a voice less loud, through its joys and fears,
> Than the two hearts beating each to each!

This poem is technically remarkable in more ways than one. Its grammar invites remark: there is no main clause, and the two stanzas present two sentences composed of dependent or 'embedded' constructions. Its prosodic form also invites remark: the stanzas are identically punctuated at the line-ends, denoting similarities of rhythmic organization. Its vocabulary, too, is remarkable, in the way that visual references (*grey, long, black, yellow, fiery*) are overtaken by tactile or auditory terms (*pushing, slushy, tap, scratch*), only to re-emerge in a single instance (*blue*) at the emotional climax of the poem. But perhaps the most remarkable element of all is the operation of phonetic metaphor in this text.

Reading the poem aloud will make apparent the general density of sound effect. From first to last there is a medley of assonances and dissonances, making up a species of background commentary on the action and changing scenery of the poem; the recurrences of /l/ in the first stanza, followed by the repeated sibilances of /s/ and /z/ in the second, can be correlated with descriptive shifts, from the seascape, the 'water feeling' of the opening, to the darkness and furtive activity of the continuation. The sound decorates the plot, as it were. But within this rather diffuse decorative ground there are passages of concentrated expression. In each stanza there is a piece of complex 'onomatopoeic argument', coinciding demonstrably with a climax in the emotional plot, a moment of tension and excitement.

One such moment comes in the last two lines of the fist stanza:

> As I gain the cove with pushing prow.
> And quence its speed i' the slushy sand.

For the reader who has never seen the poem before, these lines are the first inkling of what is going on. The impressionistic grammar of the first four lines conveys snapshot glimpses of a scene that might be observed from anywhere – from a headland, from a house, from a reminiscent fireside, even. Only at the end of the stanza is this descriptive *topic* related to a *comment*, in those subordinate clauses that tell us how the scene is observed from a boat, that the poem's narrator is the oarsman, and, what is more, that he is rowing with considerable vigour. It is left to the reader to infer a motive for this nocturnal energy: a lover's ardour drives the boat.

Then what do the two lines 'represent', phonetically? What is their 'argument'? Obviously, they evoke the sound and the sensation of rowing a boat hard ashore. The keel takes the ground with a noise quite unmistakable to anyone who has ever heard it, and the boat loses way, 'deadens', in a fashion equally familiar. Browning's lines are in the first instance a phonetic image of this experience. The image is 'argued' via three types of consonant, the stop, the fricative, and the affricate. The materials of the argument, listing the relevant words in the order of their occurrence, are:

gain	/g/	stop	velar	voiced
cove	/k/	stop	velar	voiceless
pushing	/p/	stop	bilabial	voiceless
pushing	/ʃ/	fricative	palato-alveolar	voiceless
prow	/p/	stop	bilabial	voiceless
quench	/k/	stop	velar	voiceless
quench	/tʃ/	affricate	palato-alveolar	voiceless
speed	/s/	fricative	alveolar	voiceless
slushy	/s/	fricative	alveolar	voiceless
slushy	/ʃ/	fricative	palato-alveolar	voiceless
sand	/s/	fricative	alveolar	voiceless

The orderly listing of constituents somewhat disguises the pattern, though the recurrence of certain items will be obvious enough. The stops are /g/, /k/, and /p/; the fricative-affricate group consists of /ʃ/, /s/, and /tʃ/. These two sets of items are significantly distributed across the two verse-lines. The stops generally occur in the first line, overlapping the fricatives at the beginning of the second; the fricatives generally occur in the second line, but intrude on the stops at one point in the first. This distribution corresponds significantly with what is described in the text – the vigorous impulsion of the oars followed by the hissing lurch of the hindering sand. A diagram may be helpful at this point:

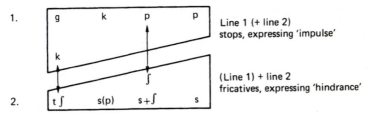

Figure 3.5

This is an abstract and somewhat simplified account of what goes on in the text. The two groups shown in the diagram are not wholly discrete; they are linked at several points, i.e. in *pushing* (/p/ + /ʃ/), in *quench* (/k/ + /tʃ/), and in *speed* (/s/ + /p/). This linking is an important part of the metaphoric process, conveying the shift from 'impulse' to 'hindrance'. An important word, perhaps the hinge-word, is *quench*. It embodies the one occurrence of an affricate (/tʃ/), and an affricate is an articulatory complex of stop and fricative. The two phonetic types so prominent in Browning's onomatopoeia converge at this point, in this word – here, one might say, the boat stops. The further significance of this is that *quench* is a crucial semantic item because of its habitual collocations with *fire* and *thirst*, which in their turn have metaphoric associations with the theme of erotic passion. The boat's *speed* (another word in which the two phonetic types meet) figuratively expresses the lover's eagerness, and these two lines come as close as Victorian poetry might dare to an avowal of the libido.

Quench is certainly a key term, but note how it falls into context with words suggesting aggression or dominance: *gain, pushing*. *Gain*, with its overtones of conquest (as compared with the neutral *reach*) is phonetically motivated, the voiced velar /g/ setting up a link with the velarities of *cove* and *quench*. This /g/, as we have already noted, is the one voiced element in the pattern. The remainder are voiceless, and this voicelessness is yet another instance of a complex, or at least ambivalent, phenomenon. It is directly appropriate to the sound a beaching boat makes, a sound more like a hiss than a hum, but it is also appropriate in a wider sense to the poem's whispering evocations of the secretive, the hasty, the illicit.

The second episode of intense phonetic activity occurs in the third and fourth lines of the second stanza:

A tap at the pane, the quick sharp scratch
And blue spurt of a lighted match

Here are two mimetic phrases, one echoing the rhythmic knocking on the window, the other representing the sound of the striking match. The first is a simple trick; the phrase *a tap at the pane* is discernibly modelled on the familiar rhythm, x / x x /, of a discreet knock. The 'beats' are expressed by the voiceless stops (/t/, /p/) in *tap* and *pane*. It is a muted, cautious signal – *a tap at the pane*, not a full-voiced *bang on the glass*.

Then, in the next line and a half, follows what is perhaps the most complex piece of sustained onomatopoeia in the whole poem. Once again, the relevant materials are stops, fricatives, and affricates, all voiceless.

quick (initial)	/k/	stop	velar	voiceless
quick (final)	/k/	stop	velar	voiceless
sharp (initial)	/ʃ/	fricative	palato-alveolar	voiceless
sharp (final)	/p/	stop	bilabial	voiceless
scratch (initial)	/s/	fricative	alveolar	voiceless
scratch (covered)	/k/	stop	velar	voiceless
scratch (final)	/tʃ/	affricate	palato-alveolar	voiceless
spurt (initial)	/s/	fricative	alveolar	voiceless
spurt (covered)	/p/	stop	bilabial	voiceless
spurt (final)	/t/	stop	alveolar	voiceless
lighted (medial)	/t/	stop	alveolar	voiceless
match (final)	/tʃ/	affricate	palato-alveolar	voiceless

What is immediately apparent from this list is the number of words containing two or three phonetic motifs. Severally and collectively, these words contain the 'argument' of match-striking, and it is not in this case feasible to separate the onomatopoeic tokens into two groups. Nevertheless, the onomatopoeia is constructed in accordance with a discernible scheme. The striking of the match involves two phenomena, a friction and a combustion – the rubbing along the sandpaper and the bursting into flame. The fricatives and affricates naturally represent the 'friction' phase, and the 'combustion' is expressed by the stops. These two phases are further differentiated, thus:

Friction:	initial	/s/
	increasing	/ʃ/
	arresting	/tʃ/
Combustion:	touch	/k/
	catch	/p/
	burst	/t/

There are in both sets, as we see, graded degrees of intensity, as the match is first touched to the box and then drawn with increasing firmness along the rough surface until it catches and bursts into flame. In word after word the vocabulary rehearses the process of match-striking, combining the constituent phonetic elements in various ways until the moment of ignition is emphatically represented in *spurt*:

quick	/k/ – /k/	'touch' – 'touch'
sharp	/ʃ/ – /p/	'increasing friction' – 'catch'
scratch	/s/ – /k/ – /tʃ/	'initial friction' – 'touch' – 'arrest'
spurt	/s/ – /p/ – /t/	'initial friction' – 'catch' – 'BURST'

Spurt is the crucial word, the central point in the pattern. *Lighted* and *match*, with their single motifs, echoically reinforce the general sound-texture, but contribute nothing to the development of an already complete phonetic metaphor.

The tactile *spurt* collocates with *blue*, a visual reference recalling the colour words with which the poem opens. In its immediate environment, *blue* makes a phonetic as well as a semantic contrast. In the third line of the second stanza there is not a single voiced consonant. Voicelessness is the rule – and then, in the fourth line, comes this word beginning with a cluster of voiced sounds (/bl/), the onset of a new 'argument':

blue	/b/	stop	bilabial	voiced
blue	/l/	approximant	lateral	voiced
lighted	/l/	approximant	lateral	voiced
match	/m/	nasal	bilabial	voiced

Colour and sonority return to the poem – even if it is only in the low luminosity of a match, the muted sonority of heartbeats and murmuring voices.

What is the sum of all this? It is, that in this poem there is no one level at which the text can be readily decoded. Its 'message' becomes available only as the reader shifts his attention back and forth from the grammar to the lexicon to the phonology to the lexicon to the grammar. In this intricate texture, the role of the phonetic component is twofold. First, it provides the 'onomatopoeic argument' that reinforces the poem's lexicon; and second, it is a designator of the structure of the poem, working within the ostensible form. In prosodic form, the poem is elegantly symmetrical; the punctuation and line-management of the second stanza exactly matches that of the first. Within this composed pattern there is an affective structure that is not quite so regular. It may be described thus:

Stanza 1	lines 1–4	Description of a scene
	lines 5–6	Psychological tension
Stanza 2	lines 1–2	Description of a scene
	lines 3–4	Psychological tension
	lines 5–6	Release of tension

It is in the episodes of psychological tension, the emotional crises of the poem, that we discover the most intense onomatopoeic activity. Sounds here have a stylistic importance which is more than decorative. They are integral to the poem's aesthetic and affective structure, and to the meanings working through that structure. The result of an analysis such as this is to leave one marvelling at the intricacy of the poetic process. Yet 'Meeting at Night' is not a particularly difficult poem, and certainly not an obscure one. It is a brief and highly competent piece of poetic discourse, and as such serves admirably to document one aspect of writing style.

Finally, and before we move from poetry to politics, it is important to underline one or two provisions about the analyses which have been undertaken in this section. We have indeed dealt only with aspects of poetic writing. We have intended no more than to lay a basis for further interpretation and certainly do not want to claim that these are the only available meanings and effects in the two texts. We should also recognize once more here a point which was stressed in our second chapter: that differently 'positioned' readers with different interests may put different meanings on the features of language we have analysed in our far from complete accounts. Furthermore, analysis at other levels of language organization may well require us to modify what we deduce as reasonable interpretations here. However, we have *seen through* some key features of language and tried to make visible what we have seen. Our aim has not been to offer an exhaustive account but a reasonable and reasonably explicit account of how closely our own intuitions are tied to the language of texts.

Our case of samples in 3.1 drew attention to the discursive or 'interactional' implications of writing; in 3.2 and 3.3 the samples were chosen to demonstrate intrinsic properties of texts; now, in 3.5, demonstration purports to be both textual and discursive. Fields as diverse (apparently) as politics and literary criticism have at least this in common, that in each there are powerful *ideologies*, involving the beliefs and attitudes a speaker or writer wishes to enjoin upon an audience. In the case of criticism, particularly, the enforcement of the ideology involves a *metalanguage*, a set of conventions for discoursing about discourse. The case of samples that thus opened with a glance at the most popular manifestations of discursive appeal here closes with a scrutiny of one of the most specialized types of discourse.

3.5   IDEOLOGIES AND METALANGUAGES

3.5.1 *Political Rhetorics*

We are beset by the language of politics; it surrounds us, we meet it every day in diverse forms and sources, in radio and television broadcasts, in newspapers, in the very conversations we have with friends or colleagues, or in the family circle. Our common discourse has its local equivalents for 'negotiating', 'budgeting', 'taking measures', 'putting forward proposals', 'referring', 'reporting', 'arbitrating', 'debating', 'legislating', and so on. Politics, indeed is a substantial part of life, and our involvements in life are interpretable as political processes. Some of these processes, however, are more obviously political than others. Institutions are created, to make a stable framework for what might otherwise be random or undifferentiated transactions; with the institutions come codes of language appropriate to institutional purposes; and with the development of recognizable institutional codes comes the evolution of political rhetorics.

The political dictionary   There is thus a primary language of politics, meaning the language required by, and immediately designating, the characteristic features and processes of the political institution. In the case of Great Britain, 'the political institution' signifies in the first instance the Houses of Parliament (as, in the United States, it would denote the Senate and Congress). There is a language of Parliament, reflecting its organization and procedures, with which the public is generally familiar. Everyone is acquainted with the vocabulary of the democratic process (the phrase 'the democratic process' is itself a piece of political rhetoric); with *platform* and *manifesto* and *hustings* and *polls* and *constituencies;* with *casting a vote* and *returning a candidate* and *giving a mandate* expressing *the will of the people.* Equally familiar is the language of the *House,* with its personages, its procedures, its peculiar rituals: its *Government and Opposition benches*, its *whips* and *back benchers*, its *Speaker;* its *tabling of amendments*, its *votes of confidence* and *motions of censure*; its formal modes of address – *my right honourable friend, the honourable member, members opposite.* In many instances the language of Parliament must now seem frozen and formulaic, however playful or prudent its origins; and yet parliamentary terminology does not lack at least a residue of rhetorical power. To say, for example, *He lied to the House,* is to say something more than 'He lied to his colleagues', and praising *the Chancellor's performance at the despatch box* is asserting something of greater import than 'the Chancellor made a good speech'. In these instances, *House* and *despatch box* are emblematic of an institution, its history and traditions, its morality, its offices; hence they imply more than a tally of personnel, or the indication of the place where the Chancellor of the Exchequer stands to deliver his budget speech. The examples present one of the recurrent characteristics of political rhetoric: a tendency to use words imposingly, implying (at times falsely) resonances beyond what the words ostensibly denote.

Institutional rhetoric is apparent in some of the formal proceedings of Parliament; for example, in the Speech from the Throne at the opening of a parliamentary session. This oration, though read by the sovereign to the assembled Lords and Commons, is in fact composed by civil servants acting for the Prime Minister. It is thus a kind of extended speech act, a piece of performative rhetoric. Here is a part of the Queen's Speech delivered to Parliament on 6 November 1985:

My government will pursue vigorously their programme of privatization as a means both of improving the efficiency of the industries concerned, and of encouraging wider share ownership. Measures will be introduced to permit the transfer of the assets of the British Gas Corporation to the private sector and to enable the Atomic Energy Authority to operate as a trading fund from April 1, 1986, with a capital structure and borrowing powers.

A Bill will be proposed to introduce private capital into the British Airways Authority, to require larger local authority airports to be formed into companies, and to regulate certain airport activities.

My Government will bring forward legislation to introduce commercial management to my Naval Dockyards, as a significant contribution to encouraging a commercial approach and securing value for money in spending on defence.

Legislation will be introduced to facilitate funding by the industry of agricultural research, advice and related services; and to implement European Community arrangements to protect areas of particular environmental sensitivity.

Measures will be introduced to establish a new regulatory framework for the financial services sector, which will enhance its efficiency and competitiveness whilst providing greater safeguards for the interest of investors, and to modernize and liberalize the law governing building societies.

Measures will be brought forward to reform the operation of wages counciles, to make provisions concerning the payment of wages and to amend the law on sex discrimination in employment.

Legislation will be introduced to encourage the sale of public sector flats to their tenants and wider private sector involvement in the ownership and management of council housing, and to improve the planning system.

For Scotland, Bills will be introduced to extend the rights of public sector tenants and to facilitate the private ownership of public sector housing stock, to improve legal aid arrangements, and to modify and extend the management structure of salmon fisheries, including further measures to combat illegal salmon fishing throughout Great Britain.

The language of this curious artefact, supposedly representative of Her Majesty's own wishes and sentiments, yet remote from human volitions in its abstraction and artifice, invites decoding. Behind the conventionally formal constructions and the portentous phraseology, it may be said, there is simply the brute fact of a party in power, announcing its power; the tenor of this document could be constructed as 'The Government hereby disposes of British Gas, discards holdings in the British Airport Authority, sells off the stock of municipal housing in England and Scotland, makes things a little easier for bankers and stockbrokers, comes down on poachers, etc.' Its purport might be even more drastically expressed – but such direct 'decoding' is foreign to the spirit of the political language game, in which expression is conventionally formal, circuitous, abstract, and sometimes figurative, but then only in metaphors which put reality at a safe distance, a little out of reach. Political language in all its forms turns all references into abstractions. When and if it becomes concrete and specific, it loses its power to suggest power.

Some aspects of the primary language of politics are well illustrated by the extract from the Queen's Speech. Examination of its use of the major form-classes, for example, will show that while adjectives and adverbs of manner are not significantly represented (phrases like *pursue vigorously* are stylistic deviants from the general texture), verbs and nouns fall discernibly into a semantic scheme of primary, secondary and tertiary functions. The primary function is the designation of a topic with the appropriate locution ('what verb do we use when we want to talk about making a law?'); the secondary function is to express the notion of regulating or arranging ('what would be the appropriate way of saying "a set-up"?'); and the tertiary function is to indicate some form of beneficent or corrective effect ('what word do we use for whatever this is intended to do?'). The three kinds of expression, the 'locutory', the 'regulatory' and the 'benefactive', occur regularly in the language of the Speech from the Throne. Thus, verbs:

Primary: *introduce, propose*
('locutory')

Secondary: *regulate, facilitate, implement, require*
('regulatory')

Tertiary: *improve, encourage, combat, support, modernize, liberalize*
('benefactive')

And, correspondingly, nouns:

Primary: *measure, legislation, Bill*
('locutory')

| Secondary: ('regulatory') | *arrangement, management, operation, framework, approach, provision* |
| Tertiary: ('benefactive') | *privatization, efficiency, competitiveness* |

What is notably absent from the Queen's Speech is the overt bias or emphasis that would normally be supplied adjectivally or figuratively. Nevertheless there are gestures of emphasis, not only in the occasional adverb (*pursue vigorously* has already been noted), but also in the construction of word-pairs such as *efficiency and competitiveness, ownership and management, modify and extend, modernize and liberalize*. In these couplings, the ostensible role of the second co-ordinate is to complement the meaning of the first; but what seems evident is that the true function is one of rhetorical emphasis.

Another feature of the Queen's Speech is its incorporation of many phrases from the (then) current politico-economic lexicon; phrases which were either in temporary vogue, or had established themselves in the political vocabulary as indispensable forms of reference to persistent social or economic facts. *Private sector, public sector housing stock, financial services sector, capital structure, management structure, share ownership, borrowing power*, are examples of such phrases. It will be noted that some of them turn on words denoting primary political concepts – e.g. *ownership, power* – and some embody vogue words such as *sector* and *structure*. Free compositions and coinages of this kind characterize discourse about the changing prominences and realities of politics. The current vocabulary may be dense with terms relating to economic policy, or defence policy, or industrial relations; a dip into any day's paper will present the current trend. The economy is often in the news: whence, *market forces, market confidence, trade deficit, balance of payments deficit, public sector borrowing requirement, gross national product, industrial base, wage policy, wage freeze, ratecapping, the poverty trap, the floating pound, spending cuts, growth*, and 'growth's antonyms, *recession* and *decline*. ('The word "decline" crept into the political vocabulary some time towards the end of the 1970s, although the condition has long been present' – Peter Jenkins, in the *Independent*, 9 November 1987.) A notable feature of this politico-economic phraseology is its proclivity towards metaphor, as suggested by *force, base, freeze, capping, trap, float, cut, growth*. Political cartoonists regularly exploit these notions of freezing, floating, or capping – presenting, perhaps, a sinking ship with a pound sign on its funnel, or a gusher marked 'domestic rates' being 'capped' by a resolute Minister. The visual, or 'experiential', component in the political lexicon is the basis of a larger rhetoric which sometimes goes comically astray:

> Consequently the Chancellor's much-vaunted new growth will not be the smooth, well-balanced creature that ministers like to parade and stroke. Instead it is likely to turn out to be a lumpy unbalanced beast whose different limbs – investment, exports and domestic consumption – grow at alarmingly different rates. (Editorial in *The Times*, 14 November 1985)

This is inspired by a physical sense of *growth*, but the 'beast' is indeed 'unbalanced'; it apparently has only three 'limbs'.

Political language transiently reflects *issues* and *initiatives*, these words having 'primary' functions, as elements in the 'locutory' lexicon (along with *measure, procedure,* and others). Typical 'issues' are *freedom of information, sex discrimination* and *civil rights*; characteristic 'initiatives' are *nuclear deterrence, arms control* and *verification.* Pursuit of initiatives and issues leads to a proliferation of *isms: monetarism, Europeanism, confrontationism, welfarism, statism, interventionism, entryism, uni/bi/ multilateralism* – the whole ideational ragbag that led a *New Statesman* contributor to submit, in wry entry to one of that journal's competitions:

> Capitalism, communism,
> Feudalism, anarchism,
> Cynicism, fatalism,
> Optimism, pessimism,
> Chauvinism, terrorism,
> Pugilism, barbarism,
> Dogmatism, egotism,
> Jingoism, masochism,
> Vandalism, nepotism,
> Rheumatism, onanism,
> Perish every single 'ism
> In a nuclear cataclysm.

(Stanley J. Sharpless, in the *New Statesman* competition for 1 November 1985; competitors were invited to compose a witches' curse for Halloween.) A concomitant tendency is apparent in the number of verbs in *-ize*, denoting political intentions or processes: *privatize, modernize, liberalize, unionize, politicize, democratize, radicalize.* Such formations are so common in political journalism that they often turn up in rhetorical pairs:

> The country seems to be caught in the grip of a militant trade union psychology, with everything politicized and proletarianized. (Peter Jenkins in the *Independent*, 9 November 1987)

The ever-elaborating *-isms* and *-izations* produce a flourishing lexicon of 'buzz-words' or 'vogue words'. Some current buzz-words are *accountability, analysis, confidence, dimension, generate, image, perception, trend, system, structure, strategy.* There are also buzz-phrases, denoting, for example, issues – *social justice, social cohesion, political stability, economic performance;* or initiators of issues – *think tank, pressure group, inquiry team;* or scenes of political activity – *the grass roots, the inner cities*:

> Those who are less prepared to compromise, or who are cut off from the centres of power, are consolidating at the grass roots, particularly in the inner cities. (*Daily Telegraph*, 14 November 1985)

(*Consolidate* is another item of buzz-vocabulary.) The last quotation shows how in political discourse, particularly as practised by journalists, the 'buzz value' of words is readily allowed to obscure their figurative implications. Here, not so much by mixed metaphor as by a progression of casual figurative contradictions, there is 'consolidation' at 'grass roots' which are found in 'inner cities'.

Inevitably, such phraseology settles into cliché. The economy regularly *overheats*, the recession *deepens*, the power of the unions has to be *curbed*, discussions are *high level*, growth is manifested in a *growth area*. With the clichés come hackneyed expressions of approval or condemnation – 'purr-words' and 'snarl-words'. Current 'purr-words' in British politics (or at least in the politics of the establishment) are *radical, innovative, flexible* and *choice*, or *freedom of choice*. Current snarl-words (in the same perspective) are *activist, militant, state, welfare, benefit* and, oddly enough, *political* – an epithet which, in such contexts as 'the Council has a political bias' or 'he's too political in his approach' almost invariably implies left-wing politics. The same slant is observable in the use of the word *politics* itself, when we are told to 'keep politics out of religion', or that 'too many teachers dabble in politics'. (This colouring of what should be a neutral word may have originated with Harold Wilson who, in one of the crises of his term as Prime Minister, spoke of the machinations of a 'tightly knit group of politically motivated men'; his hearers were allowed to infer that 'politically motivated' signified 'motivated from the left'.)

Words thus implying some sort of evaluation, the acceptance of which is taken for granted, of course change colour between parties. *Activist* is not a snarl-word on the left, but *establishment* is; and *peace* is a word of dubious import in right-wing discourse (the mocking coinage *peacenik* expresses a reaction against those who are militant in the politics of peace). The general public becomes sufficiently sensitive to the verbal tokens of political difference to be able to infer from a usage the politics of the user. This, for example:

N.S. . . . said the change was 'designed to avoid the damaging effects for young people of moving straight from school into the benefit culture'. (The *Independent*, 24 October 1987)

The speaker here has coined a phrase, *benefit culture*, the meaning of which is immediately apparent to a hearer, together with its political tenor, which is patently Conservative. (The phrase-maker is Mr Nicholas Scott, Minister for Social Security.) *Benefit culture*, with its 'anthropological' hint of tribalism and primitive practice, is not a phrase that would be used on the left, where its counterpart would be *caring society*.

The linguistic expression of contrasting philosophies is seen first and foremost in the way parties denominate themselves and each other. We have our *left* and our *right* (terms derived, curiously enough, from the seating pattern of continental legislatures, not from our own parliamentary model), and more recently our *wets* and *drys*, or, in the context of military politics, our *doves* and *hawks*. Left-wing attitudes are further differentiated into *hard* and *soft*, a usage illustrated by these extracts from different pages in one issue of the *Daily Telegraph* (14 November 1985):

(a) [Headline] The hard left's struggle for Labour's softer centre

(b) Militant is the largest such group but it is not unique. And anyone who imagines that all the other activists of the so-called 'hard-left' will now retire gracefully to their bed-sits and Poly common rooms conceding victory to Mr Kinnock is woefully mistaken. The struggle for the heart and mind of the Labour party is far from over.

(c) There is an affinity of ideas between the 'Euros' and the 'softies', and a desire to isolate wilder comrades who may spoil the show before the General Election. A recent conference on Left-wing strategy sponsored jointly by *Marxism Today* and the Labour party's equivalent journal *New Socialist*, epitomised the spirit of cross-party fertilisation.

Extract (b) illustrates incidentally the social connotations of 'hard left' as perceived by a Conservative newspaper, as well as echoing a familiar political catch-phrase, *the struggle for hearts and minds*. (Ironically, the usual context for this phrase is the diplomacy of Western powers competing with Communism for the assent of 'non-aligned' nations.) Extract (c) likewise reflects the attitude of the reporter; *Euro* (for 'European Communist') and *softy* suggest, particularly in the latter case, a dismissive refusal to take seriously an alien political breed. As *lefty* is derived from 'left', so *softy* derives from 'soft'; but in each case, what results is something more than a mere playful diminutive. 'Lefty' connotes left-handedness, and hence 'cackhanded-ness', awkwardness (it is worth remembering also that the Latin term for 'left hand' passed unchanged into English as the word 'sinister'); 'softy' suggests soft-headedness, silliness, as much as soft-heartedness. Similar inferences of imbecility and lack of resistance are to be drawn from the headline pun, in extract (a), on 'soft centre'. The common-place working terms of politics are thus inherently polemic, or can be made so, and the language of political reporting frequently presents, perhaps not always with a clear intention, the bias of the writer.

Political discourse: the deliberative rhetoric   This brings us, however, to the larger topic of political language at work in various patterns of political discourse. There are, broadly speaking, two types of rhetoric practised by politicians and political commentators. One consists of oratory and exhortation; the other, which probably has more subdivi-sions, is the rhetoric of debate, discussion, day-to-day arguing of issues – the *deliberative rhetoric*.

Political argument, as exemplified by the parliamentary routine of Question Time, or by what is conventionally called 'the cut and thrust of debate', is generally a form of verbal posturing with a pretence to logic; assertions are presented in linguistic forms that suggest reason-ing. Mr Kinnock, for example, in responding to the Queen's Speech quoted above, is reported (by *The Times*) as having said the following:

> As the Government tried to avoid the truth – that crime was historically and obviously rooted in part in social and economic conditions – it was shirking its duty and dodging the truth. (*The Times*, 7 November 1985)

The sentence is obviously a tautology – 'As the Government tried to avoid the truth it was dodging the truth' – cast in the form of propositions like 'As the sun sets the air cools', or 'As he struggled to free himself, he tightened his bonds'; the 'proposition', however, is merely an accusatory gesture, framing another gesture, the assertion made parenthetically between dashes. The parenthesis exhibits some tell-tale symptoms of the deliberative rhetoric. There is a phrase caught from the current political lexicon (*social and economic conditions*); there is the conventional metaphor ('crime' is *rooted* in 'conditions'); there is the appeal to common knowledge and common perception ('historically and *obviously*'); and there is the careful 'hedge' against counter-appeal (*in part*). This may have a semblance of reasoned argument, but its real nature is that of aggressive assertion and its characteristic verbal embodiment is not the sentence or clause, but the word, the phrase, the collocation.

Insistence on the assertive power of particular words or phrases often characterizes oral debate between political opponents. Here, for instance, is a verbatim report of parliamentary exchanges between party leaders:

> Neil Kinnock, the Labour leader, told Mrs Thatcher at Question Time: 'You are prepared to tolerate apartheid abroad, now you are prepared to encourage it at home'
>
> But Mrs Thatcher replied: 'I am interested in good education for all children. There have always been different kinds of schools.'
>
> Opening the exchange, Mr Kinnock asked if the Prime Minister shared the view of a junior education minister that if the Government's plans to allow schools to opt out of local authority control ended up with a segregated system, 'then so be it'.
>
> 'I am interested in the best possible education for parents and for their children,' replied Mrs Thatcher.
>
> 'I do not think the present system is giving the best possible education for all children. You are talking about segregation. I am talking about good education.'
>
> Mr Kinnock responded: 'Any Prime Minister who cannot give a "yes" or "no" answer to segregation condemns herself out of her own mouth. A segregated system would not provide good education either to those put into the segregated part or those excluded from it.
>
> 'If choice were to lead to segregation, segregation would be the destruction of choice and much else.'
>
> (Independent, 18 November 1987)

These exchanges (reported under the heading *Kinnock challenges school opt-out plan*) interestingly characterize the debating style of the two party leaders. Mr Kinnock's readiness to construct sentences on rhetorical figures like *parison* and *chiasmus* appears:

> You are prepared to tolerate apartheid abroad, now you are prepared to encourage it at home.
> *Parison:* a structure of clauses in parallel – 'tolerate . . . abroad', 'encourage . . . at home'

> If choice were to lead to segregation, segregation would be the destruction of choice and much else.
> *Chiasmus* or *antimetabole:* a 'cross' pattern, reversing the order of significant lexical items – 'choice . . . segregation', 'segregation . . . choice'

Mr Kinnock's 'arguments' are often patterned assertions of this kind. The Prime Minister's strategy, on the other hand, is one of simple reiteration:

I am interested in good education for all children.

I am interested in the best possible education for parents and for their children.

I do not think the present system is giving the best possible education for all children.

The rival rhetorics of the two personalities never engage with each other in anything resembling discussion or persuasion. Mrs Thatcher insists on Mr Kinnock's failure to make a semantic distinction (the strategy of 'We are talking about two different things'): 'You are talking about segregation. I am talking about education'. Mr Kinnock retaliates with his version of Mrs Thatcher's inability to formulate X in counterpoise to Y (the strategy of 'either you do or you don't'): 'Any Prime Minister who cannot give a "yes" or "no" answer to segregation condemns herself out of her own mouth'. Taken at its face value this is a very odd accusation: by not answering she 'condemns herself out of her own mouth'? The sub-text, however, seems to be that she refuses to *formulate* in a required style. Each of the opponents here offers a rhetoric which is not accepted by the other; each is consequently persuaded that the other is wrong in argument.

The rhetoric of face-to-face exchange is necessarily cruder, more doggedly assertive, than that of written political commentaries of the kind found in the editorials and leader pages of 'good' newspapers. These are often 'deliberative' in the particular sense of presenting arguments with prudent hedges of reservation and qualification. Here, for instance, is an extract from an editorial in the *Daily Telegraph*, in criticism of the controversial Anglo—Irish Agreement:

> Events in Ireland should be followed with a certain quiet despair. The agreement itself does not impress. There is a case waiting to be made that it is both flimsy and injurious, achieving very little in itself but laying down all sorts of precedents designed to bend, soften and diminish sovereignty. It can be argued very cogently that the genie of devolution in other parts of the United Kingdom may be released from a bottle in which Mrs Thatcher wants it firmly corked. It is a poor, meretricious piece of well-meant over-activity producing facile approval and problems which weren't there before. All this could have been made clear with force and restraint by Ulster Unionists and their mainland friends in the House.
>
> (*Daily Telegraph*, 23 November 1985)

Circumspect truculence is the key to this specimen of journalistic rhetoric. It urges its views hotly, yet takes a coolly distant stance in the frequent modals and other constructions suggesting non-committal (the strategy of 'it's not for me to say, but if I were you . . .', or 'mind you, I'm only saying this'). Thus events 'should be followed'; the case – which is asserted in quite intemperate language – is 'waiting to be made'; a position 'can be argued' – 'very cogently', we are told; the 'genie of devolution' – thus we raise a menace by making a metaphor – 'may be released'; and all this 'could have been' made clear, 'with force and restraint'. This prudent modality is accompanied by vague shows of confident demonstration: 'a certain quiet despair' (but how much is 'certain'?); 'a case' (perhaps there are other cases, too?); 'achieving very little' (but achieving something, probably); 'all sorts of precedents' ('all sorts' suggests 'virtually innumerable'); 'all this'. What goes on here is a kind of quantifying without exact quantities; an expression of intensity without specifications of degree. The writer is asserting, in effect, an absolute conviction that something may conceivably be the case.

If the rhetorical hedges were removed, the surviving version would be something like this:

> Events in Ireland give rise to despair. The agreement itself does not impress. It is both flimsy and injurious, and lays down precedents designed to bend, soften and diminish sovereignty. The demand for devolution will be heard again from other parts of the United Kingdom, where Mrs Thatcher wants it suppressed. It is a poor, meretricious piece of well-meant over-activity producing facile approval and problems which weren't there before. None of this has been made clear, with force and restraint, by the Ulster Unionists and their mainland friends in the House.

Part-digest, part-paraphrase, this exposes the columnist's sentiments by removing the language in which they are judiciously framed. As the piece now stands, there are very few words and phrases that do not present themselves as blatant value-judgements, immediately open to challenge from the reader. What is meant by *flimsy* and *injurious*, and how does the 'agreement' exemplify these alleged qualities? In what way are these words antonyms of possible semantic associates, as the 'both . . . and' frame would imply? 'Sovereignty' may be 'diminished', but in what senses may it be *bent* or *softened*? Are these words simply thrown in as fillers to make up a rhetorical rule-of-three? If something is *well-meant*, how is it also *meretricious*, given the Shorter Oxford Dictionary's definition of that word as '1. Of, pertaining to, befitting, or of the character of a harlot. 2. Alluring by false show; showily attractive'? Does *facile approval* denote 'approval readily given', or does it imply 'unmerited approval'? The questions mount, and it becomes increasingly apparent that this commentary, rationally framed though it may seem to be, is an exercise in political loudspeaking.

At its centre is a piece of image-making, neutralized in the rewritten version, but vital to the assertive process of the original:

> It can be argued very cogently that the genie of devolution in other parts of the United Kingdom may be released from a bottle in which Mrs Thatcher wants it firmly corked.

A reader is bound to interpret this figurative language as referring to the containment of a wayward and potentially dangerous force; devolution, it is implied, is not something for prudent governors to tamper with. Thus a view of the issue – devolution – is enjoined upon the reader, not by analysis and argument, but by the synthesis, a potentially deceitful synthesis, of metaphor. The enforcement (so to speak) of a metaphorical power turns on the simple equation of *genie* (malign strength) with *devolution*. Beyond that, it seems that the completion of figurative parallels, the consistent development of the figure, so essential in literary prose, ceases to be of much consequence. If *genie* = *devolution*, with what are we to equate the *bottle* in which the genie must be 'firmly corked'? Is it the bottle of lapsed parliamentary business? Or a bottle of bureaucratic oblivion? It hardly matters. It becomes a magically meaningless word, this 'bottle' in which Mrs Thatcher is determined to cork up devolution.

Figurative fuzziness Deliberative rhetoric of this kind is often figuratively fuzzy; images, personifications, anaologies are projected for the sake of convenience, as bearers of persuasive emphasis, and are readily abandoned or freely mixed with other figures. Two examples:

> In particularly attacking high interest rates, Mr Kinnock said the government's record was one of flop and failure. Great images had gone; sacred cows were turning out to be old bull. The strategy of shrinking the economy was obvious when one stripped the Queen's Speech of virile phrases about firm policies. It was a recipe for further rundown of the economy. (*The Times*, 7 November, 1985)

> In the last session the Government presented its programme badly. It dug pits for itself and strewed the banana skins in strategic places for ministers to fall in. The pits are still there, not least the pit marked 'fear of freeing the economy from state chains'. (Editorial in *The Times*, 7 November 1985)

These examples are taken from the same issue of *The Times*. One reports the utterances of a politician, presumably rendering his words faithfully into indirect speech. The other is the work of an editorial writer. In each, the apparent intention of the figurative language is a forceful playfulness; and in each the playfulness is clogged by a sluggish mixture of figures. Mr Kinnock, witty enough on sacred cows and old bull, then proceeds through the military implications of *strategy* to domestic notions of *shrinking*; thence to a dubious metaphor of disrobing (it is presumably Mrs Thatcher's quasi-virility that is to be exposed when the Queen's Speech is *stripped*); and finally back to the domestic scene for a *recipe*. ('Recipe for rundown' is clearly a derivative, jauntily alliterated, of that tired old phrase 'recipe for disaster).' The editorial extract is even more confused in its figurative excess. Hunters may dig pits to trap wild animals; pompous cartoon characters may slip on banana skins; doors may bear warning signs, or pictures be furnished with cautionary captions; but hunters do *not* dig captioned pits and bestrew them with banana skins to facilitate their own fall. This is worse than figurative fuzziness; this is analogy gone lunatic.

Interestingly, each of these extracts contains the word *strategy*, a current vogue word, and one round which political metaphor is regularly developed. 'Strategy' associates repeatedly with other words of military import – 'forces', 'reinforcements', 'assault', 'attack', 'counter-attack', 'position', 'capture', 're-group', 'entrench', and so on. Other figuratively productive vogue words are *dimension* (involving 'area', 'field', 'space', 'line', 'latitude', 'depth', 'breadth') *stance* (together with 'posture', 'thrust', and 'tendency'); *syndrome* (used accurately in its linkage with 'symptom', 'disease', 'remedy', or more loosely in the sense of 'commitment', 'behaviour pattern', e.g. 'the monetarist syndrome'); *perception; consensus; flexibility* (in connection with 'choice' and 'option'); *formula* (associated synonymically with 'initiative' – but initiatives can 'get under way' or 'run out of steam'; and collocationally with 'agreement', 'peace', 'settlement', etc.). These are bases for metaphoric inventions which then mingle freely with cliché metaphors of the 'uphill task', of the 'climate of opinion', of 'throwing light on' and 'nailing colours to', of 'sowing', and 'reaping', and 'rooting out'.

In journalistic commentary, mixed and fuzzed metaphor is further commingled with current buzz-, purr- and snarl-words, often with bizarre effect. Thus an article in the *Independent* concludes with the following paragraph:

> Mrs Thatcher and her ministers should now accelerate their challenge to the protectionist consensus in their own backyard. If the Prime Minister was serious in her hustings rhetoric about creating a people's government then she should truly open it to the people's inspection. A

government elected on its pledge to overturn the relatively recent cotton wool welfarism of local governments – which is more openly conducted then central government – deserves to be accused of mote and beam hypocrisy if it fails to tackle the more ancient redoubts of our bureaucratic elite. (*Independent*, 1 July 1987)

Here even the grammar is fuzzed (in the sentence beginning 'A government elected on its pledge . . .'). Littered about this paragraph are words from the institutional vocabulary (*hustings*), vogue words (*consensus*), snarl-words (*protectionist, welfarism*), literary allusions (*mote and beam*) and tokens of stock metaphor ('speed' metaphor in *accelerate*, military metaphor in *redoubt*). The lexicon generates some imposing phrasal gestures: *the protectionist consensus, cotton wool welfarism, mote and beam hypocrisy, the more ancient redoubts of our bureaucratic elite*. The accommodation of these phrases to the discourse structure of sentence and text, however, leads to some woeful metaphoric mixes. To accelerate a challenge to a consensus in a backyard is indeed a wonderful thing; even more wonderful than overturning cotton wool or tackling ancient redoubts. It is as though the writer had conceived his discourse as a collage of noun phrases ('cotton wool welfarism', 'the more ancient redoubts of our bureaucratic elite'), and had been little concerned for the semantic propriety of the verbs ('overturn', 'tackle') linking those phrases into predications. What is produced is a text of sorts; but it conveys no clear sense of the text as a rhetorical process with an overarching plan which dictates, among other things, consistency of figuration and metaphor.

Oratory Such planning is more apparent in platform oratory, though even here phrase-making is a major effect. A staple of political oratory is the kind of rhetorical figure that depends on balance, equivalence, or parallelism of constructions – the *parison* that pervades Classical and Renaissance rhetoric. This is most readily observable in speeches made by political leaders at party conferences or during election campaigns. For instance, James Callaghan, leader of the Labour party, during the General Election campaign of 1979:

> As long as there's a family without a home,
> as long as there is a patient waiting for a hospital bed,
> as long as there's a man or woman without a job
> or someone who suffers discrimination because of their colour
> so long will our work as a Labour government not be done.
> We go forward in that spirit and that resolve.

Or Neil Kinnock in 1984, referring to outbreaks of violence during the miners' strike:

I condemn violence
I abominate violence
I damn violence
– Yes I do –
All violence, without fear or favour –
And *that's* what makes me different from Margaret Thatcher.

Polemic oratory, indeed, concentrates on 'that's what makes me different'; antitheses are measured, contrasting verbal items brought into sharp focus:

Now, the Labour Prime Minister and his colleagues are boasting in this election campaign that they have brought inflation *down* from the disastrous level of 26 per cent. But we are entitled to enquire: who put it *up* to 26 per cent? (Edward Heath, 1979)

We shall find two or three million demoralised long-term unemployed who have to be put back to work in factories not that Hitler has *bombed* but that Thatcher and Joseph have *closed*. (Tony Benn, 1980)

Simple devices of repetition, emphasis and counter-emphasis are sufficient to create a kind of prosody, a rhythmic incantation that half-invites, half-enforces assenting applause.

Such devices also extend into the larger architecture of the platform oration. Here is one of the most famous of all political speeches in English, delivered by an American politician in 1863:

Fourscore and seven years ago our fathers brought forth upon this continent a new nation, conceived in liberty, and dedicated to the proposition that all men are created equal. Now we are engaged in a great civil war, testing whether that nation, or any nation so conceived and so dedicated, can long endure. We are met on a great battlefield of that war. We have come to dedicate a portion of that field as a final resting-place of those who here gave their lives that that nation might live. It is altogether fitting and proper that we should do this. But in a larger sense we cannot dedicate, we cannot consecrate, we cannot hallow this ground. The brave men, living and dead, who have struggled here, have consecrated it far above our power to add or detract. The world will little note, nor long remember, what we say here, but it can never forget what they did here. It is for us, the living, rather to be dedicated here to the unfinished work they have thus far so nobly advanced. It is rather for us to be here dedicated to the great task remaining before us, that from these honoured dead we take increased devotion to that cause for which they here gave the last full measure of devotion; that we here highly resolve that the dead shall not have died in vain, that this nation, under God, shall have a new birth of freedom; and that government of the people, by the people, and for the people shall not perish from the earth.

The 'politician' is, of course Abraham Lincoln, and the speech the famous Gettysburg Address. This composition has achieved monumental status and has secured for itself a place in the history of literary English – distinctions that may occasionally blind us to the fact that it is, none the less, a political speech, by an astute practitioner of the craft of politics. This is Lincoln's plea for the Union, at a time when the fortunes of the Union, and its future, were critically balanced; and as a speech it is none the less noble for serving pragmatic purposes.

Its most obvious rhetorical characteristic is the use throughout of rhythmically and syntactically counterpoised phrases and clauses. There is, of course, the famous closing cadence:

> government *of* the people
>   *by* the people
>   and *for* the people
> shall not perish from the earth

But also:

> whether *that* nation   or *any* nation
> *so* conceived   and *so* dedicated

And also:

> we cannot dedicate
> we cannot consecrate
> we cannot hallow this ground

And further:

> The word will little note
> nor long *remember*   what *we say* here
> but it can never *forget*   what *they did* here

And:

> It is for *us*, the living, rather to be dedicated here . . .
> It is rather for *us* to be here dedicated . . .

And:

> we *take*   increased devotion . . .
> they here *gave*   the last full measure of devotion . . .

Such structures contain and give emphatic force to the speech's essential counterpoise of *we* and *they*, the living and the dead, the survivors and the sufferers. This is a counterpoise of persons; there are also other deictic emphases, pointed up in the recurrence of *this, that,* and *those* (in 'this continent', 'that nation', 'that war', 'that field', 'those who here gave their lives') and in the insistently repeated *here,* which refers both to time (after *ago* and *now*) and place ('who here gave their lives', 'who have struggled here', 'what we say here', 'what they did here'; 'to be dedicated here', 'to be here dedicated', 'for which they have gave . . .', 'that we here highly resolve'). The text is elaborately orientated to its subject-matter and its audience, in such a way as to suggest both immediacy of experience and objectifying distance – the oneness of the addresser and those addressed, and their joint contemplation of events in which they have had no part, but from which moral resolve is to be drawn.

The vocabulary of the Address is at first glance far removed from our common notions of the political, though in fact it is cleverly politicized. There are two significant motifs in the lexicon of the text. One is that of birth and death and rebirth, notably represented at the beginning and end of the text by *brought forth, conceived,* and *a new birth.* (It is perhaps not often remarked that mothers, not 'fathers', more appropriately 'conceive' and 'bring forth'; but Lincoln's object is not biological accuracy.) The other motif is represented by a strain of what is essentially *religious* vocabulary: *dedicate, consecrate, hallow, devotion.* These words, uttered with evangelical fervour, are political converts; Lincoln, arguing for the very life and survival of the Union, does so in terms that suggest a sacret mission. The master-word in this set is *dedicate,* a term that is made to slip easily through several shifts of meaning, thus:

1 'dedicated to the proposition that all men are created equal' ('dedicated' = 'committed by belief or argument')
2 'any nation so conceived and so dedicated' (the same)
3 'we have come to dedicate a portion of that field' ('dedicate' = 'set aside for special reverence')
4 'we cannot dedicate . . . this ground' (the same, in conjunction with 'consecrate', and 'hallow')
5 'It is for us . . . to be dedicated here . . .' ('dedicated' = 'devoted (by public affirmation) to a cause')
6 'It is rather for us to be here dedicated . . .' (the same).

It appears from the above that the 'meanings' occur in pairs, 1–2, 3–4, 5–6, and that the relevant meaning in each instance is supported by other lexical items in context. Thus, meaning 1 ('committed by belief or argument') draws support from *conceived*, which is in fact a pun: 'conceive' as in 'conceive a child', and 'conceive' as in 'conceive an idea', the latter being the meaning that supports the first interpretation of *dedicate*. Meaning 2 ('set aside for special reverence') occurs in context with *consecrate* and *hallow*. Meaning 3 ('devoted to a cause') is introduced in sentences which actually contain the word *devotion*. What happens, in sum, is that Lincoln, with considerable rhetorical skill, manages to involve one word in global applications: to the life of the intellect, to religious feeling, and finally to the quickening of political resolve.

The Gettysburg Address is a noble utterance, an expression of lofty humanity; at the same time it is a masterpiece of political rhetoric. Such achievements, like other masterpieces in other genres, are rare. The language of politics is seldom uplifting, and frequently specious in its claims on our feelings and our minds. It is nevertheless a variety of language that enters our daily experiences so pervasively that we cannot afford to neglect it. Fortunately there are copious texts at hand, in the form of newspapers and television or radio broadcasts; and what they have to tell us about the rhetorics of our time – the old-new or new-old rhetorics – is well worth a little study.

(For further exploration of issues raised in this section, see Leith and Myerson, 1989; Nash, 1989.)

3.5.2 The Language of Criticism

The study of styles in criticism – the critical assessment of critical assessments of creative artists – is an odd undertaking, and one that may recall the old rhyme telling us how great fleas have little fleas upon their backs to bite 'em, and little fleas have lesser fleas, and so *ad infinitum*. But there is, after all, a point in what may at first look like an exercise in literary parasitology. Though the critic certainly depends for his livelihood on the creative artist's ability to produce work for criticism, criticism itself should not feed on art, becoming a mere client form, but should define and help to promote the conditions under which art can flourish; and stylistic investigation, by defining the verbal resources of criticism, should help us to distinguish effectively between legitimate argument and chicanery, between necessary elaboration and mere persiflage, between considered censure and showy abuse.

The functions of criticisms (1): judgement Criticism is a complex act –

socially, psychologically, politically, as well as aesthetically complex – and any discussion of it will turn up differing, possibly conflicting, views of what the critic does and what his or her professional priorities should be. On one simple proposition, however, all are agreed: the prime business of criticism is *judgement*. Etymologically the word means just that: Greek *krites* is a judge. Disagreement may break out again over the actual scope of the term, but it will hardly be controversial if we suggest that judgement involves:

a   evaluation, i.e. the assertion that a piece of work is good, bad, pernicious, wholesome, etc.

b   functional assessment, i.e. a declaration that the work is adequate or inadequate to its professed purpose – or possibly to the purpose *read into it* by the critic.

c   correction, i.e. some recommendation for improvement or re-working.

d   interpretation, i.e. some statement about the meaning of the work; this includes the act of *reinterpretation*, when a work is thought to have been misunderstood, or when time and cultural change apparently endow it with a new significance.

Among the many questions this raises, questions of language – that is, of the critic's professional idiom – are paramount. What form do 'evaluations' take? How do we recognize that the critic is making a 'functional assessment'? How is our attention focuses on corrective or interpretative statements? The answers may seem obvious, but our avowed task of studying critical styles requires that they should be explicitly made. Let us then propose that the act of judgement has regular and recurrent correspondences in language, some of which are illustrated in such simple pronouncements as these:

This work is impressive.
Mr Bloggs has written a scholarly and entertaining text.
Students will find it particularly helpful.
The bibliography might be augmented.
The book must be seen as an essay in sociology, not linguistics.

The examples are invented; but any review might yield comparable observation. The common linguistic tokens of judgement exemplified by these sentences are: the subject–complement sentence pattern 'A is B'; the evaluative adjective, whether as a predicative ('The work is impressive') or as a premodifier ('This is an entertaining work'); verbs denoting perception, e.g. *see, consider, regard*; verbs denoting recipience, acceptance, acknowledgement, e.g. *find, welcome, receive*; the modal auxiliaries that suggest a correction, an interpretation, a warning against misinterpretation (e.g. 'the bibliography *might* be augmented', 'the book *can* be regarded as a parody', 'astute readers *ought not* to be deceived by the author's artless manner'); the conjunctions that suggest an analogy, a comparison, an identifying characteristic (e.g. 'The poem reads *like* a temperance tract', 'it should be understood *as* an allegory'); the passive constructions that often accompany verbs of perception or recipience ('it *must be seen* as an essay in sociology', 'it *will be found* valuable'). These are some of the ways in which judgements are ordinarily coded into language.

The functions of criticism (2): argument   Some judgements are baldly pronounced, as generalizations assuming common support, or brooking no opposition: 'Mozart can never be dull', 'Beethoven's late quartets are works of unsurpassable artistry', 'Mr Bloggs is a spectacularly successful literary mountebank', '*Dynasty* is trash'. The purport of judgement is often a genuflection or a jeer. It is commonly assumed, however, that judgements will be supported by arguments, particularly in the domain of academic criticism. Now *argument*, like *judgement*, invites elementary analysis. Let us assume that argument involves:

a   'principial' argument, i.e. the presentation of a general thesis, the construction of a coherent investigative procedure from which judgements, and particularly interpretations, may be derived;

b   demonstration, requiring the citation, close examination, classification and comparison of details.

As before, we can look for linguistic tokens in brief statements characteristic of the critical style, e.g.:

> It is precisely because Frost's poetic language appears unremarkable that we should examine it with the greatest care.

> In this stanza, as opposed to the preceding three, there is a marked caesura in the third line, with a resultant accent on the word 'home'.

These sentences exhibit one or two symptoms diagnostic of the critical proposition and demonstration. *Because* (like *therefore, consequently, as a result, since, for, yet,* and other discourse-framing adverbs and conjunctions) is a typical mark of critical rhetoric; here, thanks to the construction in which it is set, it is sharply focused. 'Should' expresses a characteristic appeal to the non-existent or desired state of affairs, a not unusual tactic in critical language: 'we may assume', 'it might be conjectured', 'it must be supposed', etc. The processes of demonstration draw heavily on deictics and demonstratives, e.g. *this, that, these, those, such, the former, the latter, above, below*; on enumeratives and sequence-markers, e.g. *the first, the next, the preceding*; on contrastives, e.g. *as opposed to, by contrast with, in comparison*; on exemplifications, e.g. *for instance, for example, by way of illustration, thus*; on expressions of citation, e.g. *the word, the phrase, the expression*; on the existential clause pattern, i.e. *There is . . .* etc.; and of course on appropriate technical terms or abstractions, e.g. *stanza, caesura, accent*, and so on.

The affective element   In popular criticism mostly, but elsewhere in varying degres, even in the most austere essays in the genre, there is an affective or emotive element: the expression of a creative impulse, an indulgence of the critic's temperament, an outburst of pleasure or testiness, a mischievous impulse to amuse or beguile the reader. The affective impulse colours many acts of judgement:

> The part of the first murderer was played with sepulchral gusto.
> This is an abominably readable novel.
> His metres dance like a man in a surgical boot.
> It is hardly worth spilling your coffee on.
> This is a must for the really dedicated schizophrenic.

Simile; oxymoron ('sepulchral gusto', 'abominably readable'); the adjective submodified by the powerful adverbial intensifier ('abominably readable', 'gorgeously drab', 'demurely concupiscent', 'lamentably successful'); the noun not selected from the core vocabulary (e.g. 'gusto' for 'enjoyment'); the subversion of some banal collocation (for 'really dedicated performer', 'really dedicated athlete', read 'really dedicated schizophrenic'); the complement that downgrades as it understates (for 'it is hardly worth reading' substitute 'it is hardly worth spilling your coffee on'), or, conversely, upgrades while it overstates (for 'it is funny', read 'it is a mortal blow to melancholy'); these are typical 'affective' resources. Usually these devices can be seen (and enjoyed) for what they are. Sometimes, however, a critic will make an affective judgement as though it had the validity of a proposition in well-supported argument. If I declared, for example, that 'no one I respect and not many of the people I disrespect would be caught reading the novels of Harold Robbins', I may have pronounced personal judgement against Mr Robbins in a suitably acerbic style, but I have not produced an argument for not reading his work. The point may seem obvious, but there is a great deal of journalistic criticism in which affective assertions become substitutes for well-found propositions and patient demonstrations.

Three critical keys Now let us briefly indicate, before we go on to consider some specimens of criticism, three broad principles, three keys to the critical style. They are as follows.

1 *Generalization.* The critic attempts to formulate powerful general statements which, if demonstrably valid, will characterize an author, a work, a genre. (But critics not infrequently ignore the obligation to validate a general statement; and this, incidentally, is a general statement about critics.) It may be useful to distinguish between three kinds of generalization, i.e.:

a the major generalization, as exemplified by the sentence *Shakespeare is a difficult author.* The obvious grammatical symptom here is the relational verb, *to be.* A roughly instructive measure in the analysis of critical styles is to count the occurrences of *is.* In a species of minor or constrained generalization, verbs of appearance or transitional process are used: 'Shakespeare seems difficult', 'Yeats' later poetry becomes obscure', 'Dickens tends to grow sentimental'.

b the consensus generalization, expressed by *We all agree that Shakespeare is great.* There are two linguistic symptoms to look for here. First, the subject of the generalizing sentence is an inclusive pronoun ('we', 'we all', 'everybody') or a noun phrase denoting a general category of persons ('all right-thinking people', 'anyone with pretensions to literacy'); and second, the verb expresses consent, e.g. 'agree', 'consider', 'declare', 'pronounce', 'find'.

c the symptomatic generalization, pointing to some characteristic of an author, an artist, a work: e.g. *Shakespeare creates superb female characters; Mozart (always) writes good clarinet parts; Falstaff invariably provokes laughter.* The main characteristics of such statements are the verb in the present tense, denoting habitual action, custom, proclivity; and the occurrence, in many cases, of some adverb of frequency, such as 'always', 'usually', 'invariably', 'seldom', 'rarely', 'never'.

2 *Modality.* The critic deals in 'if', 'might', 'ought', 'possibly', 'preferably', and other such expressions. It is in the nature of his work to relate the actual to the possible, and so it is in the nature of his language to use expressions of condition, option, obligation, possibility, and so forth. Four types of modality are prominent in critical discourse:

a Modals of obligation or recommendation, e.g. *must, should,* in such declarations as 'If we are to understand Shakespeare we must study the history of the times in which he wrote'; 'The reader should consider the first stanza very carefully'.

b Modals of concession or supposition, such as *may, might, must*, as in 'We may, if we choose, interpret this as a joke'; 'Some licence might be allowed to Elizabethan taste'; 'Mr Archer must have been in dire straits to write this'.

c Modals of possibility, e.g. *may, could*, as in 'Donne may have intended a pun'; 'The printed version could have been a first draft.'

d Modals of assumption (i.e. assuming permissibility, feasibility, etc.), e.g. *can, could, might*, as in 'We can attempt a Marxist interpretation'; 'The case could be argued in this way . . .'; 'We might propose the following interpretation . . .'. (A symptom of such modals is that they are frequently followed by cataphoric expressions, e.g. *thus, in this way, the following, as follows*.)

3 *Affectiveness*. The critic tries to persuade, or enforce consent, or provoke debate, by pleasing and teasing his readers, or by treating what he does as a creative activity sufficient unto itself and not solely as an accessory to valid judgement and informed interpretation. Some characteristics of critical affectiveness have already been discussed. To them we may add: the frequent occurrence of metaphor and figurative language, whether with the intention of illuminating or simply enlivening the argument; a propensity towards rhetorical schemes of symmetry such as antithesis, parison, and chiasmus; recourse to hyperbole or litotes in connection with expressions of praise and invective; and the pronouncement of generalizations couched in unashamedly affective terms, e.g. 'It is plain to one and all that Mr Smith writes with the delicacy of a chimpanzee wielding a tar-brush,' 'There is hardly a sentence in the book that does not proclaim the author's impudent illiteracy', 'Schubert is simply the greatest songwriter that ever existed, and anyone who does not think so should consult his oto-laryngologist without delay'.

We might expect to find that of these three 'keys', the first two will give us the entry to most academic criticism, while the third will probably bring us into the domain of column-journalism and the periodical review. But let us test these suppositions against some extracts.

The critical style: first sample   Here is a first sample. It is by T. S. Eliot, and it is taken from the text of his lecture entitled *What is a Classic?*, delivered to the Virgil Society in 1944 and published in 1945. In this passage Eliot begins to develop the thesis that although Virgil was a

Roman poet, writing for the Roman world, he has values for other cultures, values that make him a classic author:

> If Virgil is thus the consciousness of Rome and the supreme voice of her language, he must have a significance for us which cannot be expressed wholly in terms of literary appreciation and criticism. Yet, adhering to the problems of literature, or to the terms of literature in dealing with life, we may be allowed to imply more than we state. The value of Virgil to us, in literary terms, is in providing us with a critical criterion. We may, as I have said, have reasons to rejoice that this criterion is provided by a poet writing in a different language from our own: but that is not a reason for rejecting the criterion. To preserve the classical standard, and to measure every individual work of literature by it, is to see that, while our literature as a whole may contain everything, every single work in it may be defective in something. This may be a necessary defect, a defect without which some quality present would be lacking; but we must see it as a defect, at the same time that we see it as a necessity. In the absence of the standard of which I speak, a standard we cannot keep clearly before us if we rely on our own literature alone, we tend, first to admire works of genius for the wrong reasons – as we extol Blake for his *philosophy*, and Hopkins for his *style*; and from this we proceed to greater error, to giving the second-rate equal rank with the first-rate. In short, without the constant application of the classical measure, which we owe to Virgil more than to any other one poet, we tend to become provincial.

In this austere discourse there is no room for affective play (although at one point – commented on below – there is an elegant touch of rhetoric). The stylistic keys to this passage are fairly obviously those of generalization and modality; it reads, as surely it is intended to read, like judgement backed by the qualificiations and concessions of reasonable argument. It also leaves the impression of so many abstractions unrooted in concrete example ('significance for us . . .', 'problems of literature', 'terms of literature in dealing with life', 'critical criterion', 'classical standard', 'classical measure') that the reader, arriving eventually at *in short*, is not quite sure how he and the argument got there, or why what is expressed *in short* can be summed up in the assertion *we tend to become provincial*.

The passage (in short) is more elusive than we might at first suppose. Bearing this in mind, it may be a useful exercise to list and comment on its generalizations and modalities. First, then, the generalizations. They are listed here as they occur, in sentence-context, but with relevant subordinate constructions in square brackets. The generalization itself is italicized. In one instance (no. 6) the generalization is retrieved, as a proposition, from a syntactic variant. The sequence is as follows.

1 '[If] *Virgil is* [thus] *the consciousness of Rome and the supreme voice of her language* [he must . . .etc.].' *Comment:* This has the form of a major generalization, but, as the bracketed *if* and *thus* will indicate, it depends on something that has gone before. *Thus* implies that a position has been argued, but this is in fact not so. The position has been *implied* in a number of assertions about the 'comprehensiveness' and 'centrality' of Virgil, the 'destiny' of the Latin language, and the character of Aeneas as the 'symbol of Rome'. The tenor of this first generalization is therefore 'These implications are to be stated thus', or rather 'If these implications may be summarized thus'. Its power as a generalization is compromised by an inherent modality.

2 *'The value of Virgil to us, in literary terms, is in providing us with a critical criterion.'* *Comment:* Here is a generalization of the 'symptomatic' type (as in 'Shakespeare creates superb female chracters', 'Mozart always writes good clarinet parts': then 'Virgil provides a critical criterion').

3 *'To preserve the classical standard, and to measure every individual work of literature by it, is to see that, while our literature as a whole may contain everything, every single work in it may be defective in something.'* *Comment:* This major generalization is the crux of the passage. It is based on the idiomatic pattern *To do X is to do Y,* or *To do X is to procure the consequence Y:* 'To understand is to forgive', 'To know her is to love her'. Eliot's construction is far more complex than the rudimentary pattern. His X and Y are syntactically elaborate, the latter containing a modal ('while our literature may contain everything') embedded in a parisonic structure ('literature as a whole' balanced by 'every single work', 'may contain' by 'may be defective', 'everything' by 'in something'). This density of syntactic and rhetorical activity indeed suggests that this is the most important part of the paragraph, its essential statement. The form of the generalization, however, queries its force. It suggests the proposition 'Our literature is defective by classical standards', but the form it assumes is implicitly modal. *To do X is to do Y* or *To do X is to procure the consequence Y* are paraphrasable as *If we do X we do Y, By doing X we may achieve the consequence Y.*

4 ['In the absence of this standard of which I speak, a standard we cannot keep clearly before us if we rely on our own ltierature alone] *we tend* [first] *to admire works of genius for the wrong reasons.'* *Comment:* this is a sample of consensus generalization (cf. 'We all admire Shakespeare', All good men despise bad writers'). It is tentatively expressed, and is all the more tentative for the long qualifying preamble.

5 '[as] *we extol Blake for his philosophy and Hopkins for his style.'* *Comment:* More consensus generalization, questionably imputing to

the literary public major generalizations about Blake and Hopkins. Ultimately this statement is dependent on the preceding *we tend. We tend to admire* strictly requires the consequence of *as we tend to extol* or *as we sometimes extol*, or *as we are inclined to extol*. The progress from (4) to (5) is a jump from the tentative proposition to the unqualified assertion.

6 '[and from this] *we proceed to greater error, to giving the second-rate equal rank with the first-rate.*' Comment: The immanent proposition is *We [tend to] give the second-rate equal rank with the first-rate*. So translated, it becomes another example of consensus generalization.

7 [In short, without the constant application of the classical measure, which we owe to Virgil more than to any other one poet,] *we tend to become provincial.* Comment: A consensus generalization, related, like (4), to a qualifying preamble so lengthy as to make a joke of the author's 'in short'. The dependent introductory clauses of (4) and (7) are closely linked in content: 'In the absence of this standard' in (4) is matched by 'without the constant application of the classical measure' in (7), and 'which we cannot keep clearly before us if we rely on our own literature alone' has its parallel in 'which we owe to Virgil more than to any other one poet'.

This sequence of generalizations frames the argument, in a scheme which involves the author's assertions and the assumption of the reader's consent. Briefly, the scheme is this: (a) a linking generalization, which is no more than a resumé of what has been implied in the preceding paragraph; (b) two generalizations which, taken together, constitute the author's *thesis* in this extract ('Virgil provides a critical standard; if we apply it, we see the defects of our own literature'); (c) three consensus generalizations, assuming the reader's agreement with the thesis and with what is said to be implied in it; and (d) a further consensus generalizations, summing up the preceding three but leaving an unresolved term ('provincial') to be elucidated in the paragraph that follows.

As we strip down the argument in this way, it begins to shed some of the authority conferred upon it by the reiteration of portentous abstractions like 'standard', 'criterion' and 'measure'. It suggests a mischievous paraphrase: 'If we agree – and we must agree – that Virgil is a classic, then we must agree that our literature *tends* not to be classic'. Its confident structure is wormed with conditions and qualifiers. Every critical argument can be expected to contain at least one unqualified major generalization – *This is good, This is successful:* unqualified, because it is contextually supported by reasoning and demonstration. A generalization which declares that *This tends to be good* or *This might be successful under certain circumstances* has simply lost its generalizing power – it has been overtaken by modality. And that is what has happend in this passage of critical argument; the central thesis is invaded by 'if' and 'may'. Furthermore, the shift from assertion to consensus, from 'it is the case' to 'we find', is managed with an assurance that might, in a less monumental author, be censured as sleight of hand. The transition is helped and disguised by the originating circumstances of the text, as a lecture. Speakers commonly engage audiences with the inclusive *we*, and that pronoun occurs in this extract no fewer than twelve times. (The distribution is interesting: nine occurrences in the stretch of text containing the consensus generalizations, five of these in one sentence – the sentence beginning 'In the absence of the standard of which I speak . . .', and which also contains an 'us' and an 'our'.) To understand more fully the procedural shiftiness of the argument, however, we need to consider its other important key, its modality.

Here the modal auxiliaries figuring in the text ('must', 'may', 'can', 'would') are listed, in italics, in the context of their clauses; adjacent clauses, wherever these are relevant to an interpretation, are shown in square brackets. Thus:

1   '[If Virgil is thus the consciousness of Rome and the supreme voice of her language,] he *must* have a significance for us which *cannot* be expressed wholly in terms of literary appreciation and criticism.' *Comment: Must* is ambiguous: is it a modal of obligation ('Virgil necessarily has this significance') or of supposition ('Virgil supposedly has this significance')? In such instances, the intended meaning can often be resolved by reference to other modals in the same context; but here the notion of possibility (or impossibility) expressed in *cannot* would accord equally well with the 'necessary' meaning ('He certainly has a significance which cannot be expressed . . .') or the 'supposition- al' meaning ('He presumably has a significance which cannot be expressed . . .'). The text begins, for the reader, in doubt: doubt about the validity of what looks like a major generalization; and doubt about the status of the modal assessing the consequences of that generaliza- tion.

2   '[Yet, adhering to the problems of literature, or to the terms of literature in dealing with life,] we *may* be allowed to imply more than we state.' *Comment:* To understand the status of *may* we need to paraphrase the text, which is not worded in the clearest possible way at this point. The sense seems to be: 'Virgil has an importance that goes beyond literary values. Now we have to confine ourselves to

literature. However, accepting that restriction, we may still *imply* commentary on extra-literary matters.' But the paraphrase after all leaves a problem unresolved: does *may* mean 'it is possible for us to imply', or 'it is permissible for us to imply'? Or 'it is both possible and permissible for us to imply'? On balance, this looks like a modal of assumption '(I am going to assume that I am allowed to imply'). In combination with the ambivalent *must* of the opening sentence, this equally ambivalent *may* admits several different readings of the first two sentences. ('This must be the case . . . but it is possible', 'This might be the case . . . but I intend . . .etc.')

3 'We *may*, as I have said, have reasons to rejoice [that this criterion is provided by a poet writing in a different language from our own; but that is not a reason for rejecting the criterion].' *Comment:* A modal of concession, and a rather familiar stratagem in argument, e.g.: 'You may have a point but . . .'. The ensuing *but* is essential to the construction; what follows the *but* cancels the concession ('You may have a point but it isn't really a valid point'). So here, 'I concede that Virgil's standards were set in and for another language and culture; nevertheless, I maintain that those standards apply to our language and culture.'

4 '[To preserve the classicial standard, and to measure every individual work of literature by it, is to see that,] while our literature as a whole *may* contain everything, every single work in it *may* be defective in something.' *Comment:* It is at this point, as we have already noted, that the 'modalizing' structure of the text is allowed to invade its 'generalizing' structure. This happens in two ways, one implicit, the other overt. The generalization itself, we have suggested, is covertly modal ('To do X is to procure the consequence Y' = 'By doing X we may involve Y'). Further, it contains, in a parenthetical clause and a subordinate clause embracing the parenthesis, two instances of *may*. the first of these ('while our literature may contain everything') is a concessive; the second ('every single work may be defective') expresses possibility. Despite the parisonic elegance of the wording, which may create the impression of a rather powerful assertion, the claim made here is actually quite tentative: not 'while our literature as a whole may contain everything, every single work in it *is* defective in something' – which would be a major generalization, and a sweeping judgement indeed – but simply '*may* be defective'. If we paraphrase, the cautiousness of the claim becomes more apparent: 'I concede that our literature contains everything, but I consider it possible that every work is defective in something'.

5 'This *may* be a necessary defect, a defect without which some quality present *would* be lacking; but we *must* see it as a defect, at the same time that we see it as a necessity.' *Comment:* This is a crucial sentence in the modal pattern. It comes immediately after the sentence identified as the text's central generalization, or *thesis*, and leads immediately into the sequence of consensus generalizations with which the paragraph concludes. If we are to look for a point of transition from 'This is the case' to 'we all agree', it is here. *May* and *must* are respectively interpreted (but see below) as modals of concession and obligation ('I grant you this, but all the same you are obliged . . .'). Note the tell-tale *but*; note also the tell-tale subject pronouns ('*This* may', '*we* must') pointing unmistakably to the shift from impersonal to personal. *Would*, however, somewhat colours the interpretation of *may*, suggesting possibility rather than concession: 'It is possible that if this defect were not present, some positive quality would be lacking'. The transition from (4) to (5), incidentally, is a deft piece of smudging. The end of (4) states that 'every single work may be defective' (= 'this is possible'). The beginning of (5) refers to 'This defect'; what was only a possibility is now presented as a recognized fact.

6 '[In the absence of this standard of which I speak,] a standard we *cannot* keep clearly before us [if we rely on our own literature alone . . .]' *Comment:* A modal of possibility; compare this with the earlier occurrence of *cannot,* in 'a significance . . . which cannot be expressed wholly'. Note that the wording in this earlier instance is not 'a significance which *we* cannot express wholly'; the passive transformation, 'cannot be expressed wholly', circumvents personality. Now, however, the modal is governed by a personal subject: 'we cannot keep clearly before us'. In both occurrences, *cannot* is qualified by an adverb: 'cannot be expressed *wholly*' 'cannot keep *clearly* before us'. The author, it seems, is determined at all costs to avoid categorical expressions. Everything *tends*.

The ostensible design of the argument is that the modal pattern provides the reasoning behind the generalizations. In effect, however, the modals insinuate rather than rationalize – by conceding the anticipated point, by tentatively pleading possibilities, and above all by nudging the reader from impersonal proposition to personal consent.

Eliot's judgements in this passage involve assertions of value, or functional importance (Virgil is necessary to us because he provides a standard), and his argument is principial. What is lacking is the supporting evidence of a demonstration. Some commentary, on as little as two or three lines of Virgilian text, would have given critical meaning a concrete location, and would have corrected the blurring of abstractions, the shiftiness of modality.

The critical style: second sample   For contrast, consider another passage of criticism, also by a poet. In 1954–5, Robert Graves delivered the Clark Lectures at the University of Cambridge (subsequently published under the title *The Crowning Privilege*), and in his final address, which he called 'These be your gods', launched a scathing attack on some modern poets. One of his targets was Dylan Thomas:

> In order to conceal this defect in sincerity, he learned to introduce a distractive element. He kept musical control of the reader without troubling about the sense. I do not mean that he aimed deliberately off-target, as the later Yeats did. Thomas seems to have decided that there was no need to aim at all, so long as the explosion sounded loud enough. The fumes of cordite would drift across the target, and a confederate in the butts would signal bull after bull. Nevertheless, as in double talk, a central thread of something like sense makes the incrustations of nonsense more acceptable. Listeners, as opposed to readers, are easily convinced, in such cases, that they are obtuse and slow to follow the workings of the interlocutor's mind, especially when the musical content is so rich. But professionally-minded English poets ban double-talk, except in satire, and insist that every poem must make prose sense as well as poetic sense on one or more levels. The common report that most of Thomas's poems came out of the beer barrel cannot be accepted. It is true that he drank a great deal of beer, and that beer is a splendid drink before one takes one's place in a male voice choir; but the poems show every sign of an alert and sober intelligence. The following, typical stanza is nonsense, but Dylan's golden voice could persuade his readers that he was divulging ineffable secrets:

> *If my head hurt a hair's foot*
> *Pack back the downed bone. If the unpricked ball of my breath*
> *Bump on a spout let the bubbles jump out.*
> *Sooner drop with the worm of the ropes round my throat*
> *Than bully ill love in the clouted scene.*

Now this passage begins and ends in tendentiousness, or judgement-pushing. The last sentence of the preceding paragraph reads: 'Even experts would have been deceived by the virtuosity of Dylan Thomas's conventional, and wholly artificial, early poems.' The virtuosity, the conventionality and the artifice become, in the first sentence of our extract, 'this defect in sincerity'. There is a jump to judgement here; we are asked to accept that because the young Thomas was (according to Mr Graves) a virtuoso and a master of artifice, but in a conventional style, that he was consequently *insincere*. And at the end of the paragraph we are told that a quoted stanza is 'typical' and that it is 'nonsense' – yet as far as the latter charge is concerned it is quite easy to demonstrate at least the general sense of the lines, though the interior details are obscure and confusing.

The critical method here is not argument and demonstration (in spite of the fact that Graves does quote a few lines of his poet), but rather, the attempt to persuade the reader by involving him in affective judgements. In comparison with the Eliot passage, there are very few modals, and the argument is not controlled and directed through them. There are generalizations, certainly; but these are bedded in affective language, and above all in imagery and metaphor. There are two strains of persuasive imagery in the passage, one concerning music (and roughly paraphrasable as 'I don't know what the words mean, but the music's lovely'), the other developing the theme of shooting on the rifle range (and roughly paraphrasable as 'he never hits anything, but he makes a lot of noise'). Into these amusing comparisons Graves insinuates his judgements, e.g.:

> I do not mean that he aimed deliberately off-target, as the later Yeats did. Thomas seems to have decided that there was no need to aim at all, so long as the explosion sounded loud enough. The fumes of cordite would drift across the target, and a confederate in the butts would signal bull after bull.

Who, incidentally, is the 'confederate in the butts'? An *alter ego*, or some indulgent critic?

An attempt to paraphrase the lines just quoted will show how the critical generalizations have to be retrieved from the figurative fun. Their sense may be expressed as follows:

> In his later poems, Yeats had something meaningful to say, but deliberately chose to say it obscurely. Thomas apparently did not see the necessity of saying anything meaningful. It was enough to contrive expressions that sounded poetic, and trust the reading public to assign a meaning to these.

These are essentially symptomatic generalizations – 'Yeats sometimes writes with deliberate obscurity', 'Thomas seldom tries to make sense' – but they are couched in an affective style that forces them upon us and forbids us (or begs us not) to examine them too closely. To use words like 'meaningful' or 'obscure' involves an obligation to start defining what is implied in 'meaning' and 'obscurity', as far as the art of poetry is concerned. These theoretical concerns are avoided if one talks of 'aiming off-target' or of the 'fumes of cordite' that 'drift across the target'. Metaphors are not for expounding, and only a tiresome reader would look for an exposition.

Graves' argumentative technique is macaronic, a mixture of styles and stratagems, as the following (sequent) sentences from the second half of the extract will show:

1 'But professionally-minded English poets ban double-talk, except in satire, and insist that every poem must make prose sense as well as poetic sense on one or more levels.' *Comment:* Six propositions, at least, can be retrieved from this sentence. Before we list them, however, let us note the first clause, which is a form of consensus generalization, comparable with 'All right-thinking people shun communists'. 'We all' (Graves is a professional poet) 'ban double-talk'. But what is 'double-talk'? Does Graves use this expression in the original sense of 'a babble of meaningless syllables'? Or in the later sense of 'ambiguous or deceitful expression'? Or in both senses? Is the proposition 'All good poets avoid misleading ambiguity'? or 'All good poets avoid gibberish'? This twin solution might add more propositions to our suggested list of six:

1 All good poets avoid double-talk.
2 Double-talk is allowed in satire.
3 Every poem must make prose sense.
4 Every poem must make poetic sense on one or more levels
5 All good poets insist that 3 is the case.
6 All good poets insist that 4 is the case.

Six propositions – and perhaps more could be teased out. The point is, however, that they require a high degree of consensus. The phrase 'professionally-minded poets' begs acceptance for every proposition that follows.

2 'The common report that most of Thomas's poems came out of the beer barrel cannot be accepted.' *Comment:* This is mean, a trick worthy of a tabloid journalist ('Sex Orgies in Cricket Pavilion Denied'). The syntax and wording make it suspect, as a form of denial without retraction. 'The common report' = 'What a lot of people say' (the consensus again!); and 'cannot be accepted' = 'is not supported by reliable evidence'. If we paraphrase the sentence, 'It is not true that most of Thomas's poems were composed when he was drunk', then the original is tantamount in meaning to the paraphrase, but not tantamount in intention. Graves' sentence implies that Thomas was a

drunk, but that there is no way of knowing whether he was drunk when he wrote his poems. This is not criticism; it is tattle.

3 'It is true that he drank a great deal of beer, and that beer is a splendid drink before on takes one's place in a male voice choir; but the poems show every sign of an alert and sober intelligence.' *Comment:* This sentence contains the passage's one straightforward, penny-plain expression of judgement: 'the poems show every sign of an alert and sober intelligence'. Yet the evaluative adjectives, 'alert', 'sober', are tainted by the preliminary assertion 'It is true that he drank a great deal of beer'. I may say that the writing of Robert Graves shows an alert intelligence, or that beneath his wit is a sober concern for the truth, without implying that he might sometimes be fuddled or boisterous with booze – which is what Mr Graves manages to imply about Thomas. The aside on the subject of male voice choirs is a cheap way of getting back to the music-motif and 'Dylan's golden voice'.

If in Eliot's assessment of Virgil judgements are presented with the help of a tinkering modality, here in Graves' assessment of Thomas it is the affective method, the mélange of image, metaphor, and loaded word ('nonsense', 'double-talk', 'incrustations', 'golden', 'ineffable') that pleads the case and directs the judgement of the audience. *Audience* is of course the appropriate word in this case, and we might make Mr Graves, ironically, the victim of his own pronouncement: 'Listeners, as opposed to readers, are easily convinced . . .' This kind of critical discourse can be very effective in the lecture room, but how we subsequently respond to it as readers is another matter.

The critical style: third example   Spoken discourse does not always play so mischievously with the susceptibilities of an audience. Here is yet another example of a poet lecturing about poetry. The speaker is Cecil Day Lewis; the occasion, once more, is a series of Clark Lectures, the book in which they were subsequently printed being *The Poetic Image*. In a lecture (or chapter) called 'Broken Images', Day Lewis discusses, with approval, Dylan Thomas' poem 'After the Funeral', and then goes on to comment rather less approvingly on 'Harry Ploughman', a poem by Gerard Manley Hopkins. Though the extract dealing with the latter is rather long, it is worth citing in full the text plus the critical elucidation. First, then, the poem.

> Hard as hurdle arms, with a broth of goldfish flue
> Breathed round; the rack of ribs; the scooped flank; lank
> Rope-over thigh; knee-knave; and barrelled shank –
>   Head and foot, shoulder and shank –
> By a grey eye's head steered well, one crew, fall to;

Stand at stress. Each limb's barrowy brawn, his thew
That onewhere curded, onewhere sucked or sank –
  Soared or sank –
Though as a beachbole firm, finds his, as at a roll-call, rank
And features, in flesh, what deed he each must do –
  His sinew-service where do.

He leans to it, Harry, bends, look. Back, elbow and liquid waist
In him, all quail to the wallowing o' the plough:
  's cheek crimsons; curls
Wag or crossbridle, in a wind lifted, windlaced –
  See his wind-lilylocks-laced;
Churlgrace, too, child of Amansstrength, how it hangs or hurls
Them – broad in bluffhide his frowning feet lashed! raced
With, along them, cragiron under and cold furls –
  With-a-fountain's shining-shot furls.

On which Day Lewis comments:

Now I fear this will be an outrage to persons who close their eyes and
genuflect before any piece by Hopkins, but I do not think 'Harry
Ploughman' is at all a good poem. For me, nothing emerges from thie
froth and flurry of images, neither a clear objective picture of Harry, nor
a sense that I am apprehending the real inwardness of a ploughman,
nor a monumental, symbolic figure such as Mr Thomas makes of his
Ann. If Harry *is* a monumental figure, then I get only a fly's-eye view of
it, a series of blinding close-ups, as if I were crawling laboriously from
limb to limb over the surface of a corrugated, undemonstrative statue.

 When we look into the poem, we find it is composed from a sequence
of images, some clear some obscure, often 'contradictory', descriptive in
intention rather than evocative – images for the most part visual, and
extremely compressed. What we look for in vain, I believe, is any
structure created by these images. We get the impression that one has
been merely added to another – 'broth' to 'hurdle', 'flue' to 'broth', '*rack*
of ribs', '*scooped* flank', '*rope-over* thigh', 'knee-*nave*', '*barrelled* shank' – all
added one to another by an imaginative eye peering so close at each
physical detail in turn that it never sees the whole body of the man, and
by a mind so fastidiously searching in each case for the physically
dead-accurate word that it misses the wholeness of the experience. This
experience – the impression made upon Hopkins by a ploughman at
work – is conveyed then in a succession of images bound loosely
together by the rhythm, rhyme, and internal assonance of the poem, but
otherwise, apart from the carpenter-cooper-wheelwright metaphors in
the opening lines, unrelated. There is almost none of that counterpoint
and cross-reference of image we found in the Dylan Thomas poem. Why
did so fine a writer fail to write a whole poem here? Why did the violent
centrifual force of his images disintegrate the poem? The answer, I

suggest, is that the poem contains an unresolved conflict, between the poet's enthusiasm for the ploughman's physique (the reader may decide for himself in what proportion pure aesthetic pleasure and homosexual attraction were involved), and on the other hand the Jesuit's stern repression of such homosexual feeling.

This makes for interesting comparison with Robert Graves' criticism of Dylan Thomas; both extracts make considerable use of affective imagery (in Graves, the target-shooting image, in Day Lewis the crawling fly), and in each there is speculative allusion to the relationship between a poet's proclivities (Thomas' drinking, Hopkins' latent homosexuality) and his style. Beneath these resemblances, however, the critical techniques of the two passages are strikingly different.

One very important point is that Day Lewis, unlike Graves (and, for that matter, Eliot), deals fairly with the consensus judgement. The first paragraph of his critical commentary firmly assumes responsibility for the opinions that are to be propounded and demonstrated. The linguistic token of this is, of course, the recurrence of the first person pronoun: 'I fear', 'I do not think', 'For me', 'a sense that I am apprehending', 'I get only a fly's-eye view', 'as if I were crawling'. Not until the second paragraph does the critic introduce *we*, and when he does so it is not to impose a consensus ('anybody can see this'), but rather to include the reader/listener in a process of exploration, a joint activity that may still allow an independent opinion to each of the exploring parties. Key sentences reveal this, e.g.:

> What we look for in vain, I believe, is any structure created by these images.

This expresses a judgement from which a generalization may be retrieved: 'The poem lacks a coherent structure'. The judgement, however, is not forced upon the critic's compeer, the reader/listener. With *I believe*, the critic continues to accept responsibility for his generalizations. The closing sentence of the extract provides an even more striking example:

> The answer, I suggest, is that the poem contains an unresolved conflict, between the poet's enthusiasm for the ploughman's physique (the reader may decide for himself in what proportion pure aesthetic pleasure and homosexual attraction were involved), and on the other hand the Jesuit's stern repression of such homosexual feeling.

This sentence is the final phase in a critical process that begins with the statement of an intuition ('What we look for, I believe . . .'), moves on to demonstration, and in conclusion seeks to account for what has been demonstrated, to put intuition into an interpretative frame. Yet even here the critic, with his parenthetical *I suggest* and *the reader may decide for himself*, avoids the assertion of an untested consensus. Day Lewis appears to believe that there *is* homosexual feeling in the poem – or at least that 'the poet's enthusiasm for the ploughman's physique' is tantamount to 'such homosexual feeling' – but he does not oblige the reader to believe that. Nor does he set modals impersonally working for him – 'The poem must/might/should/could be regarded as a conflict . . .'; nor does he take refuge behind the timidity of *tend* – 'The poem tends to suggest a conflict . . .'; the judgement suggested, i.e. that the poem contains a conflict between sexuality and religious inhibition, is claimed as his own, for good or ill.

What is important above all else, however, is that the judgement arises out of a demonstration, a commentary on the text which, if not exhaustive, is detailed enough for us to be able to understand how Day Lewis has arrived at his judgement that 'Harry Ploughman' is a culpably fragmented (or, to use his own word, 'disintegrated') poem. We may decide that the demonstration is mistaken or inadequate. For instance, Day Lewis is not wholly right in his assertion that 'apart from the carpenter-cooper-wheelwright metaphors in the opening lines', the poem is a succession of unrelated images. There is a strain of military imagery in the first stanza, in 'fall to', 'stand at stress' (clearly imitative of 'fall in', 'stand to', 'stand at ease'), 'rank', 'roll-call', 'service'; and towards the end of the second stanza, in '*bluff*hide', '*crag*iron', perhaps a hint of topographical metaphor. But such small corrective observations are possible only because the critic *has* demonstrated his point, *has* indicated and attempted to organize the evidence on which he bases his judgement. We can infer, from the language and technique of this passage, an attitude to its audience radically different from the attitude shown by Eliot and Graves to theirs. They speak dictatorially, even if their dictatorship is tempered and obliquely expressed in modals and affective terms; Day Lewis – hardly their equal as a poet, but in this instance at least a fairer critic – treats his readers as his fellow students and takes pains to demonstrate his good faith.

The critical style: fourth sample What we have been considering, in each of the above instances, has been literary criticism by some well-reputed man of letters. But this does not represent the common experience of criticism. For most people, a critic is a person who writes reviews of books, films, art exhibitions, musical performances, etc., reviews which, however witty, wise, or even profound, are ordinarily regarded as ephemeral essays in journalism. No account of critical styles would be complete without some notice of journalistic criticism. Here, then, is a review (by Meredith Oakes, in the *Listener*, 13 October 1983), of a music programme broadcast on BBC radio:

> *This Week's Composer* is Radio 3's only established way of giving the equivalent of a one-man show. It did at last week, with quartets, symphonies and other pieces by Robert Simpson, with a supplementary quartet on Tuesday night. Simpson is a rather impersonal composer. He can generate a teeming note-world from a two-note motif through every contrapuntal or rhythmic process known to Beethoven or Nielsen. He likes to work over large spans, getting action out of the tension between different key-centres and different pulses; using weights and counter-weights, springs and levers. He sets out, consciously in a number of cases, to write music about other people's music. Clearly the worlds he creates are worlds he can live happily in: his output and consistency show that. And there must be listeners who can be happy in them too – as regular Simpson performers like the Delmé Quartet obviously are.
>
> But he doesn't seem to have those happy finds from the subconscious – blazing new ideas out of nowhere that turn out to have some deep affinity with what is already there – that ought to arise from and illumine all that labour. There seems to be a less than perfect functional link between the procedures he uses – developed by Beethoven, whose actual musical ideas had extraordinary expressivity and immediacy – and his own simple, semi-modern, brutalist, neo-heroic language, all beat-by-beat rhythms and unmodulated tonality, thickened by sevenths and ninths, where a conflict of keys can take the form of simply playing in both of them at once.
>
> The pieces I liked best were *Volcano*, played by the Black Dyke Mills Band – a pictorial piece for once, and therefore easily within the expressive scope of the language – and the Trio for clarinet, cello and piano, played by the members of the Music Group of London, to whom it was dedicated, and full of ideas for chattering and chuffing rhythms, sometimes reduced to gossamer transparency.

Journalistic texts of this kind are produced under constraints which do not affect the composition of academic criticism. There is a deadline to be met, and only a day or two for the preparation of copy. There is a convention of 'noticing', which obliges the critic to mention places, participants, performances, and to append a brief commendation or censure: 'On Saturday last, at the Globe Theatre, the Lord Chamberlain's Men gave a performance of Shakespeare's *Hamlet*, the title part being convincingly played by Mr Burbage, while Mr Shakespeare himself made an amusing Ghost. Rain spoiled the duel scene', and so on. Most important of all, the review very often refers to an event that has passed, although the event may prompt reflection on current or abiding issues. The critic has to make observations on two levels, the level of the particular and transient event (performance, etc.), and the level of general and continuing critical principle. Such criticism is thus 'divided', in a way that academic criticism is not. For the academic literary critic, for instance, a poem is not something that happened last week or a hundred years ago; it is something that is always happening *now*, in immediate interaction with the responses it elicits. (A linguistic token of this is the general use of the present tense in academic criticism; in journalist criticism there is usually, at some point, an intrusion of past tenses, as in the final paragraph of Mr Oakes' review.)

We can see how these constraints have shaped the *Listener* review. The reviewer has mentioned the name and source of the programme (Radio 3), has worked in the names of performers (the Delmé Quartet, with a little nod of approval in ('obviously', the Black Dyke Mills Band, and the Music Group of London), and has made his act of commendation at the 'event' level ('The pieces I liked best were . . .'), using the past tense. These measures meet the basic requirements of a journalistic notice, leaving the writer to fill up his copy. This he does in two ways (yet another division of critical energies): he attempts the verbal bravura with which journalistic critics often hope to seduce or distract their readers, and he makes some general propositions about the music of the composer Robert Simpson. His piece is thus (a) a notice, (b) an entertainment, and (c) a commentary of sorts. In this last respect it has affinities with academic criticism; in its role as entertainment it is less powerfully affined, though we have Graves to remind us that scholars can write like journalists when they choose; and in its function as a notice of an event, it has no affinity at all with academic timelessness.

This reviewer uses all three of our proposed 'keys' – generalization, modality, affectiveness – but with a cheerful or hasty neglect of principle that allows affectiveness to enter generalization, and modality to wander into affectiveness. Consider this sequence of generalizations in the first paragraph of the review:

1 'Simpson is a rather impersonal composer.' *Comment:* This major generalization is apparently a key sentence, although 'rather' suggests that the reviewer is not quite sure what he means by 'impersonal'. From what follows it would seem to mean that Simpson has no personal style, but adroitly manages techniques learned from other composers. We might expect, at all events, some elucidation of 'impersonal'.

2 'He can generate a teeming note-world from a two-note motif through every contrapuntal or rhythmic process known to Beethoven or Nielsen.' *Comment:* And here the elucidation follows, in the form of a symptomatic generalization. (For a reminder: 'Mozart always writes good clarinet parts'.) The proposition is expressed, however, partly in technical terms ('two-note motif', 'contrapuntal', 'rhythmic process') and partly in affective terms ('teeming' and 'generate'). 'Generate' in particular is a striking figurative variant on the verbs of creative action ('write', 'create', 'paint', 'delineate', etc.) that generally characterize the symptomatic generalization. The image (hardly an 'impersonal' one) of the composer as the begetter of a progeny of notes presents us not so much with a mixed metaphor as with a trope labouring on an abstraction.

3 'He likes to work over large spans, getting action out of the tension between different key-centres and different pulses; using weights and counter-weights, springs and levers.' *Comment:* The intention is obviously to write another symptomatic generalization, but once again there is a mingling of technical language and metaphor, now with much blurring of meaning. A musician readily understands what is meant by 'key-centre' and 'pulse'; musician and layman together can understand how, in its range, the music may 'span' remote centres of tonality; it is also possible to see how, as in a bridge, a 'span' is also a 'tension' but *getting action out of the tension?* In the second part of the sentence, the attempt to indicate correspondences between metaphors and technical terms is abandoned, and metaphor is allowed to operate freely and vaguely. The sense of the sentence appears to be that the composer likes to use distant keys and dissimilar rhythms, in effectively contrived tonal and metric contrasts.

4 'He sets out, consciously in a number of cases, to write music about other people's music.' *Comment:* Yet again, the symptomatic generalization, and one that is not very sensibly worded. *Setting out* to do something is by definition a conscious act. ('He set out unconsciously to write a twelve-book epic'? 'Without knowing it, he set out to break the world pole-squatting record'?) And 'to write music about other people's music' cuts a smart rhetorical figure but leaves the reader groping for the sense. To imitate other people's music? To write pastiche or parody? To use devices which may remind us of other people's music? There is a serious difficulty here; the reader cannot really know, but feels he ought to know, what the author means – and in the absence of any possibility of citation and demonstration, he has no way of knowing.

5 'Clearly the worlds he creates are worlds he can live happily in; his output and consistency show that.' *Comment:* Interestingly, this at first looks like a major generalization, because of the sub-ject–be–complement form. It is in fact another symptomatic generali-zation, as a rewriting will show: 'He [clearly] creates worlds he can live happily in'. (Compare 'Shakespeare obviously creates interesting characters' and 'The characters Shakespeare creates are obviously interesting ones' or 'Obviously the characters created by Shakespeare are personalities that interest us'.) The quasi-major form disguises an assertion that may recall Wonderland argument. When Alice, chal-lenged to say what she means, replies that she means what she says, the Mad Hatter tells her she might just as well say that 'I see what I eat' is the same as 'I eat what I see', and the March Hare cites, as a further example, 'I like what I get' and 'I get what I like'. Our reviewer is on Alice's side; his assertion implies that 'He creates what he likes' is tantamount to 'He likes what he creates – which hardly seems a remarkable judgement, until we begin to consider the meaning of 'happily', which is ambiguous. Its 'strong' meaning is 'with pleasure', but it has a 'weaker' meaning, i.e. 'with convenience', 'with reassurance', 'with familiarity', 'without difficulty' (as in 'I am at home with French, but I don't cope so happily with German'). This weaker meaning seems to be indicated here, in which case the sense of the symptomatic generalization is 'He creates musical forms that do not raise technical problems for him'. The appended remark, 'his output and consistency show that', seems to support this interpreta-tion.

A sequence of five generalizations constitutes the thesis-element in this short review. The thesis is generally clear; the writer appears to be saying that Robert Simpson has no strong personal idiom in music, but adroitly uses techniques derived from other musicians to build his ingenious compositional structures. 'Generally' and 'appears', however, are tell-tale words, reflecting the fact that every one of these generalizations is in some way blurred or flawed. In following the path of argument, we do not – to put it figuratively – treat from step to step; we splash from puddle to puddle.

After the generalizations come the modalities. Here modal auxilia-ries like *must* and *ought* blend with verbs of modal tendency, in particular *seems*. The purport of these modal expressions is to modify the thesis: to suggest that Dr Simpson's 'worlds' are all very well in their way, but that they are not wholly satisfying; that they make one 'happy' in the weaker sense, but not in the stronger. Thus, the sentences following immediately after the statement of the general thesis read:

1 'And there must be listeners who can be happy in them too – as regular Simpson performers like the Delmé Quartet obviously are.' *Comment:* 'Can be happy' is picked up from the 'can live happily' of the preceding sentence. It is clearly a modal of possibility. The status of *must* is not so clear. It appears to be a modal of obligation – 'this has to be the case'; but it possibly disguises a grudging concession: 'I suppose there are people who are at home with this sort of thing – well, obviously, the Delmé Quartet are.'

2 'But he doesn't seem to have those happy finds from the subconscious – blazing new ideas out of nowhere that turn out to have some deep affinity with what is already there – that ought to arise from and illumine all that labour.' *Comment:* Ignoring for the moment the figurative mangle (blazing ideas have deep affinities with things that are already there), and the limping logic (the 'finds' come out of the subconscious nowhere, but are also said to arise from the act of composition), consider the function of *ought to* in relationship to *seem*. *Ought to* expresses an obligatory consequence not quite so strong as *must*. 'These consequences *must* ensue' allows of no exception, whereas 'These consequences *ought to* ensue' acknowledges the possibility of lapse in an imperfect world. Thus, 'He ought to be discovering new ideas' implies an underlying *if* ('if he is doing his work properly'), which concedes the possibility of human failing. In the text before us, this concession is made by *doesn't seem*. The full implications of the sentence can be spelled out: '*If* he is deeply creative he *ought to* have innovative ideas; but he *doesn't seem* to have them [and therefore cannot be deeply creative]'.

3 'There seems to be a less than perfect functional link between the procedures he uses . . . and his own [musical] language . . . where a conflict of keys can take the form of simply playing in both of them at once.' *Comment:* This is a digest of the original sentence. The meaning is that while Simpson derives many of his musical techniques from other composers, notably Beethoven, these techniques are imperfectly assimilated into his own style. Once again, *seem* is important for its modifying sense of 'if' ('If there were a functional link, we would presumably see it . . .'); the same escape from definitive statement is provided by *can*, which reduces the proposition from the status of a symptomatic generalization ('Conflicts of key [invariably] take the form of writing in two keys at once') to that of a mere modal of possibility, which might express something as strong as 'This often happens' or something as weak as 'This sometimes happens', 'This happens now and again'.

Taking the whole argument – thesis and commentary modals – we may summarize: 'Robert Simpson's music is a skilful demonstration of what he has learned from other composers. He appears to be satisfied with this mode of composition, and doubtless there are others who also find it satisfactory. But his creativeness is limited; he does not produce new ideas, and the ideas he gathers are not incorporated imaginatively into his own simple musical idiom.' It takes rather a long time for the reviewer to say this, and in every sentence he blurs his own argument.

Much of the blurring results from the attempt to beguile the reader with affective language. Metaphors are freely mixed (some examples have been given), and sometimes the mixed metaphor is bedded in squirming syntax:

> the Trio for clarinet, cello and piano . . .full of ideas for chattering and chuffing rhythms, sometimes reduced to gossamer transparency.

The syntax presents a problem of antecedence: is it the *ideas* or *rhythms* that are 'sometimes reduced to gossamer transparency'? Ideas may legitimately be called 'transparent', in the sense of being superficial, or patently simple; but this would imply pejorative criticism in what happens to be a context of compliment. In what sense *rhythms* are transparent, it is not easy to see; nor how the auditory/tactile perceptions implied in *chattering* and *chuffing* are to be reconciled with the visual image of *gossamer transparency*. But it is probably wrong to look for metaphoric consistency. In review-style the purpose of metaphor is usually to create impressionistic effects of colour and emphasis.

This decorative intention is shown by the number of descriptive/evaluative adjectives, often marked by peculiarities of semantics or form, that occur in writing of this kind. For instance:

> . . . and his own simple, semi-modern, brutalist, neo-heroic language.

Each of these adjectives is a judgement, and each implies a proposition and an elucidation ('I call his language simple. What I mean by simple is . . .') for which, however, the reviewer, in the nature of his trade, has no time or space. His only recourse is this piling-up of epithets, with the effect of a tirade that makes some affective impact. The impact is lessened only when the reader starts to ask what is *meant*, in musical terms, by adjectives like 'brutalist' and 'neo-heroic'.

Of the four samples of criticism cited here, three are in a greater or lesser degree flawed. This is not a judgement of their judgements, but a judgement of their system, or, more specifically, of their manage-

ment of the grammatical and semantic resources of criticism. It is as
valid or *in*valid to say 'Virgil is a necessary cultural standard', 'Dylan
Thomas sacrifices meaning to musicality', 'Robert Simpson's compositional idiom is a derivative construct', as it is to say 'Hopkins'
"Harry Ploughman" is an incoherent poem'. Literary and artistic
judgements do not have an inherent truth-value: they have to be
shown to be positions tenable by a reasonable human being. In only
one of the present instances (i.e. in Day Lewis's observations on
Hopkins) is this done at all successfully, and it is certainly not without
significance that this is the one case in which the critic demonstrates
his criticism on a definite object – a piece of text – the experience of
which he shares with his readers. If it is legitimate to make a stylistic
distinction in social terms, then we may say that Day Lewis is
democratic while each of the others, Eliot most markedly, is autocratic. But the comparative failure of the other three is not solely due to
this insistence on treating the reader as disciple or captive audience
rather than as a colleague. Its larger cause, comprehending the
autocratic stance, is the conscious or unconscious mishandling, by the
author, of his chosen critical tools. Eliot chooses to argue by generalization and modality, fuzzes one, fakes the other, and sometimes
mingles each in each. Graves chooses in the main to exploit techniques
of symptomatic generalization and affectiveness, and allows affective
imagery to provide the ground on which his symptomatic generalizations are made. The reviewer, Mr Oakes, already hampered by the
procedural conditions of his craft, which forbid demonstration and
require encapsulated judgements, elects to generalize and modulate,
but entangles both processes in such thickets of affective language as to
rob them of definition. If in all this there are stylistic lessons for the
critic – and therefore stylistic pointers for the reader of criticism – they
may be summed up thus: see that your thesis is clearly and unambiva-
lently defined; word your generalizations carefully, and be sure that
you know what kind of generalization you are making; understand the
scope of your modals and learn to control the ambiguities treache-
rously inherent in these items that operate on the frontier of grammar
and semantics; make your affective language, if that is what you
choose, an avenue of perception, not a blind alley, a merry-go-round,
or a hall of mirrors. And wherever possible *demonstrate*; for the chances
are that your style will be at its soundest when it is a text, a
composition, a work of art, and not simply your own creative
ruminations, that you offer for the consideration of your readers.

NOTES

1. The descriptive framework here is derived from Van Dijk (1977) and Labov (1972).
2. For further discussion of core vocabulary, see Carter (1987: Ch. 2).

4

Style, Composition and Creativeness

We have been looking at stylistics from the outside, as it were, pointing as observers to features of the language, structure, contextual function and general orientation of texts. This is a useful occupation, indeed a necessary one if we are to 'see through' language in the dual sense, of perceiving a message with the help of a medium and at the same time perceiving the ways in which the medium may obscure, distort, or condition the message. Now, however, it is time to admit that we are not wholly and exclusively observers of texts. We are also in some measure creators of texts, even if what we create is little more than a memo, a brief report or description, a personal letter, possibly a poem for our own eyes only, perhaps a few lines of doggerel to amuse a friend. It may be that we are little writers, but writers of a kind we must surely be; and thus, as potential practitioners, we come to look at stylistics from the inside.

4.1 THE WRITER'S MOTIVE

Writers are variously motivated. Some possible reasons for wanting or having to write are hinted at above, and these, together with all the other, larger, motives one might specify, bring into question the adequacy of the word *writing* as a common designation. Some writings are 'inspired', in the sense that the writer feels the compulsion to describe an experience, reflect an insight, demonstrate a connection, transmute some portion of his or her living into a satisfying anesthetic form. Some are the products of scholarship, research, or teaching, not 'inspired' in the former sense, perhaps, but nevertheless records of a kind of personal engagement. Others are the conventional perform-ances of an institution or profession – the memos, the reports, the regulations, the papers, the minutes. Others still are of an unassuming private kind; the letters, the journals, the poems-perhaps and the verse-for-fun, the little drafts of minor observations intended for limited audiences.

Common prejudice regards only the first of these varieties as 'real' writing. To the question 'Have you written anything lately?' the copywriter might reply, 'Yes, I've turned out a rather effective commercial'; the office head might respond, 'Well, as it happens, I've drafted a long and lucid report'; the scholar might venture, 'My chapter on Plato, if not a model of its kind, yet pleases me greatly'; and the journalist might say, 'Oh, yes, my column this week has brought in a sackful of mail'; and probably none of these answers would be accepted as relevant to the question. Copywriting, report-writing, scholarly exposition, journalism, all fall on the wrong side of a stereotypical fence, the side marked *composition*. The other side, called *creative writing* is where we place poetry and fiction and drama – productions calling, it seems, for more than ordinary gifts of imagination. They are haloed by the fitful glamour of art; they bear obvious 'literary' credentials. The argument for a 'cline', or gradation, of literariness (see Chapter 2) challenges the stereotype, but in practice does little to shake popular conviction. Even the practitioner feels that writing an article for a journal is 'composing', whereas writing a short story is 'creating'. There may then be little point in dissenting from the public perception of the matter. It is, however, a faulty perception if it leads us to conclude that so-called creative writing can dispense with the routines and disciplines of composition, or that composition is a mechanical process that can never invite the flair and exhilaration of creativeness.

4.2 Is 'Creativeness' Accessible?

One of the implications of the supposed contrast between creative writing and composition is that writing involves more than language. We may treat composition in wholly, or at least predominantly, linguistic terms; it is, we might argue, a matter of verbal selections and orderings, of the marshalling of texts to effect some pragmatic purpose. This may be a misconception, but if so it is a misconception on which most textbooks on composition (Usages, Rhetorics) are founded. Creative writing, on the other hand, is seen as involving non-linguistic components. The crudest form of the doctrine is the commonly heard assertion that you need to experience 'Life' (whatever that is) before you can become a writer. More subtly, it hints at parallels or deep-seated family resemblances between writing and the other arts.

Every art in its own way answers Forster's dictum, *Only connect*. The ability to make connections, to perceive significant analogies, to make new groupings and patterns out of familiar materials and arrangements, to achieve acts of mimesis that transcend mere representation and acquire a power of their own, implies a competence that may include verbal skill, but extends beyond it. By this implication, the true 'writer' is of a *genus* with the painter and the musician, rather than with the clerk, the reporter, or the composer of textbooks. Once again, it has to be said that the implication may be misleading – indeed, that even the simplest compositions, if they are to discharge their purposes effectively, require an intricate sense of design. Only to write four to five sentences in sequence, on any topic whatsoever, in a way that makes a coherent appeal to a reader, calls for not inconsiderable creative competence. We persist, however, in regarding 'creativeness' as something not readily accessible to ordinary writers, and in supposing that 'originality' must involve things entirely new and unprecedented (this is, incidentally, a post-Romantic view of creativeness, and not one that would have been shared by most eighteenth-century authors).

As a consequence, we are led (or lead ourselves) to suppose that creativeness is something that may be possessed, but is not accessible; that it may be nurtured, but not studied or taught. One of the reasons frequently given for the exclusion of creative writing from the curriculum – at least in British universities – is that it is not examinable; and it is thought not to be examinable because there appears to be no rational path of access to the subject, no methodological model, no well-forged chain of well-defined concepts, no demonstration of *knowledge* (as opposed to the manifestation of *craft*). Another reason, perhaps less often expressed, is that if there is an access to creativeness it is through play, through a sportive impulse, an apparent frivolity in little manipulations of language and perception. The object of this play is actually to disengage the observer, to 'alienate', in the Brechtian sense, in order to promote valuable insights, but inevitably it is seen, by those not engaged in it, as trivial. This perception begets in its turn a defensiveness about, and a dissembling of, one of the primary motives of human knowledge and capability.

4.2.1 *Creative Games (1): Pieces of Language*

It is possible to learn a great deal about the relationship between language and creativeness by devising writing games in which language itself provides the creative stimulus which we might normally expect to come from an extra-linguistic source (though indeed writers have frequently testified to the origin of a text in a linguistic token – a metaphor, a phrase, a word, even a rhythm). Some games reverse the ordinary supposition, that a context of reference is mapped on to language, and invite the player to infer, from the rudimentary linguistic map, a plausible terrain.

Here, for instance, is the rubric of an exercise given to students in a composition class:

> Write 'bottom lines' for these lists of items. The aim in each case is to identify a situation (there may be several possibilities) and supply a brief phrase or sentence that summarises and gives coherence to the rest. Note that you may perceive symbolic as well as literal coherences – or detect a symbolism *in* and *through* the literal pattern of coherence. Note also that perceptual inferences may depend on the order of the items, which you are free to change.

The first list read as follows:

> lipstick on a cup
> winestains on the tablecloth
> five stubs in the ashtray
> a cushion on the floor
> a ring among the roses

The expected 'bottom line' was *a lovers' quarrel*, and in fact most of the students produced a form of words pointing to such an interpretation. (Some were less ready to make inferences, and provided conclusions like 'after the party', or quasi-titles like 'midnight scene'.) The verbal cast of the interpretation varied from an automatic mimesis of the type of noun phrase employed throughout the list (eg. 'a quarrel between lovers') to declarative sentences like 'two people have broken off their engagement'. Strikingly, there was a general readiness to accept these pieces of language as clues to a coherent narrative, though no indications of verbal *cohesion* are given, apart, perhaps, from the reiterated syntactic formula, noun + prepositional phrase. Some interpreters suggested changes in the order of the items, in accordance with their perception of an underlying logic of events; all who proposed the suggested reading agreed that *a ring among the roses* must come last in the sequence. This was because the phrase itself suggested the last act of the little drama ('she gets up, knocking a cushion to the floor, flings down her engagement ring and storms out'); and also because of the readily noted allusion to the children's rhyme, ring-a-roses, with its pathetic conclusion, 'all fall down'.

Playing this game suggests, if in no more than a modest way, that creativeness *is* accessible, and that it can be stimulated through juxtapositions in language which may suggest cognitive, perceptual or narrative associations. Certain questions arise. For instance, are some word-classes (e.g. nouns and verbs) more likely than others (e.g. adjectives, adverbs) to stimulate the connective impulse? Or again, how large does a 'piece of language' have to be to promote the desired activity? Are single words enough, or are phrases required – because these often involve reference to complementary or contrasting features, as in 'ring' and 'roses'? Or, for much the same reason, are predications, involvements of subject and predicate, a still better form of stimulus?

To answer these questions with certainty might well require a carefully designed experiment in psycholinguistics, but it is possible to test them roughly. The exercise mentioned above presented further lists for bottom-lining. For instance, these three:

church	eat	carefully
fields	hate	unexpectedly
faces	watch	powerfully
chimneys	smile	ridiculously
gravestones	betray	benevolently

Here are lists of nouns ('church' etc.), verbs ('eat' etc.), and adverbs ('carefully' etc.). As expected, the major form-classes of noun and verb were readily effective in stimulating perceptions of coherence. The list of verbs, indeed, produced a unanimous response: everyone said 'Judas', or 'The Last Supper' – perhaps not a surprising testimony to the latent power of an archetypal story. Response to the adverbs was much less certain; it appeared that each item had to be related to a noun–verb structure (e.g. 'The chauffeur drove carefully', 'A child appeared unexpectedly'), before the impulse to coherence could be felt. This pointed to the stimulus-value of *predications*, e.g.:

the river flows
children play
planes drone
apples fall
the sky reddens

The phrases read in this sequence, suggested to everyone the 'story' of an aerial bombardment, and the interpreters were happy to make accommodation for any item that seemed at first not wholly congruous with the proposed interpretation. The sentence *apples fall* was an obvious case; for some students, the 'apples' were bombs, for some they were children, and some made the association with Eden and the Fall. There was some suggestion, indeed, that because of the different values or terms of reference assignable to this particular item, the 'narrative' could be read at literal and symbolic levels. The students were literary specialists with little training or interest in grammar; as a possible consequence of which they tended, in this particular instance, to concentrate on form-classes, particularly on the nouns, rather than to read implications into grammatical constructions. Thus, no one noted that all the constructions in this sequence are intransitive; or that in two cases the noun-subject is marked by the definite article while in the others there is no determiner. Sensitivity to such features might possibly have led to a more refined or more elaborate construction of a context of interpretation; 'children play' and 'apples fall', for example, might be read both as descriptions of current action and as statements of the habitual ('it is in the nature of children to play and of apples to fall'). These examples suggest, in sum, that language in near-minimal pieces can be an access to creativeness; but further, that a response based on some knowledge of linguistic categories and structures may greatly enhance that access.

What is suggested here is an enforced process of discovery – from word to construction, from construction to text, from text to containing form (stanza, paragraph, etc.). This may not be the path of 'true' creativeness (surely a much more complex matter) but it draws attention quite rigorously to the constraints and options of language in the forming of texts. Versions of the 'minimal clue' game may be devised at will. For instance, one might take the rhyme words out of a poem and attempt to versify round them. To illustrate the problem (without proposing a solution!), let us consider the rhyme-pattern of a poem already discussed in this book, Browning's 'Meeting at Night' (see Chapter 3, section 3.4.2). The line-end words in the two stanzas of that poem are as follows:

land	beach
low	appears
leap	scratch
sleep	match
prow	fears
sand	each

The object of the exercise would be to make a new poem – not necessarily on Browning's theme, or in Browning's metre, but verse of at least an intelligible kind, using at the line-ends the words set out above in the order indicated.

It is worth reflecting on what might be involved in the solution of this puzzle. It requires above all some facility in quickly relating lexical items to potential syntactic structures, in perceiving how constructions sequently predict or preclude one another, and in positing plausible relationships between linguistic structures and a context of reference – in other words, supplying a possible meaning. An important factor here is the grammatical and semantic status of the rhyming word. *Land*, for example, might be noun or verb, and its range of potential reference is quite broad – e.g., if a noun, to 'land' in general, to a particular 'land', to 'land' in opposition to 'sea' (as in Browning's text), to a figurative 'land' like the 'land of dreams'; or, if a verb, it may bear the sense 'to come to land' (from sea), 'to descend' (from the air), 'to go ashore', 'to put ashore', 'to bring ashore' (as in 'land a fish'), and so on. The linguistic scope of the word is evidently large – and would be all the larger, comparatively speaking, for its occurrence at the *beginning* of the proposed poem. In *prow*, on the other hand, we have a word of relatively diminished scope. It can only be a noun, and its reference is so restricted as to accommodate only one meaning, 'the bow of a ship or boat'; indeed, even within that limitation there is a tendency to further restriction, since 'prow', as compared with 'bow' or 'stern', suggests poetic usage and thus becomes a kind of 'register bound' item. In contrast with *land*, it leaves very little room for adaptation to a discursive frame (even the possibilities of transmutation into metaphor are limited); and there is the further drawback that its position in the proposed poem would be in the fifth line – that is, after some development of the text, with a consequent narrowing of the choices available at each stage of the development. This is a general condition of any compositional process. At first the options (of word, grammatical structure, etc.) are broad, but each choice confines the range of subsequent choices, until it may seem at certain points that the choice is 'dictated' and inevitable. In poetry, the appeal of the poem is often attributable to just such a sense, that the options of wording narrow to a single 'right' or 'inescapable' choice, occurring at the crucial or most intense moment of discourse. (And of course, the impact of both the ironic and the bawdy derives in large part from a last-minute 'swerve' away from that inescapably right word, which one's literary sensibility will have anticipated and supplied, only to be confounded by a quite unexpected lexical choice.) This narrowing is doubtless an illusion, skilfully wrought; but anyone who attempts to 're-versify' Browning's rhyme-list in the manner suggested will certainly encounter the problem of having to prepare the entry of *prow* in the first stanza and *scratch* in the seconed. The game has something to tell us about the elaborate interdependences of compositional language; what we do at any one moment is a provision, conscious or unconscious, for requirements that may arise somewhat later.

4.2.2 Creative Games (2): Parodic Models

The point of such play is to become an insider; to catch glimpses of how texts are made, and to understand how the intuitions of the practitioner relate to the formulations of the analyst. One of the most engaging ways of practising as insider and simultaneously judging as outsider is to attempt parodies of chosen or prescribed models. A parody is in effect an essay in stylistic analysis which substitutes mimicry for description. Take, for example, the text of the advertisement for the 'Maxi' car, discussed on pp. 46–7 of this book. One way to bring out the stylistic character of such a text would be to discuss it in terms of its component grammatical structures, its sentence-types, its lexicon, its layout, and so forth. Another way, bringing the analyst much closer to the practical 'feel' of a text-type, would be to propose a parodic imitation, not slavishly bound to the original, yet setting up palpable correspondences with its model. We are free, in play, to choose any topic other than the motor-car; the more absurd the topic, the more acute the sense of parody and the more sharply defined the symptoms of parodic mimesis. Thus, for the Maxi we might choose to substitute a fearsome invention, Bristlekleen:

Have you had enough of washing?
Have you better things to do with your body than immerse it in water every Friday evening?
Then brush up your pores with BRISTLEKLEEN.
Because BRISTLEKLEEN was made for speedy hygiene.
With BRISTLEKLEEN you can scrub yourself all over and never have to scrub round your night out.
Or clean up three times a week and save a fortune on soap.
And if you have to go to a wedding or a christening or a lodge meeting or someone else's funeral, that's all right.
Just relax under the roller for five minutes, or plug in the special action grater.
You've got three interchangeable working heads.
Which will turn into a lawn-mower, a guillotine, or a handyman's grindstone, should you need one.

And you have all the power you need to drive BRISTLEKLEEN's *Micropak Motor and vanadium-coated planetary gear-train with the famous *Bristlebright Nickel-Cadmium Battery Block, guaranteed to rub along without friction for at least six months.

Whether or not this is a good parody does not matter for the moment, though certainly the creative goal should be an act of mimesis lively enough at least to make a reader smile at the recognition of certain stylistic symptoms. The first stage in learning from such an exercise should be to check the imitation against the model, in order to see how far and how reliably instinctive responses to the model match the observations analysis might have to make about the graphology of the original text, its fractured sentences, its interpersonal appeal, its jocosity and punning, its slide from domestic chat to technical talk.

Parody thus employed is a mode of stylistic assessment and a form of compositional training; try to imitate a piece of advertising copy, a newspaper editorial, a sports report, a passage from a woman's magazine story, and you begin to have a better understanding of the technical requirements of these modes of writing. Parody also has a widely acknowledged power as a form of literary criticism – usually, though not inevitably, adverse. Here the parodist becomes the treacherous insider, identifying and deliberately abusing or mi directing the relevant stylistic devices. Thus Galsworthy's account of June's dinner party (see pp. 92–4) might be 'criticized' in parodic mockery:

They started to eat. The men were facing each other, and so were the women. The clock faced the window. The butler faced the clock.

Speechlessly the soup went down. It was brownish. Fish arrived. It looked fishy. No one said anything.

Bosinney said: 'It's the 23rd of April!'

Irene elaborated: 'April the 23rd!'

'23rd or April!' sneered June. 'St George's Day!'

The fish was led out, struggling, a piece of cod from Reykjavik. And Bilson bore in a barrel of Rioja, swathed in a bath-towel.

Soames said: 'This is Rioja. It comes from Spain, I fancy.'

June said: 'Why is Bilson swathed in a bath-towel?' No one answered her

Bilson was carried into the pantry.

Frilly legs of lamb came in. Soames said: 'These are frilly legs of lamb. I believe they have come here from New Zealand.'

But June pulled a face, and they were shooed away. And then Irene ventured softly: 'Has anyone heard my parrot?'

Bosinney answered: 'Rather – he swears like a billy-o, don't he? I heard him at it in the churchyard just now.'

Their eyes crossed over the Australian walnuts.

Soames said: 'This is Black Forest Gateau. It's from Marks and Spencers, they tell me.'

All silently ate their Black Forest Gateau. Bosinney ate the message passed him by Irene. June quietly ate her table napkin.

Soames said: 'But why isn't it from the Black Forest?' No one explained to him that Black Forest Gateau always comes from Marks and Spencers.

Like the 'Bristlekleen' passage, this picks up the stylistic peculiarities of its model (the construction of Galsworthy's dialogue and of literary dialogue in general is discussed on pp. 92–9). But also, as in the 'Bristlekleen' spoof, there is an element of inventiveness which is not the product of simple imitation but represents, rather, an original projection out of what has been elaborately imitated. The imitated text provides the impulse to add something new. Thus, comparing Galsworthy's opening with that of the parody:

Galsworthy: Dinner began in silence; the women facing one another, and the men.

Parody: They started to eat. The men were facing each other, and so were the women. The clock faced the window. The butler faced the clock.

The 'something new' is an elaboration of the notion of *facing*, a parodic idea that could involve more and more pairs of facers and things faced, and perhaps other meanings of *face* ('the government faced a crisis', 'the country faced an election'). A joke arises, not of Galsworthy's making, but made at Galsworthy's expense; the parodist both imitates and creates. Another example:

Galsworthy: The fish was taken away, a fine fresh sole from Dover

Parody: The fish was led out, struggling, a piece of cod from Reykjavik.

The creative addition here is somewhat pointedly represented by the word *struggling*. Galsworthy's text abounds in statements like 'The fish was taken away', 'Cutlets were handed', 'Spring chicken was removed', 'An apple charlotte came', 'Turkish coffee followed' – statements that have the curious effect of presenting inanimates as personages, or even as agents. Nowhere in the original, however, do such statements include typical linguistic strategies of personification in the form of manner adverbs or participle clauses expressing action or manner (e.g. 'Turkish coffee followed reluctantly', 'Spring chicken was removed, screaming'). The parodist, by introducing such an expression, exposes a perception of an underlying absurdity in Galsworthy's narrative, the absurdity of imbuing with participant vitality mere portions of fish or cuts of meat. In this instance, as in many others, parody can be more telling than the laborious abstractions of orthodox criticism; but the success of the parody must always depend on the creative intuitions of the parodist, the inventions not found in the original, yet prompted by it. Mere imitation is not enough.

4.2.3 Creative Games (3): Rewriting

In that respect, parody is an exercise qualitatively different from paraphrase, since paraphrase and all forms of rewriting do not call for creative addition and critical playfulness. They are, however, very useful as technical studies, exploring the structure of texts, the devices of sequencing and cohesion, the function of various sentence types, the balance of what is necessary and what is a decorative or explanatory addition.

Much can be learned by rewriting passages from editorials or centre-page articles in the broadsheet newspapers. Here, for example, are three versions of a passage from a *Times* editorial:

A. The anonymous Preface of *Crockford's* is about more than the Archbishop of Canterbury. Its central concern is with a deeper problem, the nature and identity of Anglicanism. This the Preface has discussed, fully and reasonably, and churchmen would be foolish to dismiss what it has to say just because they disapprove of the anonymity with which it assails Dr Runcie.

Presumably the Church Commissioners, who are responsible for *Crockford's*, do not approve of poison pen letters, though they must expect to the criticized for their association with this one. That being so, the Church should nevertheless not be side-tracked from considering the Preface's deeper thoughts.

Dr Runcie is accused of indecision. But what is he supposed to be decisive about? The problem is not that there are no answers, but that there are too many. The single identity of Anglicanism, following primarily from uniformity of worship, and from doctrines implied in that worship and contained in the Book of Common Prayer, has been lost.

B. The anonymous Preface to *Crockford's* is not only about the Archbishop of Canterbury. It is also about a deeper problem – the nature and identity of modern Anglicanism. This the Preface has fully and reasonably discussed. It would be foolish for churchmen to dismiss what it has to say about the problem just because they disapprove of the anonymity with which the Preface assails Dr Runcie.

Those responsible for *Crockford's* – The Church Commissioners and the General Synod's Central Board of Finance – presumably do not usually approve of poison pen letters. They must expect to be criticized for their association with this one. But the Church should not be side-tracked from considering the Preface's deeper thoughts.

To accuse Dr Runcie of indecision raises the question: what is he supposed to be decisive about? The problem is not that there are no answers. It is that there are too many. Anglicanism has lost the single identity which flowed primarily from uniformity of worship and from the doctrines stated or implied in that worship – doctrines contained in the Book of Common Prayer.

C. The Archbishop of Canterbury is not the only theme of the anonymous Preface to *Crockford's*. It also concerns the nature and identity of Anglicanism, which is a deeper problem. The Preface has discussed this fully and reasonably, and churchmen would be foolish to dismiss what it has to say about the problem just because they disapprove of the anonymity with which it assails Dr Runcie.

Presumably the Church Commissioners, who are responsible for *Crockford's*, do not approve of poison pen letters. For their association with this one they must expect to be criticized. But the Church should not be side-tracked from considering the Preface's deeper thoughts.

Accusations of indecision must raise the question of what Dr Runcie is supposed to be decisive about. That there are no answers is not the problem. The problem is, that there are too many. Anglicanism has lost the single identity which flowed primarily from uniformity of worship and from the doctrines stated or implied in that worship. These are the doctrines contained in the Book of Common Prayer.

One of these – but which? – is the passage originally printed in *The Times* on 4 December 1987; the other two are rewritings designed as far as possible to respect the wording of the primary text while experimenting with changes in syntactic organization. A close comparison, sentence by sentence, will reveal many differences of sentence-type, of sentence connection, of clause connection and subordination, of the ordering of clause elements, of the adjustment of 'theme' and 'focus' in sentences, and ultimately of rhythm in sentence and paragraph.

A brief examination of the management of the second paragraph in each of the three versions may help to indicate the compositional importance of minor or apparently casual options. Thus, in version A:

> Presumably the Church Commissioners, who are responsible for *Crockford's*, do not approve of poison pen letters, though they must expect to be criticized for their association with this one. That being so, the Church should nevertheless not be side-tracked from considering the Preface's deeper thoughts.

Here are two sentences. The first consists of clauses beginning *presumably* . . . and *though* . . . the first clause being interrupted by yet another clause, the relative *who are responsible* . . . etc. We must notice that beginning the sentence with *presumably* gives 'thematic' importance to that word, placing prior emphasis on the act of evlauating information, rather than on the information itself ('the Church Commissioners do not approve of poison pen letters'). This arrangement symmetrically matches the pattern of the subordinate clause *though* . . . etc. There is a constructional 'harness', *presumably* . . . *though*, of a kind commonly used when the underlying psychological procedure is 'evaluation' → 'concession': e.g. 'Presumably he means to come, though he's not very reliable', 'Presumably the act will become law, though many obstacles remain'. The expression of this psychological procedure, the close linking of the 'presumably' and the 'though', is the whole point of the first sentence. The other subordinate clause, the parenthetical relative 'who are responsible for *Crockford's*', is important only as an additional source of information, explaining the relevance of the 'Church Commissioners'. It is 'subordinate', we might say, in a double sense: as a syntactic structure, and as a carrier of knowledge pertaining to the discourse.

The second sentence is quite firmly locked into its predecessor by means of connective expressions, *that being so* (an 'evaluative disjunct', like *presumably*), and *nevertheless* (a 'concessive conjunct'). The two sentences are in fact constructed on parallel ideational schemes, though they are not syntactically parallel:

1 *presumably* . . . *though*
2 *that being so* . . . *nevertheless*

The grammar here is essentially dialogic, implying an awareness of, and a recurrent appeal to a readership primed with objections and alert for difficulties. Now as to version B:

> Those responsible for *Crockford's* – the Church Commissioners and the General Synod's Central Board of Finance – presumably do not approve of poison pen letters. They must expect to be criticized for their association with this one. But the Church should not be side-tracked from considering the Preface's deeper thoughts.

In this text there are three sentences, carrying the same information as version A, but presenting it somewhat differently, with different implications of emphasis, linkage, and subordination. The 'constructional harness' of *presumably* . . . *though*, incorporating into one sentence an evaluation and a concession, is not in evidence. The 'theme' of the first sentence is now *those responsible for Crockford's*, appositionally defined by the noun phrases between dashes; even the parenthesis works in a different way and encapsulates a different kind of construction. The word *presumably* occurs, but is located in a position where it modifies, evaluatively, the verb phrase only ('do not approve'), not the whole clause. And in this position of diminished scope, it does not compel any balance with a countering 'though'. Indeed, the second sentence, as it becomes in this version, is not linked to the first by any conjunctive expression. It is linked anaphorically through the pronouns *they* and *this one*. The link with the third sentence is even more perfunctory: no *that being so* or *nevertheless*, merely a simple adversative *but*. The impression arises of a confident, even authoritarian discourse, not seeking to establish its assertions through oblique appeal to its audience. There is little if anything of a 'dialogic' presence in passage B. But what of version C?:

> Presumably the Church Commissioners, who are responsible for *Crockford's*, do not approve of poison pen letters. For their association with this one they must expect to be criticized. But the Church should not be side-tracked from considering the Preface's deeper thoughts.

This appears to combine features noted in A and B. It presents, however, one strikingly new device: the marked 'fronting' or 'thematization' of the adverbial phrase *for their association with this one* in the second sentence. The paragraph now hinges round this bold rhetorical act, the effect of which is to stamp the text in the first two sentences with a chiastic design (an 'X' pattern) involving the items *approve . . . poison pen letters . . . this one . . . be criticized*. Some more concise examples of assertions similarly constructed on a chiastic frame may help to make the point:

> I don't approve of your drinking; for my own I must be deservedly criticized.

> Ted doesn't approve of our wives; Ted's wife no one dares criticize.

> Harry couldn't approve of judgement by so-called 'reviewers'; only by his fellow authors would he be criticized.

The effect of these examples, in each of which the nodal point of contrasting propositions is represented by the semi-colon, is to suggest not only a connection of ideas, but even a reciprocal relationship between *approve* and *criticize*. The words are not antonyms *per se*, but become antonymic by virtue of the construction. This is what happens in passage C, perhaps less obviously because there the nodal point, the point of balance, is located in the wider juncture between sentences. What the writer seeks is not the implication of dialogue, not the self-confident assertion of authority, but the construction of a scheme of emphases sufficiently powerful to persuade us that the connection of certain meanings (in this case, those embodied in *approve* and *criticize*) is somehow a key to the argumentative process. It is not; but version C suggests that it is, and makes the suggestion by means of what in face-to-face interaction would be a gesture or a vocal emphasis.

Behind these brief extracts of text, each conveying the same propositional message, we can discern differences of motive, of attitude to a theme, of orientation to an audience. Version A suggests the writer's awareness of the reader as listener or eavesdropper, with whom a kind of transmuted dialogue is conducted; 'are you with me?' and 'well, OK', and 'but all the same, eh?' are translated into terms appropriate to written composition. In B (incidentally the original version), the posture is that of one who is certain of the argument and is content to *state* without appealing to the reader for an evaluation. In passage C the attitude is that of the rhetorician or orator who, by manipulating the text, seeks persuasively to manipulate a response to the text. The writer is not stating a case through language, but uses language to construct a case. Our brief examples thus illustrate a single content in three psychological perspectives, each perspective being defined by the selection of technical options, mainly in syntax.

4.3   Technical Resources

An ordinary piece of composition may thus involve something more than the adequate presentation of a content. The 'something more' is the creativeness of a mind ready to impose its own will, its own interpretation of things, upon that content. The accommodation of that impulse, to create something distinctive within the limitations of a conventional task, requires no small command of the resources of language codified in dictionaries and grammars. Good composition, in fact, calls for an imaginative comprehension of the value of an array of choices under instant control, the repertoire of a craft. There is no space here to illustrate or even adequately to summarize the writer's repertoire. It may be useful, however, to outline some broad options in syntax, and to glance at the conditions under which those options might be creatively exercised.

4.3.1 Coherence and Cohesion

The first requirement of any composition is that it should 'hang together', 'make sense', 'fit', 'read convincingly' – the common tongue has common phrases expressing the desired integrity of a text within itself and in association with the matter of its reference. Now such integrity may be perceived at different levels. We recall, in a slightly different form, the text of one of our language games:

> Lipstick on a cup. Winestains on a tablecloth. Five stubs in the ashtray.
> A cushion on the floor. A ring among the roses.

Does this 'hang together'? Only, one might suggest, by virtue of associations which a reader is willing to supply. Possibly (the point has been made elsewhere) the order of the sentences has some effect in persuading the reader to attribute to this sequence of sentences the *coherence* of a narrative. Possibly the fact that each 'sentence' is similarly constructed (for they are, in fact, noun phrases) promotes the same tendency. Otherwise there is little or nothing in the actual language to indicate textual interconnections. The coherence is supplied by the reader responding to latent stimuli, including the *desire* to make a text out of almost any verbal display. In much the same way, the mind will compose a picture or a pattern from a random arrangement if disparate objects, *if* the notion of pictoriality is suggested to it.

Now suppose that we present our 'text' in this way:

> Lipstick on a cup – winestains on a tablecloth – five stubs in the ashtray
> – a cushion on the floor: a ring among the roses.

Simple marks of punctuation here impose an evident unity on the text, and suggest, furthermore, an interpretative scheme of connections that might be verbally elaborated, e.g.:

> There was lipstick on a cup; there were winestains on a tablecloth; in
> the ashtray lay five crumpled stubs; on the floor, a silk cushion; and
> lastly, sadly, gleaming among the roses, an engagement ring.

Now a perceived *coherence* has been realized in forms of language that demonstrate the *cohesion* of the text. There is a framework of punctuation; there is repetition of a sentence type ('There was . . . there were'); there is repetition of a variant structure (the adverbial-headed constructions 'in the ashtray . . .', 'on the floor . . .'); there is a parallel placing of lexical items ('five *crumpled* stubs', 'a *silk* cushion'); there is a suggestion ('lastly') of an ordered list. Such devices collectively represent only one way of making the text cohesive. There are many other possibilities, each implying a different orientation to the 'story'. For example.

> Firstly, there was lipstick on a cup; secondly, there were winestains on a tablecloth; next, in the ashtray, five cigarette stubs; then a silk cushion on the floor; and last, but by no means least, a ring among the roses.

This brings out very strongly, through the sequence of enumerative expressions ('firstly', 'secondly', 'next', 'then', 'last, but by no means least'), a sense of the text as a list, and indeed projects an image of the writer as investigator, asking 'What does all this add up to?' – by contrast with the previous example, which perhaps presents the writer as romantic interpreter. The point of these examples is not simply that texts can be organized with the help of various kinds of verbal token, but furthermore that the method of organization chosen reflects the psychological orientation of the writer to his text.

4.3.2 The Sentence: Discourse Functions

Such an orientation may also be expressed through the exploitation of discourse functions conventionally associated with different sentence types. We use sentences to make statements, ask questions, frame requests or directives, form 'metalinguistic' comments on our own discourse (e.g. 'Let me put it this way', 'Now let us proceed to another example'); and each of these functions is associated with familiar syntactic and lexical forms. We assume, as a norm of composition, that written discourse is largely cast in the form of declarative, statement-making sentences. But in some varieties of prose composition this is far from being the norm. Recall the 'Maxi' advertisement from p. 46 (parodied in the 'Bristlekleen' text on p. 181):

> Have you had the great Sunday car washing ritual?
> Have you got better things to do with a car than run round it with a rag, and show it off to your neighbours?
> Then the Maxi is for you.

Opting for interrogative sentences immediately brings the writer into the semblance of an interpersonal relationship with the reader; here we have a direct appeal, a confrontation, a challenge, the imputation of some sort of dialogue. Compare the copywriter's text with this paraphrase:

If the motorist is tired of the great Sunday car washing ritual, and considers that he has better things to do with a car than run round it with a rag and show it off to his neighbours, then the Maxi is for him.

Here the text is reorganized as a complex sentence with a straggle of conditional clauses homing on to the statement in the main clause. It is impersonal, distanced. The direct appeal expressed by the questions (and incidentally accompanied by the second person pronoun) has been eliminated from the message. A 'dialogic' text, warm in its personal appeal, has been replaced by one that is 'non-dialogic' and 'cool' (and therefore, we might add, unsuitable for the copywriter's purposes). The following, by further contrast, is 'dialogic', and yet 'cool':

Let us suppose that we are tired of the great Sunday car washing ritual, and let us postulate that we have better things to do with a car than run round it with a rag and show it off to our neighbours; then, arguably, the Maxi is for us.

A sense of dialogue is conveyed through the involvement of the reader in the first person plural pronouns; the 'coolness' is in the metalanguage of suppositions and postulates. 'Let us suppose that we are tired' is a different kind of verbal act from 'I am tired' or 'Are you tired?'. It is indeed, the kind of act we associate with academic expositions and demonstrations, or with pedagogic writings like those in this book. In compositions presuming a learner or collaborator whose assent is to be invited at each stage of discourse, we may well anticipate the frequent occurrence of 'metalinguistic' sentence formulations.

But here is an extract from a textbook, the actual opening of a chapter:

Look. Out of the distance, over the baked and burnished plain, along the rattlesnake trail that winds past red, uprearing buttes, comes the stagecoach. (Walter Nash, *The Language of Humour*)

This is an odd way of starting a discourse on narrative, and the oddest thing about it is that it begins with a *directive* (grammatically, an imperative). Ballads, folk-tales, epic recitals, prologues, operative arias, may begin with directives to the audience ('Listen', 'Your silence, pray', 'A word, allow me', 'Behold!' 'Attend!'). Academic disquisitions as a rule do not. Stylistic convention might have demanded something more like this:

Let us suppose that we are in the Wild West, looking out over a parched landscape, and that we can see approaching us, out of the distance, a stagecoach.

That is unexceptionally formulated, but for various reasons wholly inferior to the original text. One reason, probably the most important, is that the metalinguistic procedure – 'I will now outline the conditions under which a narrative might be devised' – is inappropriately defective in immediacy and vigour; the original, having some comments to make about narrative, plunges immediately into narrative, hustling the reader along willy-nilly. This intention of 'hustling the reader along', as opposed to tepidly inviting his or her assent, is expressed in the imperative *Look*, as opposed to the 'meta-comment', *Let us suppose*. The one posits an imaginative reality, the other a theoretical possibility. But of course there is no unassailable reason why the discourse in this case should begin with a directive. It might have begun with a statement, or even a question. It is for the writer to decide, and such decisions express a sense of something shared with the reader, in certain ways and on certain terms.

4.3.3 How to Make a Statement

But since, after all, the framing of statements is the commonest function in written discourse, it is worth considering the ways in which this is principally done. Here are some instances:

> The cat sat on the mat.
> There was a cat who sat on the mat.
> It is well known that the cat sat on the mat.
> It was the cat that sat on the mat.
> What the cat did was sit on the mat.

The first of these has the supposedly normal (statistically preponderant) grammatical form of the *declarative* sentence. The second answers to the description of an *existential* sentence. The third is an *extraposition* – so called because the 'that'-clause, containing the central statement, is 'extraposed', or pushed out to the end of the sentence. (But in this example it might be 'preposed' by being made the subject of the first, 'reporting', clause: 'That the cat sat on the mat is well known'. The fourth and fifth examples are instances of *cleft* sentences. (Definitions and exemplifications of these sentence types are conveniently accessible in Quirk and Greenbaum, 1973; they are extensively discussed in Quirk et al 1985.)

It is important to realize that there is a grammatical repertoire for statement making (as, indeed, there is a repertoire of choices available for other discourse functions), and that we draw on this repertoire in order to establish matters of orientation, focus and scope of reference in written composition. Very many narratives, for example, begin with statements, but not invariably with the same form of statement:

> The great bell of Beaulieu was ringing.
> (declarative form: Sir Arthur Conan Doyle, *The White Company*)
>
> There were four of us – George, and William Samuel Harris, and myself, and Montmorency.
> (existential form: Jerome K. Jerome, *Three Men in a Boat*)
>
> It is a truth universally acknowledged, that a single man in possession of a good fortune, must be in want of a wife.
> (extraposition: Jane Austen, *Pride and Prejudice*)
>
> It was Joe Ellis who introduced the Wild West to us.
> (cleft sentence: James Joyce, 'An Encounter' (in *Dubliners*))

Each of these 'statements' orientates the reader in a different way to the ensuing narratives: points an emphasis, elicits questions, makes predictions, arouses expectations, even suggests something about the character and 'tone of voice' of the story-teller. There is more in the statement than mere stating, as we might discover were we to experiment with different forms for these openings: 'It was the great bell of Beaulieu that was ringing'; 'The four of us – George, and William Samuel Harris, and myself, and Montmorency – sat in my room'; 'A single man, in possession of a good fortune, must obviously be in want of a wife'; 'The Wild West was introduced to us by Joe Ellis'.

The narrator's opening statement conditions the process of the narrative – a matter of obvious importance. No less important, however, are statements framed in the course of commonplace expositions. They, too, form part of a textual process that goes beyond the simple asseveration of a content. Consider, for instance, the role of the sentence forms in the following passage:

> It has become increasingly apparent of late that the political temper of the University is changing, at least among the students, that the left-wing militancy almost universal during the sixties has receded into legend, that many students, indeed, are openly or implicitly Conservative in their allegiances. There are several reasons for this. One is, that the ruthless dictates of the employment market forbid the old rebelliousness and encourage new attitudes of studious conformity. Another is that 'leaders' of the demagogic sort are no longer in evidence, or if in evidence no longer convince. Yet another may be that the political colour of the University tends to reflect, given a time-lag of some 5–10 years, the political mutations of the country as a whole.

The first thing to point to is the shortest sentence, lodged at a discursive turning point in mid-paragraph: *There are several reasons for this*. Might this existential sentence be replaced to advantage by any other statement-making form? Suppose that we attempt a declarative formulation, starting with 'Several reasons for this', e.g. *Several reasons for this + verb*. The verb may be 'exist' – *Several reasons for this exist*; or we might have recourse to a modal auxiliary expressing possibility, plus a passive transformation: *Several reasons for this may/can/might/could be suggested/offered/posited/advanced/put forward/indicated*, etc. Taking these alternatives into account, we have now made available three choices from the repertoire of stating:

1. There are several reasons for this.
2. Several reasons for this exist.
3. Several reasons for this may be suggested (etc.).

It may look at first as though the option here is purely aesthetic and subjective; for this writer or that, one of these will *sound* better than the others. But a preference for the existential form – or at least, a rejection of the proffered declarative forms – can be justified on other grounds. Sentence 2 above focuses attention on the verb, *exist*; sentence 3 similarly places a focus on *be suggested*. Both sentences, in fact, give some prominence to dictionary items more specific and positive than the neutral *be*. To state, for example, that 'There is a chill in the air' is to make an assertion slightly different in its implications from 'There exists a chill in the air'. (The latter might, for instance, set the statement in a context of time – 'since when', 'even now'; or might express a sense of substantial reality – 'this is not imagined' – or of perdurability.) The contrast between *are* and *can be suggested* is even more obvious' it is the contrast of *ease* and *posse*, of what is and what might be. Thus the verbs in sentences 2 and 3 nudge the attention towards components of meaning not implied in, or actually belying the tenor of, sentence 1.

Now we should look for a moment at the sentence with which our example passage opens. It is a sentence of the *extraposition* type, albeit quite a long one:

> It has become increasingly apparent of late that the political temper of the University is changing, at least among the students, that the left-wing militancy almost universal during the sixties has receded into legend, that many students, indeed, are openly or implicitly Conservative in their allegiances.

The syntactic frame may be represented thus:

It has become increasingly apparent of late   (1) that X
                                               (2) that Y
                                               (3) that Z

The accumulation of subordinate clauses doubtless accounts for the option taken in framing this sentence. There is an observable preference, among writers of English, for distributing the mass of a complex sentence towards the end rather than locating it at the beginning (e.g. for writing 'We were all sad to hear of the untimely death of Professor X, a man justly renowned in the annals of philately and known for his musical accomplishments as a performer on the spoons', rather than 'To read of the untimely death of Professor X, a man justly renowned in the annals of philately and known for his musical accomplishments as a performer on the spoons, made us all sad'). The extrapositional frame facilitates end-weighting, and furthermore accommodates the possibility of arranging the subordinate clauses in parallel, as suggested above. In short, the sentence form at the opening of the passage is a useful device for processing potentially bulky verbal material.

However, the form 'extraposes' not only its verbal mass but also its semantic content, the 'message' of the statement. And here we may revert to the existential sentence previously discussed, and ask whether it might not have been more effectively conceived in the following form:

For this there are several reasons.

The form of the sentence is still existential, but part of the original clause, the phrase *for this*, has been 'preposed', or 'fronted'. The effect is in part that of a rhetorical gesture of emphasis, but something more important is achieved. This simple turnabout strengthens the verbal linkages of the text by juxtaposing co-referential items, thus:

It has become	*that* X		for	there are		*one* is
increasingly	*that* Y	$\leftrightarrow$	*this*	reasons $\longleftrightarrow$		*another* is
apparent of late	*that* Z					*yet another*

With this structure, the progression from the extraposition into the existential sentence and from the existential sentence into the exemplifying list becomes not only clear, but, as it were, 'seamless', The emphatic *this* takes into immediate scope the 'that'-clause of the preceding extraposition, while *reasons*, at the other end of the existential structure, becomes the immediate antecedent of *one*.

4.3.4 How to Point an Emphasis

It must strike us, if we compare 'There are several reasons for this' with 'For this there are several reasons, that the first of these is 'usual' or 'ordinary' and the second 'unusual' or 'special'. The terms used by linguists are *marked* and *unmarked*, and choices of marked as against unmarked forms are more or less readily available in the structure of simple sentences, as in the following examples:

That may be unjust, but . . .	vs	Unjust that may be, but . . .
(unmarked)		(marked)
He wrote many such poems . . .	vs	Many such poems he wrote . . .
(unmarked)		(marked)
She made him a very happy man . . .	vs	A very happy man she made him . . .
(unmarked)		(marked)

In the first of these, a subject complement has been 'fronted' in the marked form in the second a direct object; and in the third an object complement. the effect of such frontings can be quite complex. That they stamp the preposed item with emphasis, whether of a corrective or an asseverative kind, is fairly obvious. It is also apparent that they affect the pscyhology of the sentence, in such a way that the phrase at the front becomes a kind of semantic subject, or 'theme'. What is possibly less obvious from the bare examples is that such frontings often have a part to play in expressing the structure and cohesion of texts, as we have already seen above in considering the effects of a simple adjustment of phrase order in an existential sentence. Here is an (invented) example:

> Objections can be heard in certain quarters that the proposed measures are cumbersome. Cumbersome they certainly are, but they are also undeniably just, and will surely serve to curb the extravagance of some non-elective institutions. Four billion pounds those institutions have squandered during the past year alone, and the public has seen no benefit from their activities. The Minister deserves our gratitude. He set out to correct an abuse, and a very good job he has made of it.

Perhaps the textual value of marked forms, together with their emphatic character, will be evident from this little exercise. It can be critically assessed by working through the passage and systematically 'unmarking' the relevant constructions (i.e. rewriting 'Cumbersome they certainly are' as 'They are certainly cumbersome', etc.). A comparison may then be made with the rewritten passage, to determine which of the two more satisfactorily answers the requirements of emphasis, the prominence of certain topics, rhetorical appeal, and textual cohesion.

The passive transformation is another element in the sentence-forming repertoire that involves the possibility of changing the informational focus and modifying the connective pattern of a text. Consider the following pairs:

Renoir painted the picture. (active)	The picture was painted by Renoir. (passive)
Mr B. tabled a motion. (active)	A motion was tabled [by Mr B.] (passive)
People may say that the action is ill-advised. (active)	It may be said that the action is ill-advised. (passive)
We saw the court do justice to all the claimants (active)	Justice was seen to be done to all the claimants. (passive)

The first of these is a standard example of the passive transformation, complete with the so-called 'by'-phrase indicative of an agent or instrument. The turnaround in word order results not only in a grammatical change of sentence subject, but also in a semantic shift of *theme*, and with it a changed perspective on the relationship of topic, actor and action. We might say, in effect, that one sentence in the first pair is 'about' Renoir, while the other is 'about' a picture.

The second example illustrates the option, commonly taken, of omitting the 'by'-phrase in the passive transformation, and thus of eliminating reference to an agency. The action, in *A motion was tabled*, becomes anonymous; there is no attribution of origin or responsibility. The passive can be used rather deviously in this way, or may be a quite innocent recourse when the 'agency' of the active form is something as vague as 'all of us', 'everybody', 'people in general'. The third and fourth examples illustrate this; note, however, in the last example, the peculiar force of the theme in the passive transformation. In the suggested active form, *justice* is a mere procedure; the passive raises it, rhetorically, to the status of a principle.

As with changes in word order in the simple declarative sentence, these manipulations of active and passive can have textual as well as semantic implications. A brief illustration.

> There was some dispute about a small painting of boats on a river. This picture was listed in the catalogue as having been painted by Renoir, but the claim had been widely challenged. There were those who said the date was impossible; there were those who said the technique was wrong; and there were those who said that if it had been Renoir's picture, he would have signed it. Allegations of forgery were made, arguments were bandied, and in one instance blows were exchanged.

The passive construction informs this text, and is virtually indispensable to its peculiar tone of voice – the tone of gossip or hearsay. Apart from Renoir, no one is named; the participants in this fictional 'dispute' are all rendered anonymous by virtue of the passive transformation and a designedly broad pronominal reference ('There were those . . .') in the existential sentences. But apart from this game of suppressing identities – of saying 'someone or other, I don't know who' – the passive construction has the further role in this passage of promoting textual continuity by juxtaposing, wherever possible, semantic antecedents and dependents. The clearest instance appears in the linkage of the first two sentences, where *a small painting* is immediately picked up by *this picture*. It is perhaps not so obvious that the cohesion of the last two sentences depends on the use of the passive. If an active form were proposed for the three clauses of the final sentence (e.g. 'Experts alleged forgery, critics bandied arguments, and in one instance two enthusiasts exchanged blows'), the implied cohesive scheme would shift from this:

    said . . .allegations
    said . . . arguments
    said . . .blows

to this:

    those . . . experts
    those . . . critics
    those . . . enthusiasts

Thus the choice of grammatical form, in this case a voice option, may affect the style of a narrative not only in matters of rhythm and accent but also in designating a line of meaning, a semantic continuity.

4.3.5 Complex Sentences

Textual continuity is one of the products of the complex sentence, which, however, also represents a response to other concerns. In compositional terms, the complex sentence fulfils one or more of four functions. These functions are: *incorporation, sequencing, co-occurrence,* and *connection.* They are reflected in patterns of co-ordination and subordination, that is to say in various ways of assembling clauses in sentences structure. First, some examples of the incorporating function:

Whatever the Government did was vain.
All their attempts failed to elicit a response.
The Minister did not relish breaking his word.
To hold an election would have been unthinkable.

In each of these instances, a clause is incorporated into a clause; thus, in the first example, a noun clause 'whatever the Government did' becomes the grammatical subject of another clause, 'X' was vain'. In the second and fourth examples, infinitive clauses are incorporated as, respectively, adverbial and subject elements ('All their attempts failed in a certain respect', 'This procedure would have been unthinkable'). In the third example, another kind of non-finite clause, a participle clause, assumes the role of direct object ('The Minister did not relish a dishonourable act'). The incorporations thus made are syntactic, but have semantic implications, the commonest of which is that the incorporated clause is a lexical item broadly summarizing a potential array of details. Thus 'Whatever the Government did' may be regarded as equivalent to 'Their measures', and may invite the reader to supply for himself the specific entries – 'They raised policemen's pay', 'They encouraged neighbourhood watch schemes', 'They reorganized the social services', and so on, according to the general topic of the discourse. Thus a syntactic incorporation may be a form of semantic ellipsis or summary. A reading is indicated rather than specified. The purpose of this might be quite simply and guilelessly to put matters as concisely as possible; on the other hand, it might be a way of allowing the writer to persist in generalizations on topics about which he is not particularly well informed.

The patterning of sentences is usually considered from the point of view of the writer, who obviously has the problem of wrestling sometimes quite intractable material into verbal shapes that satisfy the demands of logic and aesthetics. It can also be seen from the standpoint of the reader, whose interpretations are directed by the sentence pattern, particularly in the sequencing of clauses. Consider, for example, these sentences:

> They made many attempts, but none elicited a response.
> Although many attempts were made, none elicited a response.
> No attempt elicited a response, though many were made.
> No attempt, though many were made, elicited a response.
> No response was elicited, despite the fact that many attempts were made.

In the first sentence the clauses are co-ordinated by the conjunction *but*. The common characteristic of co-ordination, that the order of the clauses may be reversed without substantial modification of form or meaning, is not evident in this case. The remaining sentences exhibit various relationships between a principal and a subordinate clause. The principal clauses are: in the second sentence, 'none elicited a response'; in the third, 'no attempt elicited a response'; in the fourth, 'no attempt . . . elicited a response'; and in the fifth, 'no response was elicited'. In one respect, the fifth is the odd case. In all the others, the sequencing of the clauses embodies the semantic sequence *attempt . . .response*, with the effect always of giving a dominant emphasis to the first-mentioned item. This applies whether the first clause in the sequence is subordinate (as in 'although many attempts were made'), or principal. Only in the last sentence do the semantic priorities read *response . . . attempt*, and there only because the clauses are deliberately so ordered; it would of course be easy to restore the alternative reading by changing the clause order – 'Despite the fact that many attempts were made, no response was elicited'. The usual choice of sequence lies between A (principal) → B (subordinate), sometimes called a *right-branching* arrangement, and B → A, correspondingly known as *left-branching*. The sentence *No attempt, though many were made, elicited a response* presents us with the possibility of another arrangement, in which the principal clause is *interrupted* by the subordinate. (For this the term *mid-branching* may be used.) In this and comparable instance, the effect of the interrupting clause, in itself a throwaway or an aside, is to suggest a marked accentuation of the thematic phrase *no attempt*. In this, more than in any other example in the set, a stress pattern is projected through the written layout.

The necessity of presenting clauses in *sequence* need not imply that their content is to be interpreted *serially*. For example, between the two sentences *We lay in the sun and we read our books* and *We lay in the sun reading our books* there is this difference: that in the second instance lying in the sun and reading are obviously to be regarded as co-occurrent events, whereas there can be no such certainty about the first instance, which could imply that a period of lying in the sun preceded a period of reading books. Participle clauses very often express this aspect of co-occurrence:

> One day, swimming in deep water, he had a fit of cramp.
> (Compare the temporal sequence: One day, after he had unwisely swum out into deep water, he had a fit of cramp)
>
> Thinking she had only a few miles to go, she did not pull in at the service station.
> (Compare the cause – effect sequence: Because she thought she had only a few miles to go, she did not pull in at the service station)
>
> While I was drafting my lecture notes, an idea occurred to me.
> (Compare time-durative (the 'progressive aspect') with time-locative: When I drafted my lecture notes, an idea occurred to me)

Adverbial clauses introduced by temporal conjunctions (e.g. *while, as*) are also frequent indicators of co-occurrence. Indeed, the two clause types can often be seen to converge in a certain kind of narrative style:

> One evening while Mary was sorting through some old letters, she came across a rather grubby brown envelope with an Australian postmark. Thinking it might be of interest to her father she tossed it to one side, but as she did so a little slip of rice paper fell out. As soon as she saw it she knew instinctively that she had found something important.

In this little 'story' there is a sequence of events presented in a series of co-occurrences. Though the text as written certainly has a temporal logic, it would be possible to re-order it, without, however, being able to separate the co-occurrent pairs. Thus, for example:

> As soon as she saw it she knew instinctively that she had found something important. One evening while she had been sorting through some old letters she had come across a rather grubby brown envelope with an Australian postmark. Thinking it might be of interest to her father she had tossed it to one side, but as she did so a little slip of rice paper fell out.

This rewriting has disturbed the 'temporal logic' of the original in such a way as to necessitate the back-shifting of tenses ('had found', 'had been sorting', 'had come across', 'had tossed') to restore the underlying sense of a time-sequence. We may order and re-order sentences as we choose, but we cannot do so without making appropriate adjustment, to preserve the impression of connectedness.

To demonstrate connections is, indeed, the major compositional role of the complex sentence; connections within the sentence, between clauses and what they refer to, and connections beyond the sentence, with predecessor and successor sentences, and so with the text as a whole. This adjustment of sentence to sentence, the supplying of plausible links, the suggestion of priorities in emphasis, the gradual framing of a narrative or an argument, and ultimately the establishment of a prose rhythm, is no doubt the master-skill in composition.

There are many ways of practising this. One is to draft a short passage consisting of simple sentences, or, if that proves too drastic a demand, of simply constructed sentences. For instance:

> Should the State subsidize the Opera? It happens in some countries. In Germany, opera houses receive considerable support from public funds. Companies mount productions of the highest international standard. The price of a ticket for a good seat is within the reach of the ordinary citizen. The Opera thus becomes a force in the education of the many, and not just a privilege for the few. But the 'education' is by no means free. It would be foolish to believe that. In the end, the taxpayer foots the bill.

In itself a not unshapely piece of prose, this invites remoulding into subtler shapes made available by the repertoire of complex sentences. might, for example, be rewritten like this:

> It may be asked whether the State should subsidize the Opera, as happens in countries like Germany. There, houses receive from public funds the support that allows their companies to mount productions of the highest possible standard, while setting the price of a good seat within the reach of the ordinary citizen. Thus supported, the Opera, traditionally a privilege for the few, becomes a force in the education of the many. It would be foolish to believe, however, that the 'education' is free, since in the end it is still the taxpayer who must foot the bill.

Or like this:

> The question of State subsidy for the Opera would not arise in countries like Germany, where opera houses are generously supported from public funds, and where productions of the highest international standards are mounted by companies able to set within the reach of the ordinary citizen the price of a ticket for a good seat. Opera ceases to be a privilege for the few. And yet, though it may seem to become a force in

the education of the many, only the foolish would assume that such education is free. Someone must still foot the bill, and that someone is the taxpayer.

These are only two versions of a passage that might be re-composed several times over, with quite minor adjustments in the lexicon – idiomatic adaptations of vocabulary to syntactic frame – but fairly considerable changes of sentence length, clause order and clause type, with consequent shifts in the perception of emphases, prominences and interconnections. Through such simple studies the strategies of composition become clearer, more firmly fixed in the mind as positive principles grounded in definable choices. The practitioner begins at last to perceive relationships between the structures of grammar and the workings of the imagination.

4.4   A POSTSCRIPT

Creativeness is not a rare endowment granted only to a few. Everyone is in some measure and in some particular respect creative; able, that is, to conceive new things and, by the command of particular materials and particular techniques, to bring those things into tangible being. Of all available materials for the exercise of creativeness, the word, spoken or written, is the commonest and yet in many ways the least tractable. No writer can be sure of understanding language as a painter understands pigment, a sculptor understands clay and stone, or even as a musician – who indeed must learn a special language with its own vocabulary and grammar – understands sonority. For language, unlike other media, has a dual role. It embodies – or, if we please, 'expresses' – some feeling or attitude, some sense of relationship between the observer and the world he or she observes, which may include the world of language itself. In the same way, carved stone and painted canvas embody the personal relationship of an artist and a subject; and notes on a stave represent a musician's exploration of acoustic relationships in patterns of sound. But language also explains and analyses; a text is a demonstration of reasoning as well as the representative of a state of mind or heart. Things written can seldom be 'projected' or 'embodied' without also being *argued*; only very minor forms, for instance some kinds of short poem, escape this condition.

Furthermore, many texts have a property not assignable to sketches, sculptures or symphonies; they have a practical function. Of course this is not generally true of what poets and novelists attempt to do, but it still applies to some varieties of text composed in a spirit of creative innovation, and not specifically the 'consumer' varieties devised by the copywriter or the publicist. An academic textbook, for example, may have pretensions to substance as the declaration of an attitude or a philosophy, but at the same time seek the practical end of fulfilling an instructional role. All these considerations must suggest to us that in our use of language the interaction of creative impulse and composi-tional skill is indeed complex. It would be less than adequate to say that a study of the resources of language can do no harm if we wish to use it creatively. Such a study is forced upon us in the very attempt to be creative. It does not necessarily consist of a formal investigation of grammar, and certainly does not involve an attempt to master the lexicon by memorizing the dictionary. (The attempt at systematic acquisition of a vocabulary, day by day, is a pious practice not unknown among would-be writers.) An unreflective 'mugging up' of language, however strenuous, will probably do little to promote competence in composition, and might even impair the creative imagination. But understanding language, or *seeing through language*, as we have called it in this book, means something other than mindless rote-learning. It may oblige us, for convenience's sake, and to assist the mind in accommodating complex facts, to have at our disposal a terminology, a descriptive metalanguage; but it is not the metalangu-age that is the object of our study. Our object must be the clearest possible perception – or, sometimes, the most reliable intuition – of how thinking and imagining can be most convincingly realized in words combined into phrases composing clauses patterned into sen-tences arranged in texts. The greater part of this book has been devoted to the study of texts as we read them, and only this final section has been concerned with the evolution of texts as we write them. The two things, however, are but complementary aspects of the same process. Informed reading is part of the discipline of becoming a technically competent writer; and intelligent writing is a useful element in the education of an appreciative reader. That sounds like, and indeed is, a profession of faith, and may be as good a place as any at which to stop.

Exercises

The exercises in this section reflect the philosophy of our book as it has emerged through dealing with practical problems of content and design. It is our view that to understand the theory of language in written communication it is necessary to conduct analyses of different kinds of text; and further, to be properly acquainted with the lessons of analysis it is necessary to practise the actual making of texts. Thus composition and rhetoric are inextricably related to theory and descriptive analysis; theoretical and analytical concerns guide us towards facility in composition; composition is, in return, a kind of analysis. This explains the thinking behind the choice and ordering of exercises, which in general require our readers firstly to study the relevant sections of our text and secondly to choose or devise their own examples and compositional procedures. It does not imply that the exercises must be tackled in textbook order, although it might be interesting to discover what insights are yielded by a regular as opposed to a random progression through the material.

1 LANGUAGE, STYLE AND LITERARINESS

The exercises which relate specifically to Chapters 1 and 2 are exercises in rewriting. The rewriting tasks involve transferring the content of a text from one style to another and are designed to heighten awareness of the different functions which different types of text embrace. A number of the exercises involve rewriting with reference to clines of literariness: the purpose here is to focus attention on the properties of 'literary' language. Other exercises in this sequence invite readers to participate in and thus reflect on processes of creative composition which result directly from rewriting activity.

Exercise 1

The following opening (1a) to a novel describes a hotel. In passage
1(b) we have begun to rewrite the content of the passage as if for a
brochure describing the hotel to potential clients. Passage 1(c) is an
entry to an actual hotel guide.

i. Complete passage 1(b) in a similar style. Make notes on the
kind of changes to the styles and content of 1(a) which you have
made.

ii. Using passage 1(c) as a model construct a hotel entry for Hotel
du Lac. Write notes on the features of your entry which are
specifically non-literary.

iii. Write a commentary on passage 1(a) which draws particular
attention to the specifically literary features in the use of
language.

iv. Re-read the discussion of 'titles' to advertising at 3.2.1. Write
three one-line titles advertising the Hotel to different types of
potential clientele.

v. Re-read the discussion of narrative structure in advertising at
3.2.2. Write a narrative (using pictures or illustrations if you
wish) advertising the Hotel du Lac.

1(a) The Hotel du Lac (Famille Huber) was a stolid and dignified
building, a house of repute, a traditional establishment, used to
welcoming the prudent, the well-to-do, the retired, the self-
effacing, the respected patrons of an earlier era of tourism. It had
made little effort to smarten itself up for the passing trade which
it had always despised. Its furnishings, although austere, were of
excellent quality, its linen spotless, its service impeccable. Its
reputation among knowledgeable professionals attracted appren-
tices of good character who had a serious interest in the hotel
trade, but this was the only concession it made to a recognition of
its own resources. As far as guests were concerned, it took a
perverse pride in its very absence of attractions, so that any
visitor mildly looking for a room would be puzzled and deflected
by the sparseness of the terrace, the muted hush of the lobby, the
absence of piped music, public telephones, advertisement for
scenic guided tours, or notice boards directing one to the
amenities of the town. There was no sauna, no hairdresser, and
certainly no glass cases displaying items of jewellery; the bar was
small and dark, and its austerity did not encourage people to
linger. It was implied that prolonged drinking, whether for
purposes of business or as a personal indulgence, was not *comme il*

faut, and if thought absolutely necessary should be conducted either in the privacy of one's suite or in the more popular establishments where such learnings were not unknown. Chambermaids were rarely encountered after ten o'clock in the morning, by which time all household noises had to be silenced; no vacuuming was heard, no carts of dirty linen were glimpsed, after that time. A discreet rustle announced the reappearance of the maids to turn down the beds and tidy the rooms once the guests had finished changing to go down to dinner. The only publicity from which the hotel could not distance itself was the word of mouth recommendations of patrons of long standing.

Anita Brookner, *Hotel du Lac*
(Jonathan Cape, 1984)

1(b)   *Hotel du Lac.*
'A highly reputable hotel providing high class accommodation with a long tradition of respect for the privacy of its guests. The hotel occupies comfortable premises and provides a high standard of service unequalled by most modern hotels. The policy for some years has been to avoid tourist groups, with the result that most of the public rooms recall the quiet but luxurious calm of a former era. Staff are highly trained and attentive to detail, though for the most part unnoticed. This hotel will appeal particularly to the well-to-do traveller who dislikes piped music, and objects to the distractions of video tape and television as a constant presence.'

1(c)   CASTLE DONINGTON The Donington Thistle Hotel****
A new hotel situated in its own grounds at the entrance to the East Midlands International Airport and Aeropark and less than two miles from Donington Race Circuit with its collection of vintage cars. Visit Belvoir Castle and Holme Pierrepont – the British Watersports Centre with the historic towns of Ashby de la Zouch and Quorn nearby. The hotel leisure club, free to residents, offers a pool, whirlpool, saunas, solarium and well-equipped gymnasium.

East Midlands Airport   A Thistle Hotel

Prices per person per night in £'s	3 Nov–14 Dec & 30 Mar–3 May		15 Dec–29 Mar	
	BB 26	HB 38	BB 24	HB 36

Exercise 2

The following passage 2(a) is an encyclopaedia entry to the French city of Marseilles. Rewrite the passage into the following styles:

i.   A description of the place for a travel agent's brochure (use the discussion at 2.3 if required).

ii. A letter from Marseilles to a friend describing places you have visited and using as much content as possible from the encyclopaedia entry.

iii. The opening of a novel (about two paragraphs) set in Marseilles. Specify in some detail what the main themes of the novel are and how the style of your passage relates to those themes.

iv. Using the model for a weather forecast (see 1.2.3), write a forecast for Marseilles for a day in late July. (You may need to consult in encyclopaedia if you require more information about the location of Marseilles.)

v.   Write a commentary in the style of passage 2(b), which is the opening to Charles Dickens's novel *Little Dorrit*.

2(a) The contemporary city. Marseille is becoming increasingly a modern city of elevated highways, vehicular tunnels (including one under the Vicux Port), and tall housing developments, but the most striking change in the 1970s is more psychological than physical: the city is becoming increasingly French. Until the enormous state investments of expertise and money in the region – exemplified by improvements in flood control, navigation, irrigation, electricity, roads, schools, and hospitals and by promotion of and participation in industrial development – Marseille had felt as neglected by the central authorities as it was laughingly patronized by the Frenchmen in other regions.

The mythical Marseille did indeed have some small basis in fact: it was a sunny, noisy, gay place with a voluble population. Although the general standard of living ranged from modest to poor, the cynicism and tension of Paris was unknown. The port attracted a cosmopolitan population largely concentrated in the seething waterfront district noted for its gangsters and prostitutes. Until the intensified police action of 1971–72, it was a world centre for the illegal manufacture and shipping of drugs, especially heroin. The residential districts beyond the business centre consisted of spacious villas spread along broad avenues shaded by dusty plane trees. The countryside, flecked with tawny villages, began just outside the city.

2(b)　Thirty years ago, Marseilles lay burning in the sun, one day. A blazing sun open a fierce August day was no greater rarity in southern France then, than at any other time, before or since. Everything in Marseilles, and about Marseilles, had stared at the fervid sky, and been stared at in return, until a staring habit had become universal there. Strangers were stared out of countenance by staring white houses, staring white walls, staring white streets, staring tracts of arid road, staring hills from which verdure was burnt away. The only things to be seen not fixedly staring and glaring were the vines dropping under their load of grapes. These did occasionally wink a little, as the hot air barely moved their faint leaves.

There was no wind to make a ripple on the foul water within the harbour, or on the beautiful sea without. The line of demarcation between the two colours, black and blue, showed the point which the pure sea would not pass; but it lay as quiet as the abominable pool with which it never mixed. Boats without awnings were too hot to touch; ships blistered at their moorings; the stones of the quays had not cooled, day or night, for months. Hindus, Russians, Chinese, Spaniards, Portuguese, Englishmen, Frenchmen, Genoese, Neopolitans, Venetians, Greeks, Turks, descendants from all the builders of Babel, come to trade at Marseilles, sought to shade alike – taking refuge in any hiding-place from a sea too intensely blue to be looked at, and a sky of purple, set with one great flaming jewel of fire.

The universal stare made the eyes ache. Towards the distant line of Italian coast, indeed, it was a little relieved by light clouds of mist, slowly rising from the evaporation of the sea, but it softened nowhere else. Far away the staring roads, deep in dust, stared from the hill-side, stared from the hollow, stared from the interminable plain. Far away the dusty vines overhanging way-side cottages, and the monotonous wayside avenues of parched trees without shade, drooped beneath the stare of earth and sky. So did the horses with drowsy bells, in long files of carts, creeping slowly towards the interior; so did their recumbent drivers, when they were awake, which rarely happened; so did the exhausted labourers in the fields. Everything that lived or grew, was oppressed by the glare; except the lizard, passing swiftly over rough stone walls, and the cicala, chirping his dry hot chirp, like a rattle. The very dust was scorched brown, and something quivered in the atmosphere as if the air itself was panting.

Blinds, shutters, curtains, awnings, were all closed and drawn to keep out the stare. Grant it but a chink or keyhole, and it shot in like a white-hot arrow. The churches were the freest from it. To come out from the twilight of pillars and arches – dreamily dotted with winking lamps, dreamily peopled with ugly old shadows piously dozing, spitting, and begging – was to plunge into a fiery river, and swim for life to the nearest strip of shade. So, with people lounging and lying wherever shade was, with but little hum of tongues or barking of dogs, with occasional jangling of discordant church bells and rattling of vicious drums, Marseilles, a fact to be strongly smelt and tasted, lay broiling in the sun one day.

Charles Dickens, *Little Dorrit*

Exercise 3

Read the following passage from a book on linguistic criticism. Write a paragraph indicating the extent of your agreement with Fowler's position.

Adopting a linguistic approach to literature, as I do, it is tempting to think of and describe the literary text as a *formal* structure, an object whose main quality is its distinctive syntactic and phonological shape. This is a common approach, adopted by, for instance, the most famous of the linguistic stylisticians, Roman Jakobson (see Jakobson, 1960; Jakobson and Lévi Strauss, 1962; Jakobson and Jones, 1970). It also happens to agree with the dominant formalist tendency of the more conservative schools of modern criticism. I argue that linguistic formalism is of limited significance in literary studies, and educationally restrictive. As an alternative I shall employ some linguistic techniques which emphasize the *interactional* dimensions of texts. To treat literature as discourse is to see the text as mediating relationships between language-users: not only relationships of speech, but also of consciousness, ideology, role and class. The text ceases to be an object and becomes an action or process.

This anti-formalist approach is pretty much at odds with received opinion in conventional literary aesthetics. Among my heresies, from this point of view, are willingness for literary works to be kinetic; denial of their alleged formal autonomy; acceptance of the relevance of truth-values to literature. It is not my purpose in this paper to argue a collision of linguistics and aesthetics, however – as I said, my immediate object is methodological. Furthermore, I shall assert, without offering any formal justification, one other assumption implicit in my position – that is, that no plausible essentialist or intrinsic definition of literature has been or is likely to be devised. For my purpose, no such theory is necessary. What literature is, can be stated empirically, within the realm of sociolinguistic fact. It is an open set of texts, of great formal diversity, recognised by a culture as processing certain institutional values and performing certain functions.

R. Fowler (1981), *Literature as Social Discourse:*
The Practice of Linguistic Criticism
(London: Batsford Academic and Educational Ltd., pp. 80–1)

Exercise 4

With reference to the analysis of styles undertaken at 2.3 and at 2.4, discuss the degrees of literariness to be found in the following passages. How far is it possible to arrange the passages along a cline of literariness?:

4(a)   TALFOURD RD, SE 15. Handsome mid 19th cent. DETACHED PERIOD fmly hse. 2flrs only. Just along from CAMBERWELL GROVE. Attrac lge drawrm orig chmnypce, shutters, 24ft dble recep rm (now as studio), 4 gd bedrooms, poss space 5th bedrm, en suite bathrm. 2nd newfit white bathrm. Utility rm. Excellent lge b'fst/fmly rm & kit overall abt 24ft×13ft Gas CENT HEAT. Lovely GDN, shrubs, trees, figs etc. £85,000 FHLD. View Sun 701 5631

CANONBURY, N1. Imaginatively restored GEORGIAN ter hse, mins sq. & tube. GAS CENT HEAT, DBLE GLAZ. Gracious 30ft × 16ft 1st flr drawrm, fine chmnypce, shlvs fr bks & objet d'art. Formal dinrm. 20ft study, dble bedrm, chmnypce. 2nd dble bedrm. Dress rm/3rd bedrm. 2bathrms. Fit kit. Quiet 40ft 'country gdn', battling with nature! Lse 65 yrs. (Fhld prob avail). GR£50. £73,000. View Sun 359 2404.

4(b)   The tower is ten-sided in plan, the walls being fifteen feet thick at the ground floor, while the internal diameter at this level is thirty-four-feet. In the top-floor it is thirty-six feet, owing to the setting back of the wall faces. The floors and ceilings of these large rooms were carried on huge oak beams supported by struts from corbels, the modern beams which replace them giving a very good idea of their effect, though if the beam holes in the wall are to be trusted, the old beams were slightly larger than those now seen. The new floors and roof date from 1911–14. The tower is of four states, the lowest being a basement reached by a flight of steps from the court, and opening to the quay by a postern door on the west.

4(c)   Haddon Hall is the English castle *par excellence*, not the forbidding fortress on an unassailable crag, but the large, rambling, safe, grey, lovable house of knights and their ladies, the unreasonable dream-castle of those who think of the Middle Ages as a time of chivalry and valour and noble feelings. None other in England is so complete and convincing. It is set in gentle green surroundings, with woods above and lush fields and the meandering river below. The river in its winding course enhances the charms of the W as well as the S side. The slope up to the house on the W is steep but not high, and grassy not rocky. The towers and turrets and crenellations look exactly as if they were taken out of the background of some C15 illuminated manuscript. There is any amount of variety and no architectural system whatsoever. The architectural critic and historian would indeed be hard put to it if he were asked to define what in the sensations of a first visit to Haddon Hall is due to aesthetic and what to extraneous values.

4(d)   The house stands back from the road and there's a lot of black soil packed down hard that must have been a garden at one time. It's big and square, the house, and it looks a lot like a broken-down Working Men's Club. I reckon it must have been standing right there the best part of a hundred years because the stone's all grey-black and the flags round it are all sunk and sticking up in the corners any-old-how. There's a bit of a porch with some coloured glass windows in it, red and yellow and green, round the door, and I go along the path and knock, still thinking somebody's slipped up and given me the wrong address. There's a kind of rising sun in frosted glass in the top half of the door and I give it a push and go into the porch when nobody answers my knock. Inside there's the house door and a mat that's worn nearly to strings on the step. There's a pile of sacks and a rusty old paraffin stove and a crate of empty stout bottles as well. Everything smells damp and you get the idea it's all rotting away here and nobody cares a hang. It's a real rum do. I don't like it much.

Exercise 5

i.   Describe and account for the stylistic 'mixing' or 'borrowing' of James Joyce in the extract below from the novel *Ulysses*. The extract from the 'Court Circular' is included for purposes of contrast with the *Ulysses* extract.

ii.   What are the functions of style mixing in James Joyce's story 'A Painful Case' published in the collection *Dubliners?*

William Humble, earl of Dudley, and Lady Dudley, accompanied by lieutenantcolonel Hesseltine, drove out after luncheon from the vice-regal lodge. In the following carriage were the honourable Mrs Paget,

COURT AND SOCIAL

Court ⚜ Circular

WINDSOR CASTLE, April 21.
Today is the fifty-seventh anniversary of the birthday of the Queen.

The Duke of Edinburgh was present this morning at the start of the third stage of the Sealink International Cycle Race 1983 at Barry Avenue, Windsor.

Mr Brian McGrath was in attendance.

KENSINGTON PALACE, April 21.
The Duchess of Gloucester this morning opened the Greater Manchester Police, Manchester International Airport sub-divisional headquarters and later as President, visited the Princess Christian College. In the afternoon Her Royal Highness opened the Wallness Gamma Camera Unit at the Royal Manchester Children's Hospital, Pendlebury, Sulford.

The Duchess of Gloucester travelled in an air-craft of the Queen's Flight.

Mrs Euan McCorquodale was in attendance.

YORK HOUSE, April 21.
The Duke of Kent, Vice-Chairman of the British Overseas Trade Board, this morning visited Quest Automation Ltd at Ferndown, Dorset, and in the afternoon, as President of the Royal Masonic Benevolent Institution, opened 'Zetland Court', the Institution's new home in Bournemouth.

His Royal Highness, who travelled in an aircraft of the Queen's Flight, was attended by Capt. John Stewart.

The *Daily Telegraph*,
Friday 22 April 1983

Miss de Courcy and the honourable Gerald Ward, A. D. C. in attendance.

The cavalcade passed out by the lower gate of Phoenix Park saluted by obsequious policemen and proceeded past Kingsbridge along the northern quays. The viceroy was most cordially greeted on his way through the metropolis. At Bloody bridge Mr Thomas Kernan beyond the river greeted him vainly from afar. Between Queen's and Whitworth bridges Lord Dudley's viceregal carriages passed and were unsaluted by Mr Dudley White, B. L., M. A., who stood on Arran Quay outside Mrs M. E. White's, the pawnbroker's, at the corner of Arran street west stroking his nose with his forefinger, undecided whether he should arrive at Phibsborough more quickly by a triple change of tram or by hailing a car or on foot through Smithfield, Constitution hill and Broadstone terminus. In the porch of Four Courts Richie Goulding with the costsbag of Goulding, Collis and Ward saw him with surprise. Past Richmond bridge at the doorstep of the office of Reuben J. Dodd, solicitor, agent for the Patriotic Insurance Company, an elderly female about to enter changed her plan and retracing her steps by King's windows smiled credulously on the representative of His Majesty. From its sluice in Wood quay wall under Tom Devan's office Poddle river hung out in fealty a tongue of liquid sewage. Above the crossblind of the Ormond Hotel, gold by bronze, Miss Kennedy's head by miss Douce's head watched and admired. On Ormond quay Mr Simon Dedalus, steering his way from the greenhouse for the subsheriff's office, stood still in midstreet and brought his hat low. His Excellency graciously returned Mr Dedalus' greeting. From Cahill's corner the reverend Hugh C. Love, M.A., made obeisance unperceived, mindful of lords deputies whose hands benignant had held of yore rich advowsons.

James Joyce, *Ulysses*

Exercise 6

How would you characterize the effects of the use of language in the following extract from a travel guide book? What kinds of style mixing can you detect? What are the writer's interests? What are the reader's interests? (See in particular discussion at 2.5 and 2.5.1) What lexical and grammatical choices serve to encode the writer's point of view and ideology?

Population. Kenya was subjected to a census in August 1979. From the national total of 15,320,000, 0.4% are European, 1.5% have Arab or Asian origins, and 2% pay income tax.

While any remarks about the last class would be rash, it is no secret that the minuscule European percentage represents the tail-end of the large-scale white immgiration in the first half of this century. First the Germans in Tanganyika; next the Boers, poor but experienced pioneers from South Africa: then in the 1910s the first shipments of wealthier British immigrants to follow Lord Delamere's colonizing lead: 'British East Africa – Winter Home for Aristocrats' fast became the permanent home of some 80,000 Europeans. Developments in Europe – wars, depressions, international gerrymandering – made the influx cosmopolitan.

Independence put an end to this 'white exploitation', which was far more beneficial and far less unscrupulous than Africa's hotheads insist. Unlike America's reservation Indians, East Africans now control their territory entirely. Large numbers of European landowners, feeling themselves increasingly to be a foreign body and unused to the tenor of new African trade unions, sold up and left. But in other fields many remain, 'settlers' of second or third generation, East African citizens perforce. Kenya in particular has benefited sensibly by barring discrimination: 'Europeans' here still run the best hotels and lodges, manage the national parks, operate travel agencies and occupy sensitive Civil Service posts. Along with the still numerous missionaries, the older generation continues to display the secondary pioneer talents that choral concerts, amateur dramatics, fêtes and flower-shows imply, while their offspring are more for motor rallies, race-courses and drive-in cinemas.

Nairobi, as capitals go, is a comely upstart. The Uganda Railway surveyors arrived at the turn of the century to find little more than the 'Swampy place' which the name in Kikuyu supposedly means. (Masai maintain that *Nairobi* is their word for 'Place of cool Waters' but Muthaiga, a suburb, may mean 'Place by the Swamp'.) Water, anyway, was why Sergeant Ellis RE in 1899 chose this site in the Masai-Kikuyu No Man's land, and disease that the Nairobi River's water brought, in 1900 and 1902, explains the rapid replanning of the one-street, tin-shack 'Nyarobe Nyrobi'.

The World Bank's recent K£31-million loan from a new city water uspply points to the contrast today. The central Avenue – first 'Sixth', then 'Delamere', now 'Kenyatta' – was built so broad that twelve-span ox-carts could turn: today you will see it a Big City thoroughfare, with zebra crossings and parking meters to clinch the modernity. The shanties, bazaars and marshalling yards have given way to clean streets and plate-glass façades: cinemas, stores and neon-glossy arcades: government offices and neat green lawns. Bank and insurance blocks dominate the skyline, for Nairobi's monuments are not to the past but to present prosperity.

Exercise 7

Describe and explain the stylistic contrast in this text. If necessary re-read section 2.3 in which a range of other texts about Malaysia are examined. A useful essay on style mixing in advertising/informational brochures is Fairclough (1987).

MALAYSIA

Malaysia. The country where great cultures meet. An exotic blend of Malay, Chinese and Indian people is reflected in the history, customs and traditions of the country. This is the land of intriguing contrasts. From secluded, palmfringed beaches to festivals packed with colour and excitement. From warm tropical seas to cool, refreshing hill resorts. From ancient jungles to bustling bazaars. It's all here in Malaysia. We're just north of the Equator, at the heart of South East Asia. And we're served by many major international airlines. Come holiday in this wonderful land. We have so much to offer. From luxurious hotels to well-planned tours, just the way you like. Malaysia welcomes you now or at any time of the year.

ENTRY FORMALITIES

Passport: Visitors to Malaysia must be in possession of a national passport or other internationally recognized travel document endorsed for travel to Malaysia.
Visa: Commonwealth citizens. British Protected persons or citizens of the Republic of Ireland and citizens of Switzerland, Netherlands, San Marino and Lichtenstein do not need a visa to enter Malaysia. Citizens of the United States, West Germany, Italy, Norway, Sweden, Denmark, Belgium, Japan, Austria, Finland, Luxembourg, Iceland, South Korea and Tunisia do not require a visa for a visit not exceeding three months except for employment.
Fourteen Day Visa Free Visit: Citizens of ASEAN countries, International tourists, both transit and non transit except those from Albania, Chinese People's Republic, German Democratic Republic, Israel, Mongolia, Kampuchea, Laos, Taiwan, North Korean, Vietnam, South Africa, Rhodesia and Republic of Transkei are elligible for the fourteen day visa free vist to Malaysia.
Seven Day Visa Free Visit: Citizens of Bulgaria, Czechoslovakia, Hungary, Poland, Rumania, Russia and Yugoslavia are allowed to enter Malaysia for the period up to seven days only except for employment.
Health Regulations: Cholera – No cholera or smallpox vaccination is required for travellers entering Malaysia.
Yellow Fever – Vaccination is required for arrivals from infected areas and from yellow fever endemic zones except for children under 1 year of age.

TRAFFICKING OF ILLEGAL DRUGS CARRIES A DEATH PENALTY

2 STYLISTIC SAMPLES

Exercise 1

To what extent do the following Letters to the Editor conform to the proposed descriptive framework for such texts outlined in section 3.1.2? After your examination, would you propose any changes to the *problem* (argument) *solution* (counter or 'real' argument) structure of such letters? Do you see any parallels between the structure of these texts and the examples of the language of criticism discussed in section 3.5.2?

PROFESSOR Morten Cohen is wrong (Review Guardian, August 4). The Merchant of Venice is undoubtily an anti-Semitic and racist play. Any modern reader immediately perceives it as such and no amount of special pleading in the historical context will change that.

Professor Cohen defends Shakespeare on two counts. First, Shylock was originally designed to be a figure of fun rather than a tragic character. Secondly, since Shakespeare probably didn't know any Jews, he was writing from hearsay with an ignorance of their culture. Much the same sort of argument could be mustered in defence of the so-called comedians who propagate more recent racial stereotypes in the pursuit of easy laughs. Surely the essence of prejudice is that it arises from ignorance? Shakespeare was a great writer and was a product of his society. As Morton Cohen points out, that was an anti-Semitic society and the Merchant of Venice is a testament to that fact.

P. Main.
18 Premier Road,
Nottingham.

Is The Merchant of Venice an anti-Semitic play? If it is how does one come to terms with it? asks Morton Cohen. This begs the question, what is there to come to terms with?

The play has been around for the best part of 400 years and to my knowledge it has never made any claim to be anything other than what it is.

Perhaps what we should really be coming to terms with is our own received liberal shibboleths, as a banal, uncomplex and inadequate critical response.

Michael Toomey.
7 Goldsmith Court,
London WC2.

I quite agree with Sir Peter Hall that the Merchant of Venice is "the most pro-Semitic play ever written," and Professor Morton Cohen is right that it is necessary to realise its historical context to appreciate this — but there is more to be said.

The play was written about 1596. In 1594, London had witnessed a particularly ugly outbreak of anti-Semitism, deliberately whipped up by the Earl of Essex to get his revenge on the Queen's physician, Lopez, who happened to be Jewish by birth, though a Christian in belief and practice. Essex examined him for "treason" in his own house at first, but removed him to the Tower on February 5, 1594 — where more "persuasion" could be applied to obtain a "confession"

from him. The day before, February 4, Sussex's Men revived Marlowe's Jew of Malta at the Rose Theatre. As Essex's cronies later persuaded the Chamberlain's Men to revive Richard II on the eve of his rebellion in 1601, one wonders if these players, too, were not bribed.

The Queen herself appears not to have believed in the "guilty" verdict at his trial, and delayed the execcution. However, the London mob — no doubt encouraged by further performances of the Jew of Malta at the Rose — was now beyond control. Lopez was executed on June 7, amid howls of derision when he said "he loved the Queen as he loved Christ".

Shakespeare's Gratiano is "holding the mirror up" to Essex's young followers who were responsible for this outbreak. This, and Shylock's "Hath not a Jew eyes?" speech need to be seen in this context.

As for Marlowe's Jew of Malta, it would be anti-Semitic if it was really about a Jew, but there were very few about when it was written, about 1590, and they didn't go in for money lending.

The money lenders were Christians. 10 per cent interest was regarded as fair, more was "usury," and pamphleteers of the day castigated those who extorted it as "worse than Jews".

Margaret Hotine.
5 Albert Street,
London NW1.

One of the reasons why Shakespeare was such a genius is because there is no "wrong" way to interpret his plays. Morton Cohen suggests, justifiably, that The Merchant of Venice is often viewed as an anti-Semitic play. But Peter Hall has every right to direct it as a pro-Semitic play.

Where Sir Peter falls down is in the drama of the thing. By making Shylock such a sympathetic character he has thrown the whole thing off balance. Jessica can only seem an ungrateful and uncaring daughter in siding with the Christians when her father is portrayed as such a tender and affectionate parent. We wince uncomfortably at the open anti-Semitism meted out by the Venetians to such a cuddly Shylock, and when he insists on the meat, rather than the moolah, we can almost see his point.

Sir Peter doesn't have to see the play as anti-Semitic, but we would have had a much more interesting evening if he had made it anti-Shylock.

Alister Cameron.
Swan Island.
Twickenham, Middx.

Exercise 2

It could be said that the main function of a newspaper editorial is to explore situations which imply problems which in turn require solutions. Collect examples of editorials from two or three different daily newspapers. With reference to these editorials consider the following questions about the structural organization and function of the language of editorials:

  a   How important is the category of evaluation in these texts? How pervasive is evaluation? Are some editorials exclusively evaluative? Does an evaluative style vary from one newspaper to another?
  b   How regularly are solutions proposed to particular problems?
  c   Is it possible to detect differences in any of the newspapers between reporting styles and editorial styles?
  d   It has been proposed that there is an underlying structure to editorials. This consists of a three-part structure:

Lead	=	A description of a situation and problem
Follow	=	A follow-up to the lead in which current contexts and specific examples are presented
Valuate	=	An evaluation of the problem with reference to future action.

How far are you able to detect such a structure in the proceding and following examples? What features of language use are typically associated with each part of the structure? Is any one part more or less dominant in the production of ideology? Does the notion of core vocabulary (3.1.1) help you?

Re-read 3.1.1 and the discussion of the front page report 'Canute Kinnock'. Does this report contain any features which would be more normally associated with an editorial?

Exercise 3

In the following passages, which are examples from Women's magazines, women are represented in particular ways. What is the part played by the writer's use of language in effecting this representation?

"Ms Cowley —" Teri opened the door with composure, but the greeting died on her lips. This tall, solidly-built man was not the sharp-eyed female reporter she'd been expecting.

He grinned disarmingly. "Sorry to disappoint you," he said, "but I'm Kim Cowley!"

Teri frowned slightly.

"Won't you come in?" She spoke primly, leading the way into the living-room.

He didn't sit down as she suggested, but roamed around the room disconcertingly, examining the large collection of framed photographs on the walls.

"I remember this one," he announced abruptly. "It was taken when *Forever Love* was first released, wasn't it?"

"That's right," she admitted, surprised. It had been the first song she'd written for the band. Impressed by the lyrics, Cal had suggested she join them as lead singer, and the combination of the song, her sweet husky voice and the vibrancy of his guitar accompaniment had led to their "discovery" and the first of many hits. *Forever you, forever me, forever love*, promised the words — it was their song, hers and Cal's. She had been nineteen then.

"You haven't changed!"

Kim's voice startled her. For a moment she'd been back there, lost in the excitement, the glamour of that first year at the top.

"Tell me about it," he asked quietly. He'd been watching her — maybe he'd caught a hint of nostalgia in her face — so she went to stand beside him and made her voice determinedly bright.

"What do you want to know?"

"Everything," he replied promptly, and she laughed.

"That's a tall order — but I'll try!"

She talked for ten minutes or so, painting a vidid picture of the kaleidoscope days when they'd been on the road, when "home" had been a hotel room in any town, any city which had a stage big enough to accommodate them and the capacity to seat the thousands of screaming fans they drew. Wonderful days spent driving from gig to gig, she and Cal huddled together on the front seat of the big trailer — talking, laughing but mostly singing. She could count off the months by the songs she'd composed then, like a string of bright beads —

"Did you enjoy the life?" He interrupted her train of thought.

She looked up at him but her eyes didn't really see him.

"Oh, yes," she said softly. "The rehearsals, the gigs, the parties — I loved it all."

from "The Love Song"
LOVE STORY. May 1989

*M*ONDAY NIGHT 7.30pm — Sandy crushed further back in the narrow shelter of the doorway, as the rain battered relentlessly off the pavements in front of her. It didn't really help — she was already soaked. Her fringe stuck to her forehead in trickling wet clumps, and she sniffed miserably to herself as she looked up and down the road for the hundredth time for any sign of Nick. So far, he was half an hour late. Knowing Nick, that shouldn't have been a surprise, but after the promises he'd made at the weekend, she'd hoped for more.

Her heart lurched — what if there had been an accident? He wasn't used to the new car yet, he'd only had it a week. Maybe it had gone out of control on the wet, slippery roads, maybe he was lying hurt somewhere, alone in pain, and calling for her . . .

She stopped and shook herself. She was just cold and miserable and letting her imagination run overtime. But there had to be a reason, surely?

"Sandy," she could imagine her mother saying for the umpteenth time, "Sandy, that boy is just messing you about. And he's let you down. Again."

But, no Mum wasn't right this time. Okay, so there'd been problems in the past, but this time they'd talked it over. They'd sorted things out at Jamie's party on Saturday night; he'd listened to how she felt, and what's more, understood. Hadn't he promised to be more thoughtful, more considerate?

from "Tears in the The Rain"
True Romances. May 1989

Exercise 4

It has been observed that advertisers are making increasing use of narratives to sell their products. For example, there are advertisements for luxury cars, bank loans, whisky and aftershave lotion which involve the users of these products or facilities in narrative action. Make a collection of advertisements from recent magazines, journals, newspapers and newspaper colour supplements which make use of narratives. When you have a collection of 6–10 examples attempt the following examples:

1 Using the descriptive framework outlined at 3.2.2 attempt an account of the effects of the advertisement. Which of the advertisements is the most successful and why? What part is played by non-linguistic factors such as colour, print size, photographs etc.?

2. To what extent does the descriptive framework assist you in accounting for the relative successes of these texts, particularly in the way language is used? Suggest modifications and extensions to the descriptive framework if you wish.

3. Write a short narrative which is intended to sell (a) an expensive camera, (b) an inexpensive camera.

4. Write a short narrative which advertises a holiday in Malaysia (refer closely to material discussed at 2.3).

It has also been observed that advertisements are designed to provide solutions to problems (see discussion at 3.1.2). Using advertising material you have collected for narrative analysis, as well as other examples you obtain, attempt the following exercises.

a Rewrite an advertisement which has a narrative structure into one which has a more overt S.P.S.E. structure (*Situation, Problem, Solution, Evaluation*). What have you had to change and why? What does this reveal about the nature and use of narrative structure in the promotion of products?

b Write an advertisement for a hair shampoo which makes use of S.P.S.E. structure but which is cast in the form of an agony aunt letter.

What kinds of relationship are set up between the content of your advertisements, the products themselves and the chosen style of writing?

Exercise 5

Here are some projects for the study of style in popular fiction. Our chapter section 3.3.3 will provide guidelines that can be usefully extended.

I The 'realism game'. Get hold of some samples of current best-selling fiction in the 'thriller' or 'adventure' genre; e.g. of books by Frederick Forsyth, Jack Higgins, Wilbur Smith, Robert Ludlum, Desmond Bagley, or any other obviously successful 'bookstall' author (new names are made almost month by month). Take soundings in your chosen material, collecting evidence for the stylistic importance of: (a) *names and epithets*; (b) *technical specifications* (i.e. of machinery, weapons, cars, planes, substances, etc.); (c) *measurements and statistics*.

Secondly, compare these passages:

(a) A wide plain, where the broadening Floss hurries on between its green banks to the sea, and the loving tide, rushing to meet it, checks its passage with an impetuous embrace. On this mighty tide the black ships – laden with the fresh-scented fir-planks, with rounded sacks of oil-bearing seed, or of the dark glitter of coal – are borne along to the town of St Ogg's, which shows its aged, fluted red roofs and the broad gables of its wharves between the low wooded hill and the river-brink, tinging the water with a soft purple hue under the transient glance of this February sun.

(b) The River Floss in Lincolnshire is one hundred and twenty yards wide, broadening to a quarter of a mile as it reaches the confluence of its rapid, six-knot current with the inrush of a tide capable of generating, at the springs, a twelve-foot bore. This bore, which the locals, for reasons best known to themselves, call the *aegre*, is ridden from seawards by the sturdy black-hulled coasters, serviceable vessels, but smallish – 5,000 tons displacement at the most – that ply along the English coast and also between Britain and the Scandinavian ports of Bergen, Gothenburg and Malmo, carrying coal, timber for construction or pulping, and some twenty thousand sacks per annum of oil-bearing seed. Jud Eliot was the master of one of these ships, the *Adam Bede*.

Jud was heading for St Ogg's, an inland port with a population of 73,000 people and wharfage for a dozen ships of moderate tonnage, like the *Adam Bede* or her sister ship, the *Silas Marner*, under the command of Jud's fiery-tempered brother, Tom 'Old Possum' Eliot. Many a disagreement, sometimes coming near to blows, had the gruff, broad-shouldered skipper of the *Bede* had with his carrot-polled sibling, but on this February day, with the roofs showing red in the sunlight where the town nestled on the banks of the river, sheltered by the hills with their 200-year-old plantations of *Quercus robur*, all was peace and tranquillity.

The first of these two passages is the opening of George Eliot's *The Mill on the Floss*. The second uses this classical material as the base for a parodic structure, exploiting the resources of the 'realism' game. Only the first two sentences of George Eliot's narrative have been used. Now find a copy of *The Mill on the Floss*, read carefully the remainder of the first paragraph, and on the basis of that material, continue the spoof begun in passage (b) above. (Your third paragraph might begin, for instance, 'Spinning the wheel with easy mastery, Jud had time to cast an appreciative glance at the well-cultivated landscape . . .'.) Enjoy the parodic exercise, but at the same time keep account of the devices you use to convert George Eliot's lyrical opening into a specimen of pop fiction.

II   The 'keynote' game. First consult half a dozen examples of stories in women's magazines, together with some romantic novels of the kind published by Mills and Boon. Select ten (or more, if you wish) representative passages, each of 100–200 words in length; include in your selection some specimens of description as well as of dialogue. Taking your cues from Chapter 3.3.3, investigate the role played in your chosen passages by: *verbs of action; verbs used in reporting dialogue; descriptive adjectives; participle clauses; adverbs and adverbials; clauses or sentences with non-human or non-animate 'agents'; figurative language.*

Compare the following passages:

(a) Alice was beginning to get very tired of sitting by her sister on the bank and of having nothing to do: once or twice she had peeped into the book her sister was reading, but it had no pictures or conversations in it, 'and what is the use of a book', thought Alice, 'without pictures or conversations?'

(b) Alice was beginning to feel bored – bored in every fibre of her slim, vibrant, 22-year-old being, bored of just sitting here on her first day in the bank with absolutely nothing to do. Once or twice she glanced enviously at her friend Cindy, utterly absorbed in columns of obviously important figures, unable, it seemed, to give any part of her mind to the intimacy of talk. A pang of uneasiness seized Alice by the throat. 'Would I have applied for an important post in a well-known bank,' she mused, distractedly running her fingers through the lustrous mass of her blonde hair, 'if I had known that no one was going to talk to me?'

The first of these passages is the well-known opening of *Alice's Adventures in Wonderland*. The second is a parody of women's magazine style, with minimal reference, as far as content goes, to Carroll's story; it builds, in fact, on the proposition 'Alice was beginning to get ery tired'. What are the stylistic elements that characterize the parody? Try writing your own version of the opening of what is obviously going to be a romantic tale. Then look at the next paragraph of the original *Alice*, in which the White Rabbit is introduced. With reference to this, write a further paragraph of your romance, introducing *either* 'fussy old Mr Roberts, an awful stick-in-the mud but rather sweet, really, or so everyone said', *or* 'devastatingly handsome Jeremy de Courcy, whose laughing eyes could blaze with cold scorn at the least hint of careless work'.

III Structures: description and dialogue. Collect from your source material in 'adventure' fiction a number of passages describing scenes, persons or objects. To what extent do these extracts conform to what we have called 'topic holding' and 'topic skipping'?

Rewrite the following in dialogue form, as though for a romantic novel; you are of course free to enlarge the details, or any hint implicit in the text:

> Simon was packing an overnight bag when Sally came home. In reply to her question, he said he was going on business to the Edinburgh office and would not be back until late on the following evening. He would be travelling alone, he said. Sally knew that both of these statements were false, and decided to confront him with her knowledge. At first he blustered, and then grew spiteful and aggressive. Sally, too, became very angry. When he left the house she told him he need not return. By this time she was in tears.

IV Comparisons. Here are two openings from novels which have classic status and yet continue to exercise the popular appeal intended by their authors:

> (a) I will begin the story of my adventures with a certain morning early in the month of June, in the year of grace 1751, when I took the key for the last time out of the door of my father's house. The sun began to shine upon the summit of the hills as I went down the road; and by the time I had come as far as the manse, the mist that hung around the valley in the time of the dawn was beginning to arise and die away.
>
> Mr Campbell, the Minister of Essendean, was waiting for me by the garden gate, good man! He asked me if I had breakfasted; and hearing that I lacked for nothing, he took my hand in both of his and clapped it kindly under his arm.

(b) No one who had ever seen Catherine Morland in her infancy, would have supposed her born to be an heroine. Her situation in life, the character of her father and mother, her own person and disposition, were all equally against her. Her father was a clergyman, without being neglected, or poor, and a very respectable man, though his name was Richard – and he had never been handsome. He had a considerable independence, besides two good livings – and he was not in the least addicted to locking up his daughters. Her mother was a women of useful plain sense, with a good temper, and what is more remarkable, with a good constitution.

Do these passages (respectively by R.L. Stevenson and Jane Austen) bear any of the stylistic marks of popular fiction as described in 3.3.3? Jane Austen is actually making fun of some of the popular conventions of her day. Try to rewrite this extract as she might have done had she been writing quite seriously (e.g. making the father poor and tyrannical, the mother sickly); to complicate the exercise, attempt the rewriting *first* in the style of Jane Austen, and *next* in modern magazine-story style.

Stevenson introduces his hero setting out on his travels. Try to find examples in current popular fiction of story-openings on this theme. If examples are wanting, try rewriting Stevenson's opening in the style of (a) Raymond Chandler, (b) Ian Fleming, (c) Frederick Forsyth.

V Oratory. Collect examples of platform oratory, like those cited in 3.5.1. Try to determine for yourself whether such patterns in speech are merely ornamental, or whether there is a strategy of rhetorical devices.

Make an oration out of the following text, which merely sets out to state its basic propositions as 'factually' as possible.

This is supposed to be an age of general prosperity. It is therefore disturbing to learn that many are homeless. They are not homeless in the sense that they cannot afford to buy a house, or even to rent accommodation. They are homeless in the quite drastic sense that they have nowhere to go and nobody to whom they can turn for shelter. By day they wander the streets aimlessly, or beg from passers-by, or sit in parks drinking whatever alcohol they can lay hands on. At night, the lucky ones find a bed in hostels like those run by the Salvation Army, but most 'sleep rough'. This means dossing down in derelict buildings, in doorways, under bridge arches, or on benches in the open air. For many, the only protection from the cold may be a large cardboard packaging box, and perhaps a layer of newspaper for insulation. This is not a novelist's fantasy. It is a real state of affairs, and a grim one, and our government appears not to take it very seriously.

Exercise 6

Chapter 3.5.1 suggests that some ways of looking at the language of politics. The observations made there are quite easily documented from the pages of the daily press, particularly of the so-called 'broadsheet' newspapers – for example, in Britain, *The Times*, the *Daily Telegraph*, the *Independent* and the *Guardian*. Make use of these everday sources to collect material on the following themes:

I   The political dictionary. The relevant section of 3.5.1 suggests that the primary political lexicon – its code of institutional operations – can be divided into words of 'locutory', 'regulatory' and 'benefactive' import. Explore this theme further, with the help of your newspaper extracts. Are the suggested categories adequate, or do they need to be in some way altered or refined?

With reference to your material, what general observations are you able to make about the following?: *word formation in political language; vogue words; 'purr'-words and 'snarl'-words; the evaluative vocabulary.*

II   'Deliberative' rhetoric. After collecting material, as suggested above, from reports and political articles in newspapers, make observations on the following: *the typical style of political propositions and assertions: the role of metaphor, especially mixed metaphor; the importance of figures of speech based on repetition, counterpoise and antithesis; the use of 'hedges' (i.e. expressions such as 'virtually', 'in effect', 'to all intents and purposes', 'in most cases', 'surely', 'most would agree', rendering the otherwise absolute assertion defensible in the event of objections or counter-arguments).*

Exercise 7

Chapter 3.5.2 is devoted to some studies of the language of criticism in literature and the arts. Here is a type of writing readily accessible to university and college students, who can easily make their own anthologies of extracts from academic textbooks, articles in learned journals, essays and review pieces in periodicals, notices and reviews in the daily and Sunday press. It is important to realize that there is a range of styles, all described by the word 'criticism'.

1   Critical keys. First, make your own collection, then examine your chosen extracts with close reference to the 'three critical keys' described in 3.5.2, i.e. *generalization, modality* and *affectiveness*. Is it apparent that these 'keys' are differently used in different styles of criticism? For example, does the ordinary newspaper review (let us say the kind of film and theatre review we might find in the *Daily Telegraph* or the *Guardian*) make greater use of affectiveness and less use of modality than might be apparent in the writing of an academic critic?

II Modality. For a fairly demanding special study, choose some writings by any academic critic with whose work you are familiar, and examine in detail the writer's use of modals and associated features. Our comments in 3.5.2 on a passage from T. S. Eliot's *What is a Classic?* indicate a possible line of enquiry. If modality indeed turns out to be a dominant feature of your writer's critical style, what are your conclusions about its function?

III Affective language. An ostensibly easier enquiry (but beware!) might be based on review articles taken from the 'Arts' sections of Sunday newspapers. Make some extracts, and then study them carefully with the intention of describing types and functions in the 'affective' lexicon. Are there any standard devices, such as the deliberately abrupt juxtaposition of 'core' and 'non-core' items (see 3.1.1)? Are certain semantic categories, for instance the sensory vocabulary, favoured? Is metaphor much used, and in what way? This is in fact as difficult as the proposed exercise on modality, but for a different reason. A study of the modals in critical language requires intensive observation of a definite feature; whereas a study of affectiveness calls for an *extensive* consideration of matters that cannot be specified in advance.

3   COMPOSITION

I   Language games

Exercise 1

Here are lists of nouns, verbs and adverbs, presented in random order. Determine in each case a sequence indicative of a story or a narrative episode, and write a paragraph composing the narrative:

(a) gale   hat   smile   cry   meeting
(b) stretch   rise   stumble   curse   rinse
(c) suspiciously   carefully   cautiously   timidly   thankfully

Now write *either* a brief cautionary tale *or* a newspaper report derived from the following set of sentences (which you may order as you please):

The policeman is watchful
The child is curious
The traffic is heavy
The gate is open
The mother is busy

The object of this exercise is twofold. One aim is to discover stimuli that may nudge you into composition. The other is to prompt a critical review of your compositional procedures. Try to understand the relationship between a proposed function (e.g. 'cautionary tale', 'newspaper report') and the language you select to express that function. Does your writing imply an appeal to a reader? If so, how is that appeal exercised? Do you find yourself using certain sentence types, for example question forms? What is the average length of your sentences? Do you tend to keep a mean length, or are there stylistically significant variations – e.g. through the abrupt introduction of a shorter-than-average sentence? Are the sentences notably complex in structure or do you confine yourself to fairly simple constructions? What have you done to make the text 'read' cohesively? How have you guided a potential reader through the text – what are its principles of design? Are there indications in your text of an orientation to time and place? Or to events, phenomena, and personalities 'outside' the text? What of the vocabulary? Are form classes like the adjective and adverb prominent in your writing, or do you prefer to make nouns and verbs do most of the communicative work? Is the vocabulary 'bookish' or 'colloquial', or a mixture of these? Is the appeal of the vocabulary sensory and emotive, or abstract and intellectual? Do you make much use of figurative language? Are your metaphors and the like conventional, or do they reflect your own figurative invention? These are some of the questions you should try consciously to explore after *every* attempt at composition.

Exercise 2

Blank filling. Here is an outline for a piece of verse, in which line-beginnings and line-endings have been supplied. The line-beginnings are represented by various grammatical operators or structure words (articles, auxiliaries, pronouns, conjunctions); the line-endings present a rhyme pattern turning on words some of which are semantically related (such as colour words) while the remainder are random selections. Complete the verse by filling in the intervening blanks in each line. You are free to choose your own line length, metre, and prosodic stanza pattern.

There was	green
Whose	brown
His	queen
And	town
But though	red
Was	yellow
The	said
That	fellow

NB. Poetic quality is not required, though the verse should be metrical and make sense. The exercise demonstrates two kinds of constraint: the semantic limitations imposed by rhyme, and the syntactic constraints determined by the grammatical elements at the beginning of each line. If the task as it stands proves too difficult, try (a) cancelling the rhymes in favour of others of your own choice, while keeping the grammatical cues, then (b) keeping the suggested rhymes but framing the verse in accordance with your own grammatical scheme.

II   Parodies

Exercise 1

Make parodic imitations of any variety of popular communication. Specifically, you may care to try: *advertisements for cars; tourist brochures; guide books; property ads (i.e. estate agents' advertisements); letters to the press.*

Exercise 2

The following is the first paragraph of a well-known story, 'Cat in the Rain', by Ernest Hemingway:

> There were only two Americans stopping at the hotel. They did not know any of the people they passed on the stairs on the way to and from their room. Their room was on the second floor facing the sea. It also faced the public garden and the war monument. There were big palms and green benches in the public garden. In the good weather there was always an artist with his easel. Artists liked the way the palms grew and the bright colours of the hotels facing the gardens and the sea. Italians

came from a long way off to look up at the war monument. It was made of bronze and glistened in the rain. It was raining. The rain dripped from the palm trees. Water stood in pools on the gravel paths. The sea broke in a long line in the rain and slipped back down the beach to come up and break again in a long line in the rain. The motor-cars were gone from the square by the war monument. Across the square in the doorway of the café a waiter stood looking out at the empty square.

Write a parodic imitation of this paragraph, beginning as follows:

There were only two Liverpudlians staying at the hotel. They did not recognize any of the people they kept passing on the corridor as they tried to find their way out. Their room was on the third floor, facing the old brewery. It also faced the gasworks and the fish-and-chip shop . . .

Or write a guide-book entry, beginning:

Conveniently situated not far from the town centre, this quiet hotel offers excellent amenities for the discerning traveller . . .

Or rewrite the piece in the style of D.H. Lawrence *or* Raymond Chandler *or* Jerome K. Jerome. To do this, you will have to look into the work of these authors and come to grips with their style, whether by imitation or analysis or a combination of these. You will then have to integrate your mimetic impressions of Lawrence, etc., with your understanding of Hemingways' stylistic mannerisms. This is not easy, but it is fun and has much to teach about literary style.

III   *Rewriting and Paraphrase*

Exercise 1

Rewrite the following passages, putting them into modern English and taking as your model the editorial style of a 'quality' newspaper:

(a) Studies serve for delight, for ornament, and for ability. Their chief use for delight, is in privateness and retiring; for ornament, is in discourse; and for ability, is in the judgement and disposition of business; for expert men can execute, and perhaps judge of particulars, one by one; but the general counsels, and the plots and marshalling of affairs come best from those that are learned. To spend too much time in studies, is sloth; to use them too much for ornament, is affectation; to make judgement wholly by their rules, is the humour of a scholar; they perfect nature, and are perfected by experience: for natural abilities are like natural plants, that need pruning by study; and studies themselves do give forth directions too much at large, except they be bounded in by experience. Crafty men condemn studies, simple men admire them, and wise men use them; for they teach not their own use; but that is a wisdom without them and above them, won by observation. Read not to contradict and confute, nor to believe and take for granted, nor to find talk and discourse, but to weigh and consider. Some books are to be tasted, others to be swallowed, and some few to be chewed and digested; that is, some books are to be read only in parts; others to be read but not curiously; and some few to be read wholly, with diligence and attention. Some books also may be read by deputy, and extracts made of them by others; but that would only be the less important arguments and the meaner sort of books; else distilled books are, like common distilled water, flashy things. Reading maketh a full man; conference a ready man; and writing an exact man; and therefore, if a man write little, he had need have a great memory; if he confer little, he had need have a present wit; and if he read little, he had need to have much cunning, to seem to know that he doth not.

(Francis Bacon, Of Studies)

(b) I have been told that late marriages are not eminently happy. This is a question too important to be neglected, and I have often proposed it to those, whose accuracy of remark, and comprehensiveness of knowledge, made their suffrages worthy of regard. They have generally determined, that it is dangerous for a man and a woman to suspend their fate upon each other, at a time when opinions are fixed, and habits are established; when friendships have been contracted on both sides, when life has been planned into method, and the mind has long enjoyed the contemplation of its own prospects.

It is scarcely possible that two travelling through the world under the conduct of chance, should have been both directed to the same path, and it will not often happen that either will quit the track which custom has made pleasing. When the desultory levity of youth has settled into regularity, it is soon succeeded by pride ashamed to yield, or obstinacy delighting to contend. And even though mutual esteem produces mutual desire to please, time itself, as it modifies unchangeably the external mien, determines likewise the direction of the passions, and gives an inflexible rigidity to the manners. Long customs are not easily broken: he that attempts to change the course of his own life, very often labours in vain; and how shall we do that for others, which we are seldom able to do for ourselves?

(Samuel Johnson, Rasselas, Prince of Abyssinia)

Exercise 2

Rewrite the following passage, attempting to convey its sense while changing as far as possible the length and construction of its sentences and paragraphs, and the ordering and prominence of the information it conveys. Changes in syntax may occasionally necessitate changes in vocabulary, to raise the overall formality of the style:

> Los Angeles – An 11-year-old girl noticed a 3-foot-tall marijuana plant growing in the back yard here this week and turned in her parents. Police are holding the girl in protective custody lest her parents speak sharply to her while an investigation continues.
>
> This is evidence of drug abuse hysteria, as if the nation is on a high from its crackdown on crack.
>
> No wonder. News magazines have been conducting a circulation-building war on drugs for months; television networks are finding prime-time slots for documentaries deploring the crisis; newspapers vie for the most lurid series on the local angle of the issue now in vogue.
>
> Politicians know they can get on the air and in print by railing at the pushers at home and the producers abroad. Pollsters tell candidates that interest in drug abuse is number one in the voters' hit parade, and every commercial turns otherwise serious legislators into apoplectic cops demanding death penalties and bombing runs. With this media-political symbiosis running rampant at campaign time, news junkies ask: Is drug abuse worse now than a year ago?
>
> (Syndicated article by William Safire,
> *Seattle Post-Intelligencer*,
> 13 September 1986)

Your revised piece might begin thus:

> In order to forestall retaliatory action during the course of their enquiries, Los Angeles police have taken into protective custody an 11-year-old girl who this week reported her parents after noticing a 3-foot-tall marijuana plant growing in the back yard. If this instance appears merely to support a general impression that the intensive campaign against 'crack' has produced a national state of hysteria over the abuse of drugs, there can be no wonder.

On the other hand, the aim of the rewriting might be to make the piece even more familiar and colloquial in tone. It might then begin thus:

> That plant in your back yard. Three feet tall and flourishing. Have you ever thought what it might be? Better yet, have your *kids* ever thought what it might be? Just suppose it's marijuana, and let's pretend the little dears decide to turn mummy and daddy over to the law. No so funny, eh? But that's exactly what happened in Los Angeles this week. An 11-year-old girl reported her parents for drug abuse. Now she is in custody. Protective custody. While mum and dad are under investigation. Just in case they get mad with her. And want to get even.
>
> There's only one word for this sort of thing. HYSTERIA. And who is to blame? . . .

Exercise 3

Taking Wordsworth's 'Westminster Bridge' sonnet:

Earth has not anything to show more fair:
Dull would he be of soul who could pass by
A sight so touching in its majesty:
This City now doth, like a garment, wear
The beauty of the morning; silent, bare,
Ships, towers, domes, theatres, and temples lie
Open to the fields, and to the sky;
All bright and glittering in the smokeless air.
Never did sun more beautifully steep
In his first splendour, valley, rock, or hill;
Ne'er saw I, never felt, a calm so deep!
The river glideth at his own sweet will:
Dear God! the very houses seem asleep;
And all that mighty heart is lying still!

a Attempt a prose paraphrase; then study the compromises and
   necessary defects of paraphrase.
b Make a prose version, faithful to the content of the poem but
   composed as though for an encyclopaedia entry ('the city is most
   advantageously viewed from one of the bridges, preferably in the
   early morning before traffic builds up'), *or* for a travel book ('we
   were struck by the almost rural calm of our surroundings'), *or* for
   a commercial ('you'll THRILL to the stupendous views!')

Further reading in this area and further examples of parodies,
paraphrases and creative writing exercises may be found in Nash
(1980, 1985, 1986).

Further Reading

Readers should consult the notes at the end of chapters as well as the bibliography for material with which to follow up and extend the discussions in this book. This section contains a short annotated bibliography of supplementary material which students using this book as a textbook may find helpful. All the suggestions are for books which contain extensive analysis and discussion of texts.

Birch, D. (1989), *Language, Literature and Critical Practice: Ways of Analyzing Text* (Routledge: London). A useful introduction to language-based criticism of texts in the twentieth century. Contains powerful arguments for the relationship between text analysis and ideology.

Birch, D. and O'Toole, L.M. (eds) (1987), *The Functions of Style* (Frances Pinter: London). A collection of essays covering some similar ground to this book, though at a more advanced level. A mixture of analyses of literary and non-literary texts. Essays include: analysis of poetry (Tennyson), prose (George Eliot), agony aunt columns, a comparison of medical advertising and a doctor–nurse romance novel, an analysis of style mixing in an advertising circular for credit cards. The descriptive frameworks draw almost exclusively on systemic linguistics.

Carter, R.A. (ed.) (1982), *Language and Literature: An Introductory Reader in Stylistics* (George Allen & Unwin: London). An introduction to literary stylistics with analysis based on canonical literary texts. A main focus on grammatical structures. Collection of essays.

Carter, R.A. and Simpson, P. (eds.) (1988), *Language Discourse and Literature: An Introductory Reader in Discourse Stylistics* (Allen & Unwin: London). A companion volume to Carter (ed.) (1982) with a main focus on structures of discourse. Useful introduction to analysing dialogue in fictional and dramatic texts.

Coupland, N. (ed.) (1988), *Styles of Discourse* (Routledge: London). A collection of essays analysing different kinds of discourse in literary, non-literary and media texts. Some essays quite advanced.

Crystal, D. and Davy, D. (1969), *Investigating English Style* (Longman: London). A classic volume which examines style in many different varieties of

English, spoken and written, including sermons, scientific reports, sports commentaries. Introductory textbook.

Davies. H. and Walton, P. (eds.) (1984), *Language, Image, Media* (Blackwell: Oxford). Useful case studies of newspaper, media, advertising discourse. Collection of essays.

Durant, A. and Fabb, N. (1989), *Literary Studies in Action* (Routledge: London). A unique activity-based introduction to the study of texts. Extensive coverage includes material on recent literary theory, literatures in English and procedures of interpretation as well as chapters oriented to stylistic analysis.

Fairclough, N. (1989), *Language and Power* (Longman: London). An extensive discussion of the ways in which language mediates structures of social and political power. Contains relatively advanced discussion of social theory. Useful and extensive analysis of spoken and written texts, including (chapter 7) an analysis of 'Thatcherian discourse'.

Fowler, R. (1986), *Linguistic Criticism* (Opus/Oxford University Press: Oxford). An introduction to stylistic analysis of literary texts with particular attention to the insertion of the texts into socio-cultural, linguistic and historical contexts. Strong argument for the analytical techniques to be extended beyond the study of canonical texts.

Fowler, R., Hodge, R., Kress, G. and Trew, T. (1979), *Language and Control* (Routledge and Kegan Paul: London). A detailed discussion of the relationship between language and ideology in a range of texts including newspapers and transcriptions of interviews. Quite advanced in level.

Freeborn, D. (1986), *Varieties of English* (Macmillan: London). An introduction to a range of spoken and written styles of English. Mainly non-literary texts. Contains some useful introductory discussion of the role of language and ideology in newspaper front-page reports.

Kress, G. (1985), *Linguistic Processes in Sociocultural Practice* (Deakin University Press: Victoria, Australia). A book aimed largely at teachers and students of education and containing therefore extensive discussion of the language of school textbooks and children's writing. Valuable for its discussion of the operation of ideology through texts and for helpful theoretical distinctions between text and discourse.

Leech, G.N. and Short, M.H. (1981), *Style in Fiction* (Longman: London). A linguistic introduction to style in canonical English prose texts. Discussion at a range of linguistic levels.

Nash, W. (1980), *Designs in Prose* (Longman: London). A discussion of compositional processes in the construction of texts. A useful extension to discussion in Chapter 4 of this book.

Nash W. (1985), *The Language of Humour* (Longman: London). An exploration of style and technique in comic discourse in a range of texts from one-line jokes to comic novels.

Toolan, M. (1988), *Narrative: A Critical Linguistic Introduction* (Routledge: London). Discusses a range of narrative texts, including canonical literary narratives, narratives in news reports and narratives for and by children.
Traugott, E. and Pratt, M.L. (1980), *Linguistics for Students of Literature* (Harcourt Brace Jovanovich: New York). A textbook in which several descriptive frameworks from generative grammar to sociolinguistic variation studies are applied to a range of literatures in English.

Van Peer, W. (ed.) (1988), *The Taming of the Text* (Routledge: London). A collection of essays devoted to linguistically oriented discussion of a range of literary and non-literary texts, including drama texts.
Vestergaard, T. and Schroeder, K. (1985), *The Language of Advertising* (Blackwell: Oxford). Not particularly detailed as a linguistic study but helpful discussion of the interface of language, gender, culture and ideology.

Wales, K. (1989), *A Dictionary of Stylistics* (Longman: London). A very useful resource for students of language and style, containing extensive explanations of key terms and concepts.

Bibliography

Attridge, D. (1988), *Peculiar Language: Literature as Difference from the Renaissance to James Joyce* (Methuen: London).

Bally, C. (1925), *La Langue et la Vie* (3rd edn) (Geneva).

Bennett, T. (1983), 'Texts, Readers and Reading Formations', *Literature and History*, 9, 2, 214–27.

Carter, R. A. (ed.) (1982), *Language and Literature: An Introductory Reader in Stylistics* (Allen & Unwin: London).

Carter, R. A. (1985), 'A Question of Interpretation', in T. D'Haen (ed.), *Linguistic Contributions to Literature* (Rodopi: Amsterdam).

Carter, R. A. (1987), *Vocabulary: Applied Linguistic Perspectives* (Allen & Unwin: London).

Carter, R. A. (1988), 'Is there a Literary Language?', in R. Steele and T. Threadgold (eds), *Language Topics: Essays in Honour of Michael Halliday* (Banjamins: Amsterdam), pp.431–50.

Carter, R. A. and Long, M. N. (1987), *The Web of Words: Exploring Literature Through Language* (Cambridge University Press: Cambridge).

Carter, R. A. and Nash, W. (1983), 'Language and Literariness', *Prose Studies* 6, 2, 123–41.

Carter, R. A. and Simpson, P. (eds) (1988), *Language Discourse and Literature: An Introductory Reader in Discourse Stylistics* (Allen & Unwin: London).

Chatman, S. (1971), 'The Semantics of Style', in J. Kristeva et al. (eds), *Essays in Semiotics* (Mouton: The Hague).

Cluysenaar, A. (1976), *Introduction to Literary Stylistics* (Batsford: London).

Crystal, D. and Davy, D. (1969), *Investigating English Style* (Longman: London).

Culler, J. (1975), *Structuralist Poetics* (Routledge and Kegan Paul: London).

Culler, J. (1981), *The Pursuit of Signs* (Routledge and Kegan Paul: London).

de Beaugrande, R. and Dressler, W. (1981), *Introduction to text Linguistics* (Longman: London).

Dillon, G. (1981), *Constructing Texts: Elements of a Theory of Composition and Style* (Indiana University Press: Bloomington, Indiana).

Eagleton, T. (1983), *Literary Theory: An Introduction* (Blackwell: Oxford).

Fairclough, N. (1987), 'Register, Power and Socio-semantic Change', in D.

Birch and L.M. O'Toole (eds), *The Functions of Style* (Frances Pinter: London).

Fish, S. (1980), *Is There a Text in This Class?* (Harvard University Press: Cambridge, Mass.).

Fowler, R. (1981), *Literature as Social Discourse* (Batsford: London).

Fowler, R., Hodge, R., Kress, G. and Trew, T. (1979), *Language and Control* (Routledge and Kegal Paul: London).

Ghadessy, M. (1983), 'Information Structure in Letters to the Editor', *International Review of Applied Linguistics* 21, 1, 46–56.

Halliday, M. A. K. (1964), 'The Linguistic Study of Literary Texts', in H. Lunt (ed.), *Proceedings of the Ninth International Congress of Linguists* (Mouton: The Hague).

Halliday, M. A. K. (1971), 'Linguistic Function and Literary Style', in S. Chatman (ed.), *Literary Style: A Symposium* (Oxford University Press: Oxford).

Halliday, M. A. K. (1983), Introduction to J. Cummins and R. Simmons, *The Language of Literature* (Pergamon: Oxford).

Hasan, R. (1971), 'Rime and Reason in Literature', in S. Chatman (ed.), *Literary Style: A Symposium* (Oxford University Press: Oxford).

Havránek, B. (1932), 'The Functional Differentiation of Standard Language', in P. Garvin (ed.), *Prague School Reader in Esthetics, Literary Structure and Style* (Georgetown University Press: Georgetown).

Herrnstein–Smith, B. (1978), *On the Margins of Discourse: The Relation of Language to Literature* (University of Chicago Press: Chicago).

Hodge, R. and Kress, G. (1981), *Language and Ideology* (Routledge and Kegan Paul: London).

Hoey, M. (1983), *On the Surface of Discourse* (Allen & Unwin: London).

Holub, R. (1984), *Reception Theory* (Methuen: London).

Jakobson, R. (1960), 'Linguistics and Poetics', in T. Sebeok (ed.), *Style in Language* (MIT: Cambridge, Mass.).

Kress, G. (1985), *Linguistic Processes in Sociocultural Practice* (Deakin University Press: Victoria, Australia).

Labov, W. (1972), 'The Transformation of Experience in Narrative Syntax', *Language in the Inner City* (University of Pennsylvania Press: Pennsylvania).

Lakoff, R. and Johnson, M. (1980), *Metaphors We Live By* (University of Chicago Press: Chicago).

Leech, G. N. (1969), *A Linguistic Guide to English Poetry* (Longman: London).

Leitch, T. (1983), 'To What is Fiction Committed?', *Prose Studies* 6, 2, 159–76.

Leith, R. and Myerson, G. (1989), *The Power of Address: Explorations in Rhetoric* (Routledge: London).

Levin, S. (1962), *Linguistic Structures in Poetry* (Mouton: The Hague).

Moeran, B. (1984), 'Advertising Sounds as Cultural Discourse', *Language and Communication* 4, 2, 147–58.

Mukařovsky, J. (1932), 'Standard Language and Poetic Language', in P. Garvin (ed.), *Prague School Reader in Esthetics, Literary Structure and Style* (Georgetown University Press: Georgetown).

Nash, W. (1980), *Designs in Prose* (Longman: London).

Nash, W. (1985), *The Language of Humour: Style and Technique in Comic Discourse* (Longman: London).

Nash, W. (1986), 'The Possibilities of Paraphrase', in C. J. Brumfit and R. A. Carter (eds), *Literature and Language Teaching* (Oxford University Press: Oxford).

Nash, W. (1989), *Rhetoric: The Wit of Persuasion* (Blackwell: Oxford).

Nash, W. (1990), *Language in Popular Fiction* (Routledge: London).

Ohmann, R. (1971), 'Speech Acts and the Definition of Literature', *Philosophy and Rhetoric* 4, 1–19.

Pratt, M. L. (1977), *Towards a Speech Act Theory of Literature* (Indiana University Press: Bloomington, Indiana).

Quirk, R. and Greenbaum, S. (1973), *A University Grammar of English* (Longman: London).

Quirk, R. et al. (1985), *A Comprehensive Grammar of the English Language* (Longman: London).

Riffaterre, M. (1960), 'Stylistic Context', *Word* 15, 154–74.

Riffaterre, M. (1964), 'The Stylistic Function', in H. Lunt (ed.), *Proceedings of the Ninth International Congress of Linguists* (Mouton: The Hague).

Short, M. H. (1973), 'Some Thoughts on Foregrounding and Interpretation', *Language and Style* 6, 2, 97–108.

Sinclair, J. (1966), 'Taking a Poem to Pieces', in R. Fowler (ed.), *Essays on Style and Language* (Routledge and Kegan Paul: London).

Sinclair, J. (1982), 'Lines on Lines', in R. A. Carter (ed.), *Language and Literature: An Introductory Reader in Stylistics* (Allen & Unwin: London).

Tambling, J. (1988), *What is Literary Language?* (Open University Press: Milton Keynes).

Thibault, P. J. (1986), 'Metaphor and Political Oratory in Ronald Reagan's Acceptance Speech', in B. Bosinelli (ed.), *US Presidential Election 1984: An Interdisciplinary Approach to the Analysis of Political Discourse* (Pitagora Editrice: Bologna, Italy).

Thompson, J. B. (1984), *Studies in the Theory of Ideology* (Polity Press: Cambridge).

Todorov, T. (1973), 'The Notion of Literature', *New Literary History* 5, 1, 5–16.

Todorov, T. (1981), *Introduction to Poetics* (Harvester Press: Brighton).

Toolan, M. (1988), *Narrative: A Critical Linguistic Introduction* (Routledge: London).

Van Dijk, T. A. (1977), *Text and Context* (Longman: London).

Waugh, L. R. (1980), 'The Poetic Function and the Nature of Language', *Poetics Today* 2, 1, 57–82.

Werth, P. (1976), 'Roman Jakobson's Verbal Analysis of Poetry', *Journal of Linguistics* 12, 21–74.

White, Hayden (1981), 'The Fictions of Factual Representation', in *Tropics of Discourse* (John Hopkins University Press: Baltimore).

Widdowson, H. G. (1972), 'On the Deviance of Literary Discourse', *Style* 6, 3, 294–306.

Widdowson, H. G. (1975), *Stylistics and the Teaching of Literature* (Longman: London).

Williams, R. (1976), *Keywords* (Fontana: London).

Winter, E. (1977), 'A clause-relational approach to English texts: A study of some predictive lexical items in written discourse', Instructional Science 6, pp. 1–92.

Winter, E. (1982), *Towards a Contextual Grammar of English* (Allen & Unwin: London).

Glossarial Index

The purpose of this index is threefold: (a) to list references to the principal themes of the book in the usual way, with page numbers indicating the main entries; (b) to amplify or further elucidate some themes with brief definitions and commentaries; and (c) to provide information on topics, mainly grammatical and semantic, not of central importance to the book, but usefully accessory to the discussion of language as the vehicle and medium of our perceptions. In the latter regard, it has no pretensions to comprehensiveness, though we have tried to cover basic concepts in grammar, phonology and lexis.

Cross references are indicated in **bold type**

Active *see* **voice**

Adjective Adjectives constitute a **form class** of words which regularly **modify** nouns, e.g. 'an *attractive old* house', and which may be modified by **adverbs**, e.g. 'an *extremely pretty* cottage'. They are *gradable*, i.e. can be made to express degrees of comparison, whether through the addition of a **suffix** ('old*er*', 'old*est*'), or the use of the adverbs 'more', 'most' (a *more attractive/ most attractive* old house'). An adjective occurring in the **predicate** as a **complement**, e.g. 'Sarah looked quite ravishingly *beautiful*' is called a *predicative adjective*.

Adjunct An adjunct is an **adverbial** integrated into the structure of the **clause**, expanding the meaning of the **verb**. In 'the old man who sat in the corner', 'he jumped for joy', and 'she received the flowers with great pleasure', the phrases *in the corner, for joy*, and *with great pleasure* are adjuncts.

Adverb Adverbs constitute a major **form class** of somewhat diverse items. 'Manner' adverbs are words like 'happily' and 'fast', which occur as **adjuncts**. 'Intensifiers' are words like 'very', 'rather', 'extremely', which are used to **modify adjectives**, e.g. 'An *extremely* pleasant journey.' Other types express place ('here', 'there') and time ('now', 'then', 'afterwards'). Like **adjectives**, adverbs are *gradable*, i.e. have degrees of comparison: 'well, better, best', 'much, more, most'; but 'happily, more happily, most happily'.

Adverbial   An **element** in the structure of the **clause**, commonly **realized** by an **adverb**, or by an **adjunct** in the form of a prepositional phrase. In 'We arranged to meet on Saturday', 'We arranged to meet then', and 'Afterwards we set up another meeting', *on Saturday*, *then* and *afterwards* represent the adverbial element in the clause.

Adverbial phrase   A **phrase**, the **head** of which belongs to the **form class** of adverbs, e.g. 'very quickly', 'quite happily', 'soon afterwards', 'just then', 'almost here'.

Advertisements, narrative structure in 81–6

Affricate   125–6   A class of **consonant**, the articulation of which resembles a **stop** at its onset and a **fricative** in its release, e.g. the 'tch' and 'dge' sounds in 'scra*tch*' and 'bri*dge*'.

Agent deletion 57   'Agent' is a semantic term signifying 'doer', 'performer' of the action, process, etc., denoted by the *verb*. Though 'agent' and grammatical **subject** frequently coincide, they are not co-terminous. In 'John planned the garden', *John* is the agent, and his name **realizes** the grammatical role of **subject**; but in 'the garden was planned by John', *John* no longer represents the grammatical subject, though he is still the agent. 'Agent deletion' denotes the omission of any reference to an agent, e.g. in 'The garden was carefully planned', 'An order was promulgated', 'The text lays this down quite clearly'. *See also* **voice**.

Alliteration 120   Alliteration involves **consonants** occurring at the beginning of syllables. It should not be confused with *assonance*, which refers to **vowels** or syllables of similar sound, e.g. 'A stitch in *time* saves *nine*', '*morning*'s minion, *king*dom of daylight's *dauphin*'. The word *consonance* is sometimes used to describe the play of consonants in both alliterating and non-alliterating positions, e.g. 'the *sessions* of *sweet silent* though*t*'.

Alveolar 125   A type of **consonant** formed by the tongue in contact with or in close proximity to the *alveolum*, or 'teeth ridge' (the ridge of gum behind the upper front teeth). The initial consonants of the English words *t*in, *d*ark, *n*eck, *s*ip and *z*inc are alveolar articulations.

Anaphoric 109, 112 'Anaphoric' denotes reference to something occurring earlier, or 'above', in a **text**. In 'A few people had made reservations, but most arrived without tickets. Only the former gained admittance to the ground', the function of *the former* is anaphoric, in its reference to 'a few people etc.'. **Pronouns** and **demonstratives** frequently have anaphoric functions in **texts**. In classical rhetoric, *anaphora* is a **figure of speech** in which the first word of a **phrase** or **clause** is repeated in successive constructions: 'strong in faith, strong in friendship, strong in fight'. *See also* **cataphoric; endophoric**.

Antecedent 198 An antecedent is the verbal forerunner to which a word or **phrase** is subsequently linked. In 'Americans are always being criticized, but I like them', the antecedent of *them* is *Americans*; in 'Some people detest lemons, but I like them', the antecedent of *them* is *lemons*; in 'They thought we were laughing at their accents, but we took them very seriously', the antecedent of *them* could be either *they* or *accents*; in 'After her brothers had caught several fish, Mary gutted them', the real antecedent is *fish*, but there is a comically lurking 'false antecedent' in *brothers*.

Antonym In the **lexicon**, a word perceived as standing in opposing correspondence to a word belonging to a different set of **synonyms**. The word 'love' may be seen as antonymic to the word 'hate'; but 'fear' might also be perceived as 'love's' antonym.

Apposition Words or phrases are said to be *in apposition* when two **realizations** of one and the same **element** are juxtaposed. The element concerned is often the **subject** or the **object**, and the apposed expressions are usually **nouns** or **noun phrases**. In 'Martin, his youngest son, was a very successful lawyer', the noun phrases *Martin* and *his youngest son* are in apposition.

Approximant 122 A term used to describe types of **consonant** articulation which are not characterized by total closure (like **stops**), or by obvious constriction (like **fricatives**), but in which the tongue, as the main articulating organ, 'approximates to', or approaches, a closed/constricting articulation. The *l* in *l*ine is described by some phoneticians as an approximant, as are the *r* in [southern British] English *r*ed, and the *y* (/j/) of *y*oung.

Article A **closed form class**, comprising the words *the* (called the *definite article*), and *a(n)* (called the *indefinite article*). In the construction of **noun phrases**, the articles function as **determiners**. Semantically they relate in various ways to expressions of *generic* and *specific*, as well as to *count*ability and *non-count*ability. *See also* deictic, deixis.

Aspect A grammatical/semantic category associated with the **verb phrase**, indicating the way in which a speaker views a situation with reference to stretches and lapses of time. English has two aspects, the *progressive* ('continuous', 'durative') expressing action, event, etc., over a period of time ('I was working in London in those days'), and the *perfective*, expressing action or event completed either in recent or more distantly past time ('I have finished my work', 'I have lived in Seattle', 'I had waited for three months before I decided to give up'). Progressive and perfective aspects are often co-occurrent, e.g. 'I have been waiting for ages', 'They said they had been expecting you'.

Automatization 4 This term, which we owe to the Czech **formalists**, means the everyday, banal use of language, with no features so unorthodox or unpredictable as to enforce attention. *See also* **background**; **foregrounding**.

Auxiliary A **verb** subordinate and supportive in function to the main **verb** in the **verb phrase**, expressing time or **modality**. 'Be', 'have', 'must', 'ought to', 'have to', 'may', 'might', 'can', 'could', 'shall', 'will', 'should' and 'would' are auxiliaries.

Background 4, 10 In the usage of the Czech **formalists**, this apparently refers (a) to the 'standard' language, the *norm* against which *deviant* features are perceived (*see* **automatization; defamiliarization**), and (b) the aesthetic traditions of expression and form handed down in the literary canon – e.g. the sonnet form, the rhetorical pattern of the essay. *See also* **foregrounding**.

'Benefactive' expressions in the political dictionary 132

Bilabial 125 A type of consonant formation, made by the closure of the lips; the *p* in to*p*, *b* in *b*oat, and *m* in *m*ap are bilabial.

Caesura 150 In traditional metrics, the point at which a measure or line of verse is considered to be balanced by a 'cut' which may or may not correspond to a syntactic/semantic division. In 'To be or not to be, that is the question', the caesura is marked by the comma before *that*. In 'A little learning is a dangerous thing', the caesura comes after 'learning', though it is not formally marked and perhaps not even perceived by anyone other than the **prosodic** analyst.

Case A grammatical category associated with **nouns** and **pronouns**, expressing their status as **subject, object,** etc. In so-called *inflected* languages (e.g. Greek, Latin, Russian, Finnish), case is principally expressed by **suffixes**. English has a possessive or *genitive* inflection, and distinguishes between *subjective* and *objective* forms of pronoun ('I', 'he', 'she', 'they'; 'me', 'him', 'her', 'them'); otherwise the notion of case has to be retrieved from some recurrent syntactic patterns, e.g. 'He gave his watch to his brother', where *to his brother* has a 'dative' sense, or from an underlying semantic structure, e.g. as in 'The poor man had his watch stolen', where *the poor man* must be 'dative' rather than 'subjective' ('from the poor man his watch was stolen').

Cataphoric   'Cataphoric' denotes reference to features that occur 'below', i.e. that 'follow' in a **text**. *Here* in 'Here is my reason – I have no money' is cataphoric. *See* the companion terms **anaphoric**; **endophoric**.

Clause 117, 124   The clause is a major unit of **syntactic** form, the only higher instance being the **sentence**. In the formal hierarchy, a sentence is regarded as consisting of one or more clauses, a clause of one or more **phrases**, a phrase of one or more words, and a word of one or more *morphemes*. The **elements** of structure in the clause are **subject, verb** (or *predicator*), **complement** ('subject' or 'object' complement), **object** ('direct' or 'indirect') and **adverbial**. The ordering of these elements in **declarative** sentences is generally fixed for subject and verb, but with some options of placing for the other elements. (*See* **fronting; marketing**). Clauses in sentence structure are related to each other in patterns of dependence or *subordination*. Clauses in which the predicator takes the form of a **participle** or an **infinitive** construction are called *non-finite clauses*; non-finite clauses are always subordinate (*see also* **embedding**). Clauses without a predicator (through reduction or deletion, e.g. '*Though full of regret*, he had nothing practical to offer') are called *verbless clauses*.

Clause relations (defined) 69

Cleft sentence 192   A sentence divided into three parts, i.e. a 'proposing' formula, consisting of 'It' + the verb 'be'; a 'proposed' *phrase*, on which emphasis falls; and a *that-*, *who-*, or *which-* clause. Thus. 'It was / the dog / that died', 'It was / Mozart / who wrote *Don Giovanni*', 'It is / at Christmas / that we remember our friends'. Such sentences are 'cleft' because they represent a grafting of one proposition upon another, e.g. 'The dog died' and 'It was the dog'.

Cline, of literariness 41, 43, 47, 49, 205   The term 'cline' may have been borrowed into linguistics from the language of biological science, where it signifies the range of variations of form displayed within a species. In stylistics it refers to a gradation of text types, according to the density of certain formal and **semantic** constituents.

Closed class   In grammar, a 'closed class' contains a finite number of items, to which no more can be added. **Articles**, for example, are a closed class, unlike **nouns**, which constitute an **open class**, containing all the English nouns that ever were, and accepting all that come along.

Code 39   A code is basically a set of rules for producing a sign-system, e.g. morse, semaphore, cryptograms. Language itself is a sign-system, requiring from its users acts of encoding, which other users decode. However, the word 'code' in the sense used in this book refers principally to the production of text systems, or **text conventions. Texts** are encoded and decoded by **readers** who have the **competence** to interpret their underlying rules.

Coherence   A **text** is perceived as coherent when it makes consistent sense, with or without the help of devices of **cohesion**. 'The term ends next week. I have a pile of essays to mark', might be considered coherent, even in the absence of connectives and commentary items, such as 'unfortunately', 'still', and 'before then'. *See also* **metalanguage, metadiscourse**.

Cohesion   'Cohesion' is the demonstrable pattern of the **text**'s integrity, the marks of its 'hanging together'. Two principal types of cohesion (there are others) are *syntactic* and *lexical*. The cohesion of the following short passage is expressed in part through **lexical** items ('Head', 'masters', 'staff', 'employer'), and also through grammatical items ('that', 'them', 'their'): 'The Head decided that the masters, as well as the boys, should be granted a holiday. That pleased the staff and made them think better of their employer'. See also **antecedent**; **discourse**; **metadiscourse**; **metalanguage**; **text**.

Collocation   A collocation is a fixed or conventional sequence or textual association of words: 'alluring' collocates with 'woman', not with 'man'; 'shabby' collocates with 'clothes' or 'treatment', rather than with 'meal' or 'typewriter'; the **verb** that regularly collocates with 'bee' is 'buzz', or with 'bicycle' is 'ride', and so on. 'Alluring woman' is a *high frequency collocation*; 'voluptuous boxer', 'shabby sausage', 'the bees were bellowing', and 'I sailed my bicycle home' are not. *See also* **norm and deviation**.

Comment *see* **topic and comment**.

Competence 27–8   The term 'competence' is particularly associated with the model of language and grammar propounded by Noam Chomsky and his associates and called *transformational-generative*, or simply *generative*. It attributes to human beings the innate ability – the competence – to recognize and process the 'rules' that 'generate' symbolic systems, above all the system of language; so that children can produce in their native language sentences they have not heard before or acquired by imitation. Literary scholars and stylisticians have taken up this term and applied it to the ability to recognize literary devices and structures, decode literary texts, and even generate literary forms. Whether such 'literary competence' can be described as 'innate' is, however, a matter for question.

Complement 196   In grammar generally, a construction that is required to complete the sense of another. In **clause** structure specifically, a complement is a word or **phrase** completing the reference of a **subject** ('whence 'subject complement') or **object** ('object complement'). In 'The policeman turned quite pale', *quite pale* represents the subject complement +. In 'The committee elected him president', *president* complements the direct object, *him*.

Conjunct 186   A word belonging to the general class of **adverbs**, but having some affinity with **conjunctions**. Conjuncts express links between **sentences**, rather than connections within **clauses**, or between the constituent clauses of a sentence. In 'I don't trust him, although he seems friendly', *although* is a conjunction; in 'I don't trust him. He seems friendly, though', *though* is a conjunct.

Conjunction   Conjunctions are a **form class** of linking words, indicating relationships of *co-ordination* or *subordination* between the constituents of clauses and sentences. The words 'and', 'but', and 'or' are *co-ordinators*, linking units of equal status; words like 'although', 'because', 'therefore' and 'if' are *subordinators*, linking units which are of unequal status because one is **dependent** on another. In 'If you don't accept this, the deal's off', the word *if* is the subordinator indicating the dependence of 'you don't accept this' on the *main clause*, 'the deal's off'.

'Connection', compositional function of complex sentence 199.

Consonant 122   A type of **speech-sound**, the articulation of which is characterized, (a) by the formation of some closure or constriction impeding the airstream proceeding from the lungs through the larynx and into the oral or nasal cavities, (b) by diverse ways of managing the onset and the release of the closure or constriction, and (c) by the presence or absence of

voice, a resonance brought about by the closing of the vocal cords. In our sound system there are regular contrasts of 'voiced' and 'voiceless' consonants. Phonologically, the consonant ('con + sonant') is marginal to sounds of greater **sonority**, i.e. vowels; thus in a syllable the central, prominent sound is a vowel. *See* **affricate; alveolar; bilabial; dental; fricative; nasal; palatal; palato-alveolar; stop; velar**

Context   Generally, the environment in which words are written or spoken. This may be the environment of other words – the verbal context; or of the physical circumstances in which the words are uttered – the context of situation; or of the intention the words are designed to serve – the functional context. *Stylistic context* 6–7; *internal context* 6; *interactive context* 15.

'Co-occurrence,' compositional function of complex sentence 199

Co-ordination, co-ordinator *see* **conjunction**

Core vocabulary 122

Count noun *see* **noun**

Creativeness 175–6

Criticism, 'keys' to critical style 151, 225; language of 148–72

Declarative   A term denoting the type of **sentence** that frames a statement, e.g. 'Many people speak English', 'I'm disappointed', 'The wind has blown down our trellis'. In such sentences the **subject** normally precedes the **verb**. *See also* **imperative; interrogative; mood.**

Defamiliarization 31, 36   *See also* **norm and deviation.**

Definite article *see* **article**

Deflection 5   *See also* **fronting; marking; norm and deviation; well-formed.**

Deictic, deixis   'Deixis' is the textual function of 'pointing', retrospectively, prospectively, or extra-textually. In 'This above all, to thine own self to be true', *this* is a deictic. What is pointed to may be in the verbal **context**, or may be in the context of situation, e.g. 'over there', in 'I'd like to pop into the little shop over there'. *See also* **anaphoric; cataphoric; cohesion; demonstrative; endophoric**.

Demonstrative 150   In grammar, a demonstrative is an **adjective** or a **pronoun** having **deictic** reference usually to a **noun** or **noun phrase**. Typical demonstratives are *this, that, these, those*: 'A fair trial – that was his stipulation'; 'I should like you to observe these few simple principles.'

Dental   A type of **consonant** articulation, in which the tongue makes contact with the teeth, e.g. *th* in *th*is, ten*th*.

Dependent 196   In grammar, **sentences** and **clauses** are said to be *independent* when they are potentially free-standing, complete in themselves, but *dependent* if they require the presence of another, governing construction. In 'I don't want to do it *because I can't afford it*', 'I'm doing my best *to meet your demands*', and 'I can't imagine myself *keeping up with the payments*', the italicized constructions are all dependent, or *subordinate*. *See also* **embedding**.

Determiner 179   In **noun phrases** determiners mark the onset, or *terminus a quo* of the construction. They are often **articles**, but may be indefinite **pronouns** ('some'), interrogative pronouns ('which?') or **demonstratives** ('those', 'such'): 'The prettiest little house', 'Some rather pretty houses', 'Which rather pretty house?', 'such undeniably pretty houses'.

Deviation *see* **norm and deviation**.

Dialogue, in fiction 92–9.

Diphthong   A type of **vowel**, during the articulation of which the speech organs, notably the tongue and lips, gradually change their posture, producing the acoustic effect of a 'glide'. In *tyke* (transcribed / taik/, the tongue is at first roughly in the position required for the *a* in *tack*, but then moves fractionally in the direction of the *i* in *tick*. In British (southern) English, there are almost as many diphthongs as *monophthongs*; they outnumber the long vowels.

Directive   Semantically, a directive is any form of words issuing a request for action. The commonest form is an **imperative** sentence, but directives can take other forms: 'I'd like you to write an article for me' is no less directive than 'Write me an article'.

Discourse 9, 86–7 This word is loosely used as a convenient general description for language in action. In some usages it refers specifically to conversational exchanges and the rules underlying them; in others it refers to the properties of **texts** designed by a **writer** and interpreted by a **reader**. Although a single **sentence** or a minimal conversational exchange might be described as 'discourse', the term usually presupposes some more extensive process, exhibiting a structure, the symptoms of an authorial intention and (particularly in the case of conversation) some rules of procedure and participation.

Discourse function 190.

Disjunct 109, 186 a type of **adverbial** expression not integral to the **clause** to which it is attached, and not, like a **conjunct**, serving as a link between clauses. Disjuncts are expressions like 'fortunately', 'hopefully' (as in 'he's coming tomorrow, hopefully'), 'as things turned out', representing the speaker's commentary on or evaluation of what is said.

'Displaced interaction' 41.

Domain Sometimes called *field*; refers to the type of activity in which language is used, e.g. the law, advertising.

'Dossier' epithets (in popular fiction) 101.

Element A constituent of **sentence** or **clause** structure; essentially a 'position' or abstraction, open to **realization** by an actual choice of words. Thus the **subject** of a clause might be realized by 'He', or 'John', or 'the little boy', or 'whatever you say' (as in 'whatever you say is wrong'). *See also* **adverbial**; **complement**; **object**.

Embedded, -ing 117–18, 124 In grammar, the term *embedding* denotes the incorporation of one construction into another. Thus in 'a good meal is what he needs', a **clause**, *what he needs*, is embedded, as **complement**, in another clause.

End weight The principle that longer units come after shorter units, in the absence of special stylistic constraints. English sentences are commonly end-weighted. 'What we need is a system of taxation that will take into account the circumstances of individuals and their ability to pay' is end-weighted from *is* onwards. It would be possible to give the sentence *front weight:* 'A system of taxation which will take into account the circumstances of individuals and their ability to pay is what we need'. *See also* **left branching; right branching; sequencing**.

Endophoric 'Endophoric' reference, of **deictics, pronouns**, etc., is to any item within the **text**, backward reference being **anaphoric** and forward reference **cataphoric**. References to extra-textual phenomena (i.e. in the **context** of situation) are called *exophoric*.

Evaluative adjective 102; in the language of politics 135–6.

Event verb (dynamic verb)   Semantically, 'event' verbs describe actions of happenings. There are several sub-types: activity verbs ('work'), *transitional event* ('arrive'), *momentary event* ('wink', 'drop'), *process* ('become', 'change', 'grow'). *See also* **state verb**.

Existential sentence 150, 192   An existential sentence has the structure THERE + BE + NOUN PHRASE, e.g. 'There is a God', 'There were three men waiting in the living room', 'There can be no reason for going to war'. Such sentences may involve verbs other than *be*, e.g. 'appear', 'occur', 'arise'. Existential sentences help to create *end* **focus** and **end weight**.

Extraposition 192   The construction of a **sentence** so that, for purposes of *end* **focus**, its information-bearing **clause** comes at the end, after a formula of the type 'It is the case (that)', 'It is well known (that)', 'It was unfortunate (that)'. In the sentence 'It was unfortunate that you could not come', the clause *that you could not come* is extraposed.

Fiction, narrative structure in 86–90.

Figurative language in political discourse 134–5, 141–3; in popular fiction 107–9, 113–14.

Figure of speech   Traditionally, 'figures of speech' are of two kinds: figures of language', or *schemes*, which are essentially devices of word-order, and 'figures of sense', or *tropes*, which depend on transferences of meaning. *Antimetabole* ('look after your car and your car will look after you') is a scheme; *metaphor* ('the wind is prowling round the house') is a trope.

Focus 185   The directing of attention to a part of the **sentence** or **clause** containing some important piece of information. English sentences commonly have *end focus*, i.e. present the important or 'new' part of their message at the end of the sentence. In 'Carlos ate all the plums', *Carlos* is informationally the **theme** or **topic**, the 'given' part of the message process, and 'ate all the plums' is the *rheme* or **comment**, in which first 'all the plums' and then, specifically, 'plums' are focused. End focus may be transformed into *front focus* – All the plums old Carlos ate'. *See* **fronting; marking; theme; topic and comment**.

Foregrounding 4–10   *See also* **automization; background; defamiliarization; norm and deviation.**

Form class 178–9   The older term for 'form class' is 'part of speech'. Modern English is considered to have, as 'major' form classes, **noun, verb, adjective, adverb**; and as 'minor', **article, conjunction, demonstrative, interjection, preposition, pronoun**. *See also* **closed class; open class**.

Formalism, -ist 30–2.

Free indirect speech *see* **speech**.

Fricative 122   A type of **consonant** in which the release of air is audibly constricted. The *f* of *f*at and the *v* of *v*at are fricatives, as are the *sh* of spla*sh* and the *s* of lei*s*ure, the *th* of *th*in and *th*ese, the *s* of *s*in and the *z* of *z*inc.

Front weight *see* **end weight**.

Fronting 196   The movement of an **element** from its place in the **predicate** of the **clause** and its relocation as the first element in the construction. Taking the **sentence** 'I gave those people three hours of my precious time', we may 'front' (or *pre-pose*) the **object** *complement*: 'Three hours of my precious time I gave those people'.

'Fuzziness' in figurative language 141–3.

Generic *see* **noun**.

Genitive *see* **case** *and* **noun**.

Gradable *see* **adjective; adverb**.

Graphology   This is to writing what **phonology** is to speech sounds; graphology is the system of signs representing language on paper (or other surfaces); its rules include the convention that an English written **sentence**

begins with a capital letter and ends with a full stop. Strictly speaking, 'graphology' should designate the principle and 'graphetics' the practice, but the two words, like *phonology* and *phonetics*, are often used interchangeably. The graphology of a **text** may be taken to include layout in advertisement and lineation in verse.

Head 189   In a **phrase**, the essential word, or the one that specifies its syntactic role, e.g. *house* in 'the very first really inexpensive prefabricated dwelling house'. 'House' is the head of a **noun phrase**.

Holonym   Literally 'whole name'; in the **lexicon**, a word denoting the complete phenomenon, organization, mechanism, etc., e.g. 'body', 'aircraft', 'tree'. The words denoting the parts or associated constituents of such wholes are *meronyms*, e.g. 'hands', 'nerves', 'wings', 'undercarriage', 'branch', 'root'. *See also* **hyperonym; hyponym**.

Hyperonym   In the **lexicon**, a superordinate term denoting a species or general class, e.g. 'vegetation', 'furniture', 'emotion'. *See also* **holonym; hyponym**.

Hyponym   A word specifying an item in a set or class generally denoted by a **hyperonym**, e.g. 'chair', 'stool', 'table', 'bed', 'cupboard', etc., are all hyponyms of the general term 'furniture'.

Ideology 21–4, 50–7, 129–47.

Imperative sentence   A sentence form used to frame commands and **directives**. Its **theme** is usually the base form, or **infinitive**, of the **verb**, with no preceding **subject**: 'Leave whenever you like', 'Take your belongings with you'.

Incorporation, compositional function of the complex sentence 199. *See also* **embedding**.

Indefinite article *see* **article**.

Infinitive   The 'base form' ('dictionary form') of the **verb**; *go* in 'I may go' is the *bare infinitive*; the *marked infinitive* is introduced by *to* in 'I would like to go'. The marked infinitive can be the predicator in non-finite **clauses**, e.g. 'To pay off my debt I would have to work day and night'.

Inflection, inflected *see* **suffix.**

Interjection Oh. Well. Hi! Look here! My word! A very minor **form class**.

Interrogative sentence A sentence form used for asking questions. The sentence begins with an interrogative word ('who', 'what'?), or the operator *do* precedes the verb: 'Who told you?' 'To what extent is that correct?' 'Do you understand what I mean?'

Isomorphism 7 A condition expressed by the popular **phrase** 'in so many words'; it assumes the exact fit of utterance (the form of words) and reference (the content), with no room for implications, ambiguities, expansions, etc.. Thus 'All healthy men have two kidneys' can be taken to mean just what the words say and no more; on the other hand, 'All philanthropic socialists have two kidneys' appears to imply things unspoken. *See also* **polysemy**.

'Keynote game' in popular fiction 104, 222.

Labio-dental A **consonant** formed by the contact of the upper teeth with the lower lip. The *f* of *fat* is a labio-dental.

Left branching 200 A left branch places a dependent construction before its principal, or peripheral information before central information: *after . . . calm* is a left branch in 'After we had washed, changed our clothes, collected our mail and in general regained a little calm, the conference began'. The same construction placed after 'began' would be a **right branch**.

Level 8, 39 The linguistic levels are **phonology**, grammar and the **lexicon**. Phonology concerns the representation of language, i.e. the conversion of its ideal (mental) forms into concrete, perceptible sounds; representation in the form of written sounds is called **graphology**. Language at each of its levels has a complex structure, and the levels themselves have complex interrelationships. The organization of **discourse** and **text** adds further levels.

Lexicon (lexis) 9, 115 (in poetry). A **level** of language involving (a) the formation of so-called 'lexical items' (words, compounds, **phrases**, 'idioms') and (b) the relationship between these items and the phenomena – ideas, feelings, 'things' – to which they refer. Lexical items have meanings which derive principally from **contexts**, and which may be codified in various ways; *see* **antonym; collocation; holonym; hyperonym; hyponym; synonym.**

Lineation 35

Literariness 16–18, 29–51.

'Locutory' expressions in the political dictionary 132.

'Macro' and 'micro' patterns 69–81.

Marking, marked form 5; stylistic effect of 196 The marked form of a construction is that which, for purposes of special emphasis, or to draw attention to some contextual relationship, acceptably changes the 'normal' word order. 'Liver I can't abide', 'She's coming when?' and 'All day long they toiled' are marked forms of 'I can't abide liver', 'When is she coming?', and 'They toiled all day long'. *See also* **deflection; foregrounding; fronting**.

Medium dependence 38, 43.

Meronym *see* **holonym**

Metalanguage, metadiscourse 129–91 The prefix-element *meta* in these recent formations has the sense of 'alongside', 'accompanying', rather than the nuance of 'change' which it has in, for example, 'metamorphosis' or 'metabolism'. A metalanguage is what we use to discuss language itself; the terminology of grammar, for instance, is a metalanguage. This is not quite the same as *metadiscourse*, though the term 'metalanguage' is often used (indeed, in this book) in describing discursive structures. Metadiscourse is language actually incorporated with discourse, guiding a listener/**reader** to its plan and development. In 'To begin with I shall talk about fifth-century Athens; later we shall examine the Roman concept of law', *to begin with* and *later* are metadiscursive items.

Mid-branching 200 A mid-branch is a type of parenthesis in which a **dependent** clause interrupts a superordinate construction, e.g. *swimming . . . seas* in 'The two boys, swimming with difficulty in the huge seas, struck out for the shore'.

Modality 117, 151 (in critical discourse), 226 This grammatical and semantic term refers to the description of unrealized states and possible conditions – the 'must be', 'should be', 'ought to be', 'might be', 'could be' of everyday situations and discourse. Typical meanings of modality are *obligation, option, permissibility, possibility*, expressed as a rule by so-called modal **auxiliaries**, e.g. *must, have to, ought to, may, might, can, could, will, would, need, dare.* A modal **verb** may express more than one kind of modality, according to **context**. Thus, 'Why isn't he here? – He must be in bed', expresses a conjecture, whereas 'Give Johnny his supper now – he must be in bed by nine' expresses obligation. Linguists call the former *epistemic* modality, the latter *deontic* or *root* modality.

Modifier, modify Modifiers limit, specify or elaborate the meanings of other words, as **adjectives** modify **nouns**, or **adverbs** modify adjectives. In 'a fur coat', the **head**, 'coat', is *premodified*; in 'a coat of fur', it is *postmodified*.

Monosemy is the **antonym** of **polysemy**, and signifies 'having only one meaning. Many technical terms are monosemic, e.g. 'aileron', 'carburetter', 'sphygmomanometer'.

Monovalence, -lent *see* **monosemy.**

Mood In traditional grammatical terminology, *mood* is the category that purports to reflect the attitude of the speaker to the utterance. The *indicative* mood characterizes **declarative** and **interrogative sentences** (i.e. statements and questions), as well as exclamations. The **imperative** mood characterizes commands; and the **subjunctive** mood the expression of conditions, options and uncertainties. *See*, however, **modality.**

'Motif', phonetic (in poetic style) 127.

Multivalence *see* **polysemy.**

Nasal 122 A type of **consonant** articulation in which the airstream is released through the nasal passages. The final sounds of 'da*m*', 'fu*n*' and 'pi*ng*' are nasal consonants.

Non-countable *see* **noun.**

Norm and deviation 3–7 The *norm* is the supposedly 'ordinary' or 'expected' pattern of language, the *deviation* the extraordinary usage, perceived against the **background** of the expected norm. However, the definition of the 'norm' and the perception of what is 'deviant' presents problems. *See also* **deflection; foregrounding.**

Noun A major **form class**, regularly *inflected* for plural **number** ('book*s*', child*ren*') and for the *genitive* case ('student*'s*', parents*'*). Some nouns form their plural by a change of **vowel** ('man-men', 'mouse-mice'), and some normally indicate the possessive relationship with an *of*-phrase rather than the *'s* form (e.g 'the contents of the appendix', rather than 'the appendix's contents'). Nouns normally taking a plural **suffix** (e.g. 'boys', 'chairs', 'examinations') are called *count nouns*; others, such as 'blood', 'bread', 'decency', which are not normally used in the plural are *non-countable* (sometimes called *mass* nouns). A noun or **noun phrase** referring to a whole class of objects, e.g. 'monkeys' in 'Monkeys are difficult to train', are *generic*; those referring to a particular example of the class, e.g. 'his pet monkey' in 'He gave it to his pet monkey to eat', are called *specific*. Names of persons or places are *proper nouns*; all others are *common nouns*. In form, nouns may be *derived*, through the use of prefixes or **suffixes** ('*in*sanity', 'mad*ness*'), or be compounds of two words ('bank-book', 'washing machine').

Noun phrase 177–8, 189 A **phrase** with a **noun** as its **head**, with or without **modifiers**. 'Cricketers', 'Some very famous cricketers', and 'Cricketers the world over' are noun phrases.

Number The grammatical expression of oneness (*singular*) or moreness (*plural*), represented in the *inflections* of the **noun**. In **clause** structure, number in the **subject** *phrase* must be 'in agreement' or 'concord' with **person** in the verb. Thus 'His youngest son like*s* chocolate', ('third person singular'), but 'All his son*s* like chocolate ('third person plural').

Object, direct and indirect In **clause** structure, a direct object is an **element** following a **transitive** *verb* and completing the sense 'something affects something'. In 'I like ice-cream', the direct object of 'like' is 'ice-cream'. In 'The nurses gave him ice-cream', the direct object is still 'ice-cream', but 'him' is also a kind of object, called the indirect object. *See also* **adverbial; clause; complement; phrase; subject.**

One liners (captions) 78

Onomatopoeia 121–3 Onomatopoeia is an aspect of the larger topic of *phonaesthesia*, meaning the decorative or figurative use of **speech-sounds**. Phonaesthesia includes the kind of sound symbolism here described as

onomatopoeic argument, and also the deployment of sounds in patterns of **alliteration**, *assonance*, and *consonance*.

Onomatopoeic argument 123, 128

Open class   An open class admits a theoretically infinitive number of items. **Nouns** are an open class; personal **pronouns** are a **closed class**.

Oral   Used to describe sounds in forming which the airstream is released through the mouth; in contrast to **nasal** sounds. The **consonants** *b* and *d* (as in 'buy', 'dose') are oral; the corresponding *m, n,* (as in 'my', 'nose'), are nasal.

Oratory 143

Palatal   A type of **consonant** articulation in which the body of the tongue approaches or touches the hard palate – the 'domed' roof of the mouth. The *y* [/j/] of English *y*oung, and the *ch* of German I*ch* are palatal.

Palato-alveolar   A type of **consonant** formation in which the tongue forms a closure or constriction of a position in the roof of the mouth between the alveolum (teeth-ridge) and the palatal dome. The final sounds in 'spla*sh*', 'gara*ge*', are palato-alveolar.

Parallelism 4

Paraphrase, as a creative exercise 229, 232

Parison 143, 156   A **figure of speech** requiring the **parallelism** of **phrases** or **clauses**. In 'The vicar told the sexton and the sexton tolled the bell', where sequent clauses have the same surface pattern, **subject – verb – object**, the rhetorical arrangement is parisonic.

Parody, compositional exercise 181–4

Participle   One of the constituent forms, called *non-finite*, of the **verb**. There are two participles: the present, ending in -ing, as in *working*, and the past, generally ending in -ed, as in *worked*, but sometimes with other endings, e.g. 'eat*en*', 'sle*pt*'. In some verbs the **vowel** in the past participle differs from the vowel in the **infinitive**, e.g. 'think' – 'thought'; and in a few cases the infinitive and past participle forms are identical, e.g. '(to) put', '(I have) put'. Participles can function as **predicators** in non-finite **clauses**: 'Turning away from us, he greeted the chairman', 'Accused of petty theft, she denied all knowledge of the purse and its contents'.

Passive *see* **voice**

Periphrasis 101   This is the device of calling policemen, roses, tennis players and others by roundabout names, e.g. 'the stern guardian of the law', 'the pride and glory of the English garden', 'the master of the big serve.' A standard resource in poetry from classical times down to the eighteenth century, it has gradually fallen into literary disrepute, and is now more likely to be found in journalism, copywriting and popular fiction than in 'serious' literature. But it would be imprudent to consider the device wholly discredited.

Phonaesthesia *see* **onomatopoeia**

Phology 9   The study of speech-sounds, particularly of their distribution in language and their relationship to meaning, whether in the **lexicon**, (e.g. a difference in the articulation of one segment of speech distinguishes the meaning of *t*in from that of *d*in), or in the functions of **discourse** (a difference of intonation may distinguish the function 'question' from that of 'statement'), or in aesthetic representations (e.g. of 'resonance', 'shrillness', etc.). Strictly speaking, phonology is a study of systems, as opposed to *phonetics*, which studies the articulatory and acoustic properties of speech-sounds; the two terms, however, are often used interchangeably. *See also* consonant; **graphology**; **onomatopoeia**; prosody; vowel.

Phrasal verb   A lexical **verb** (main verb) consisting of two words, the second of which is a particle, e.g. *give in, turn out, look after, stand by.* Some phrasal verbs permit the separation of the particle from the *head*, e.g. *call on*, in 'the man I called on', which allows the transformation 'the man on whom I called'. In others, the particle is not separable; thus *call up*, in 'the man I called up' cannot be rewritten 'the man up whom I called'.

Phrase   A word or bounded sequence of words **realizing** one or other of the **elements** in a **clause**. The various types of phrase are the *noun phrase*, the *verb phrase*, the *adjective phrase*, the *adverb phrase* and the *prepositional phrase*. Prepositional phrases are so called because they are introduced by a **preposition** (e.g. 'in the corner', 'after the game'). The other phrase types are named after the grammatical category of the principal item, or **head**.

Politics, language of 129–47

Polysemy 41, 46, 49 The **antonym** of **monosemy**, as *multivalence* is the antonym of *monovalence*. Words, or more broadly, **texts**, are polysemic (or polysemous) when they have more than one meaning. The word 'form', for example, is polysemic, its meaning varying with the **context** in which it occurs. Polysemy in literary style usually implies the simultaneous presence of two or more meanings, collectively and individually relevant to the text.

Possessive *see* **case**

Predicate In the structure of a **clause**, the predicate consists of the **verb** plus any **element** dependent on the **verb** (e.g. an **object** or **complement**). In 'Billy cried', *cried* is the predicate; in 'Billy hit the dentist', *hit the dentist* is the predicate.

Predicator A word sometimes used to indicate the role of the **verb** in **clause** structure. This usage distinguishes the **element** from its **realization** (or *representation*).

Preposing 195 *See also* **fronting**.

Preposition Prepositions are a **form class** of particles used to introduce **noun phrases** and to link them to other syntactic constituents, e.g. 'I left your book *on* the coffee table', 'We need to leave *after* the presentation', 'Mary was told to be here *by* five o'clock'.

Problem-solving structures 69

Pronoun 117 A **form class** of words used as substitutes for **nouns** or **noun phrases**. There are sub-classes of pronoun, e.g. *personal*, ('I', 'you'), *impersonal* ('some', 'any'), *demonstrative* ('that, this'), *reflexive* ('myself', 'yourself', etc.), *possessive* ('mine', 'yours', 'his', 'hers').

Proposition 62 Loosely used of any assertion or **declarative** sentence, this term may be defined more strictly as a **sentence** in which the **predicate** affirms or denies something about the **subject** or **theme**, and which can be declared true or false. 'The King of France has three wives' is a (demonstrably false) proposition; 'France is a nice place to spend your holidays' is a declarative sentence, but not a proposition in the stricter sense, since its truth or falsehood cannot be demonstrated.

Prosody, prosodic 128, 144   In poetics, 'prosody' refers to the principles of metre and rhythm, 'metre' being the fixed measure, like the bar system in music, and rhythm the varied disposition of accents within the measure. In linguistics, 'prosody' is sometimes used to refer to so-called *suprasegmental* aspects of speech, i.e. rhythm and intonation.

Reader, function of in text creation 57

'Realism game' in popular fiction 221

Realization   The choice of words to represent a given linguistic role. In 'Printers sometimes make mistakes', the element called **subject** is realized by the word 'printers'.

'Re-registration' 98

Rewriting, as a compositional exercise 184–8

Rheme *see* **theme; topic and comment**

Rhyme, as organizing principle in poetry 120

Right branching 200   *See also* **left branching; mid-branching.**

Semantics   Generally, that **level** of language and linguistic analysis that concerns itself with 'meaning' (as opposed to, though inextricably bound up with, 'form'). It is commonly associated with the **lexicon** (i.e. with 'word-meaning'), but semantic distinctions are also apparent in grammar and **phonology**.

Sentence   A major unit of grammatical form containing one or more **clauses**. Clauses in their turn are perceived as containing **phrases**, which contain one or more words, which contain one or more *morphemes*. A sentence containing only one clause is a *simple sentence*. Sentences composed of a linked series of independent clauses ('the men went to the pub, the women chatted, and the children played tennis') are *multiple sentences*; sentences with one or more **dependent** clauses are called *complex*. A 'fragmentary sentence' is one from which some element has been deleted, e.g. 'Thursday night', for 'He came on Thursday night', in response to the question 'When did he come?'.

Sequencing composition function of the complex **sentence** 199

Sonority 121, 122, 128   In acoustic phonetics, 'sonority' refers to the resonant qualities of **speech-sounds**, deriving from their inherent harmonic structure – i.e. a mathematical relationship among the sound's constituent wave-frequencies. **Vowels** in general have greater sonority, and are perceived as more prominent, than **consonants; nasal** consonants have greater sonority than **oral** consonants; voiced consonants are more sonorous than voiceless consonants.

Speech, direct and indirect   In direct speech, the words actually used are quoted: 'He said, "Can we expect an improvement in trade figures?" '. In indirect speech, the speaker's words are reported but not exactly repeated, 'He asked if an improvement in trade figures might be expected'. In fiction, much use is made of so-called *free indirect speech* ('free' in the absence of a reporting **verb**), to express a character's unspoken musings. 'It was a difficult situation. Some action might be urged. Perhaps there would be an improvement in trade figures'.

Speech act 33–4   The term 'speech act' is primarily associated with the philosophers J. L. Austin and J. Searle. A speech act is a form of words which is regarded either as socially equivalent to an action, or as committing the speaker to the action implied in the words. 'I declare the meeting closed', 'I now pronounce you man and wife', 'I promise to pay the bearer the sum of £5 on demand', 'I protest', 'I take it all back', are all speech acts.

Speech-sounds, aesthetics of 119–29

State verb (stative verb)   State verbs denote receptive or inert conditions, e.g. of *perception* ('see', 'hear', 'feel'), of *cognition* ('think', 'realize', 'remember'), or *relation* ('be', 'belong to', 'contain', 'comprise'), of bodily *sensation* ('itch', 'ache', 'burn'). In some cases state verbs are not compatible with the 'progressive' (-*ing*) form (e.g. we do not say 'I was perceiving it immediately', or 'Hang around and you will be hearing something to your advantage'). Some state verbs have corresponding **event verbs**, e.g. 'see' (as against the event of 'look', 'watch'), 'hear' (as against 'listen'). Verbs like *grow* are state verbs in some constructions, e.g. 'How you've grown!', but event verbs (with a difference meaning) in others, e.g. 'You've been growing tomatoes, I see'. Verbs like *desire* may be interpreted as 'event' ('I desired him to leave me in peace') or state ('I desired only peace', where 'desire' = 'want').

Statement, ways of framing 192

Stop 122   A type of **consonant** involving a momentary occlusion, or 'stopping' of the airstream. The *p* of 'repose' and the *b* of 'debate' are stops; so, too, the *t* of 'tin', the *c* of 'cat', the *d* of 'din' and the *g* of 'dog'. Strictly speaking, the term 'stop' refers to the onset of the sound, i.e. the initial closure. Another term, *plosive*, properly refers to the audible, 'breathy' release of stops on certain positions. The *t* of 'tin' can be described both as a stop and as a plosive; but the *t* of 'mat' is commonly pronounced without plosion, although it is a stop.

Style 2, 13–16   In this book, a property of **texts**, characterized by (a) the patterning of language at distinct yet coordinated **levels**, (b) the choice of language in relationship to a functional **context**, and (c) the designing of linguistic expression to appeal to, or control the responses of, a **reader**. *The relational concept of style 7, 16; style as deviation 6; style as evaluation 16; style as ornamentation 7; text-dependent view of style 6.*

Subject   In **sentence** and **clause** structure, the **element** that usually comes before the **verb** *phrase* in a **declarative** sentence, and after the *operator* (e.g. 'do', 'has') in an **interrogative sentence**. This element is represented by 'the boy' in 'The boy stood on the burning deck' and 'Where did the boy stand?'. *See also* **adverbial; complement; object**.

Subordinator, subordination *see* **conjunction**

Suffix   A particle added to the stem of a word to form a new word, e.g. *-ful* in 'hopeful'. Some suffixes are *inflections*, expressing grammatical relationships (e.g. **number, person, tense, aspect**, as in 'two boy*s*', 'he hate*s* beer', 'we work*ed* all night', 'the children were play*ing*').

Suprasegmental   Suprasegmentals, sometimes called **prosodic** features, accompany the 'segmental' sequence of sounds making up an utterance, and principally take the form of intonation, stress, and 'juncture', or pause.

Synonym   In the **lexicon**, a word belonging to a set of words with similar but not completely identical denotations or references. The words 'fat', 'plump', 'stout' and 'obese' are synonyms, appropriate to different **collocations** and **contexts**. *See also* **antonym; core vocabulary; hyperonym; hyponym**.

Syntax 115   Syntax is the branch of grammar that deals with word order and with the signalling of relationships between constructions. *See also* **antecedent; apposition; clause; left branching; mid-branching; phrase; right branching; sentence**.

Tag-question 'You're coming on Sunday, are you?' could also be 'You're coming on Sunday, aren't you?' 'Are you?' and 'aren't you?' are question tags; also 'did they?', 'has he?', 'wasn't she?', 'could I?' In modern colloquial [British] English, the tag-question is often used emphatically, to stress an assertion, rather than interrogatively: 'Where've you been?' – 'I've been shopping, haven't I?'.

Technical language, in popular fiction 102–4

Tense A grammatical category associated with the **verb**, expressing time. English has two primary tenses, present and past. The so-called 'compound tenses' ['will leave', 'have read', 'had worked', 'am compiling', 'have been eating', etc.] are to be explained in terms of **aspect** and **modality**. *Tense in poetry* 116.

Text Here, a piece of written language, having (a) **coherence**, in that its constituent parts make collective sense, (b) **cohesion**, in that the linguistic relationships between constituents are adequately demonstrated, and (c) completeness, in that it may be assumed to encompass a process of meaning. 'He was drunk, but aren't clothes expensive?' lacks coherence, yet has cohesion. 'He was drunk. Magistrate's court', lacks cohesion yet is discernibly coherent. 'He was drunk and so . . .' is obviously incomplete. 'He was drunk, and so next day found himself in the Magistrate's Court' is coherent, cohesive, and complete'. Texts may also be perceived as encoding certain **ideologies**, in which case their design involves an attempt to promote some interpretations and suppress others. *See also* **reader; writing**.

Text conventions 10–15

'Text-intrinsic' 86 Features which are notably associated with certain types of text, perhaps so closely as to be regarded as indispensable, are said to be text-intrinsic'. Imperatives, for example, are 'text-intrinsic' to cookery recipes.

Theme 185 Semantically, the 'theme' is the first **lexical** element in a **sentence**, frequently but not always coinciding with the grammatical **subject**. In 'Mr Kipling makes exceedingly good cakes', *Mr Kipling* is the 'theme' as well as the grammatical **subject**; but in 'Exceedingly good cakes Mr Kipling makes', the phrase 'exceedingly good cakes' has become the theme, although the grammatical subject is still 'Mr Kipling'. *See also* **agent deletion; focus; fronting; marked; preposing; topic and comment**.

Theme and rheme *see* **topic and comment**

Topic and comment   The sequence of information in a **sentence** may be interpreted as first, the announcement of what the sentence is going to be about – the topic – and second, a brief-narrative, the comment. Thus in 'the latest storm is said to be the worst in living memory', *the latest storm* is the topic and *is said to be* etc. the comment. Some grammarians describe this information-pattern as *theme and rheme*. A specific form of topic-comment structure is seen in A. E. Housman's line 'The gale, it bends the saplings double', as well as in sentences like 'What we are going to do now is, we are going to saw this lady in half'.

Topic holding, in popular fiction 109–10

Topic skipping, in popular fiction 109–10

Transitivity 179   A semantic property of the **clause**, specifically associated with the **verb**. In a clause constructed from the **elements subject – verb – direct object**, the verb is said to be transitive: thus, in 'John/smokes/those awful cigars', *smokes* is a transitive verb. But in constructions of the type subject – verb – **adverbial**, subject – verb – **complement**, the verb is intransitive, e.g. 'John smokes', 'John smokes heavily', 'John is a heavy smoker'.

Velar 125   A type of **consonant** formation in which the back of the tongue touches or approaches the soft palate, or *velum*. The initial sounds in '*k*eel', '*g*ood', and the final sounds in 'ha*ng*' and (Scots) 'lo*ch*' are velar.

Verb   A major **form class**, as a rule **realizing** the central **element** in **clause** structure. Verbs are *main* (lexical) or **auxiliary**, the main verb being the **head** of the *verb phrase*. Main verbs regularly have four forms, covering the *inflections* for the infinitive, third person singular present tense, present participle, past tense, and past participle, e.g. 'work', 'works', 'working', 'worked', 'worked'). There are also 'five form' and 'three form' patterns ('prove', 'proves' 'proving', 'proved', 'proven'; 'put', 'puts', putting, 'put', 'put'). *See also* **phrasal verb**.

Voice   A grammatical category affecting the structure of the **verb** *phrase* and its role in the **clause**. The active voice is exemplified by 'Dr Poole gave a lecture'; the passive transformation of which would be 'A lecture was given by Dr Poole'. In the latter instance, the 'by-phrase' (*by Dr Poole*) might be omitted – 'A lecture was given' – thus deleting all reference to an **agent**. In composition, the choice of active or passive form is often related to questions of **theme**, focus, **agent**, and **cohesion**.

Voiced, voiceless *see* **consonant**

Vowel 121, 122 A type of speech sound characterized by (a) voicing, i.e. the closure of the vocal cords, producing **sonority**, (b) the absence of any occlusion or constriction of the emergent airstream, (c) the modification and contrast of sonorities by altering the shape of the oral cavity, and (d), phonologically, its central position and superior prominence in the syllable. The articulation of vowels is described primarily in terms of tongue height and advancement, and secondarily in terms of lip-rounding. In the word 'feet', the vowel ('ee') is pronounced with the front of the tongue high in the mouth, and is called a 'high front' vowel'; the vowels in 'h*a*t', 'm*oo*n' and 'l*aw*' are respectively 'low front', 'high back' and 'low back'. The vowel in 'b*i*rd', being neither 'front' nor 'back', 'high' nor 'low', is called a 'mid-high central' vowel. The vowel in French *plume* is a high front rounded vowel. There is also a type of complex vowel articulation known as a **diphthong** (e.g. the *oi* of 'join'). Vowels vary in length and **sonority**, and have acoustic colorations which poets readily exploit.

Word games, creative value of 226

Well-formed sentence 6 In grammatical theory, a **sentence** constructed in accordance with the rules of the language, and accepted as meaningful (or potentially meaningful) by a native speaker, is 'well formed'. A sentence may, however, be well formed without being intelligible. 'I've just been hoomering the crast-wallops in case the bloobat breaks' is a well-formed sentence, in accordance with the rules of English grammar. 'Just I be paint flower tub in case weather she break' is not.

Writing 58 (the writer's function in text making); 174 (the writer's motive)

Index of Extracts

This index is a guide to passages used for illustration and commentary. It does not list minor quotations, repetitions, or incidental allusions. References follow page-order, except in citing poems, fiction, and critical writing, under which headings they follow the alphabetical order of the authors' names.